WHAT THE TARIFF
MEANS TO
AMERICAN INDUSTRIES

SOME PUBLICATIONS OF THE

COUNCIL ON FOREIGN RELATIONS

FOREIGN AFFAIRS (quarterly), edited by Hamilton Fish Armstrong.

THE UNITED STATES IN WORLD AFFAIRS (annual). Volumes for 1931, 1932, and 1933, by Walter Lippmann and William O. Scroggs; for 1934-1935, 1936, 1937, 1938, 1939 and 1940, by Whitney H. Shepardson and William O. Scroggs; for 1945-1947, 1947-1948 and 1948-1949, by John C. Campbell; for 1949, 1950, 1951, 1952, 1953, and 1954, by Richard P. Stebbins.

DOCUMENTS ON AMERICAN FOREIGN RELATIONS (annual). Volume for 1952, edited by Clarence W. Baier and Richard P. Stebbins; for 1953 and 1954, edited by Peter V. Curl; for 1955, edited by Paul E. Zinner.

POLITICAL HANDBOOK OF THE WORLD (annual), edited by Walter H. Mallory.

UNITED STATES SHIPPING POLICY, by Wytze Gorter.

RUSSIA AND AMERICA: Dangers and Prospects, by Henry L. Roberts.

STERLING: Its Meaning in World Finance, by Judd Polk.

KOREA: A Study of U. S. Policy in the United Nations, by Leland M. Goodrich.

FOREIGN AFFAIRS BIBLIOGRAPHY, 1942-1952, by Henry L. Roberts.

AMERICAN AGENCIES INTERESTED IN INTERNATIONAL AFFAIRS, compiled by Ruth Savord and Donald Wasson.

JAPANESE AND AMERICANS: A Century of Cultural Relations, by Robert S. Schwantes.

THE FUTURE OF UNDERDEVELOPED COUNTRIES: Political Implications of Economic Development, by Eugene Staley.

THE UNDECLARED WAR, 1940-1941, by William L. Langer and S. Everett Gleason.

THE CHALLENGE TO ISOLATION, 1937-1940, by William L. Langer and S. Everett Gleason.

MIDDLE EAST DILEMMAS: The Background of United States Policy, by J. C. Hurewitz.

BRITAIN AND THE UNITED STATES: Problems in Cooperation, a joint report prepared by Henry L. Roberts and Paul A. Wilson.

TRADE AND PAYMENTS IN WESTERN EUROPE: A Study in Economic Cooperation, 1947-1951, by William Diebold, Jr.

THE ECONOMICS OF FREEDOM: The Progress and Future of Aid to Europe, by Howard S. Ellis.

WAR AND THE MINDS OF MEN, by Frederick S. Dunn.

PUBLIC OPINION AND FOREIGN POLICY, by Lester Markel and Others.

THE PRICE OF POWER, by Hanson W. Baldwin.

OUR FARM PROGRAM AND FOREIGN TRADE, by C. Addison Hickman.

THE FOREIGN AFFAIRS READER, edited by Hamilton Fish Armstrong.

THE STUDY OF INTERNATIONAL RELATIONS IN AMERICAN COLLEGES AND UNIVERSITIES, by Grayson Kirk.

FOREIGN AFFAIRS BIBLIOGRAPHY, 1932-1942, by Robert Gale Woolbert.

THE UNITED STATES IN A MULTI-NATIONAL ECONOMY, by Jacob Viner and Others.

THE FAR EASTERN CRISIS, by Henry L. Stimson.

THE STRUGGLE FOR AIRWAYS IN LATIN AMERICA, by William A. M. Burden.

LIMITS OF LAND SETTLEMENT, prepared under the direction of Isaiah Bowman.

SURVEY OF AMERICAN FOREIGN RELATIONS (in four volumes, 1928-1931), prepared under the direction of Charles P. Howland.

INTERNATIONAL AIR TRANSPORT AND NATIONAL POLICY, by Oliver J. Lissitzyn.

What the Tariff
Means to
American Industries

By
PERCY W. BIDWELL

Published for the
COUNCIL ON FOREIGN RELATIONS
by
HARPER & BROTHERS
New York
1956

The Council on Foreign Relations is a non-profit institution devoted to the study of international aspects of American political, economic and strategic problems. It takes no stand, expressed or implied, on American policy.

The authors of books published under the auspices of the Council are responsible for their statements of fact and expressions of opinion. The Council is responsible only for determining that they should be presented to the public.

WHAT THE TARIFF MEANS TO AMERICAN INDUSTRIES

Copyright, 1956, by Council on Foreign Relations, Inc.
Printed in the United States of America

All rights reserved, including right to reproduce
this book or any portion thereof in any form.

For information address Council on Foreign Relations,
58 East 68th Street, New York 21

FIRST EDITION

The Colonial Press Inc., Clinton, Mass.

Library of Congress catalog card number: LC 56-10523

COUNCIL ON FOREIGN RELATIONS

PREFACE

IN WRITING this book the author derived much benefit from his association with a small group made up of members of the Council on Foreign Relations and others chosen because of their competence in matters of trade and tariffs. The group's membership is listed below:

ELLIOTT V. BELL, *Chairman*—McGraw-Hill Publishing Company

WILLARD L. THORP, *Deputy Chairman*—Merrill Center for Economics, Amherst College

JOHN R. PETTY, *Rapporteur*—Chase Manhattan Bank

SOLOMON BARKIN—Textile Workers Union of America

RAYMOND A. BAUER—Center for International Studies, Massachusetts Institute of Technology

CARL D. CORSE—Office of Economic Defense and Trade Policy, U. S. Department of State

PRENTICE N. DEAN—U. S. Department of Defense

J. FREDERIC DEWHURST—Twentieth Century Fund

WILLIAM DIEBOLD, JR.—Council on Foreign Relations

SOLOMON FABRICANT—National Bureau of Economic Research, Inc.

JOHN FAYERWEATHER—Graduate School of Business Administration, Harvard University

A. U. FOX—American Thread Company

DAVID M. FREUDENTHAL—Financial consultant

EDWARD R. GAY—St. Regis Paper Company

KERMIT GORDON—Williams College

WYTZE GORTER—University of California at Los Angeles

HEMAN GREENWOOD

JOHN K. JESSUP—*Life*

HOWARD S. PIQUET—U. S. Library of Congress

JUDD POLK—California Texas Oil Company, Ltd.

ITHIEL POOL—Center for International Studies, Massachusetts Institute of Technology

MORRIS S. ROSENTHAL—Business consultant

John H. Stambaugh—Vanderbilt University

Ralph I. Straus—Capital management

Arthur R. Upgren—Amos Tuck School of Business Administration, Dartmouth College

Raymond Vernon—Hawley & Hoops, Inc.

Howard Whidden—*Business Week*

Jacques D. Wimpfheimer—American Velvet Company

The collaboration of author and study group, a standard feature of the Council's research undertakings, proved in this project unusually fruitful. Members of the group, individually, read drafts of chapters of the book and gave me many useful suggestions. Collectively, the group, under the able leadership of Elliott Bell and Willard Thorp, served as a panel, or forum, which considered major issues of fact and opinion.

In a series of private, informal meetings extending over two years, the group dealt systematically with the tariff in its relation to eight industries selected as case studies. At each meeting, manufacturers of the product under discussion explained their need for protective duties. Importers of competing foreign products presented the opposing point of view.[1] In the ensuing discussion, both parties commented on a working paper, received in advance of the meeting, and responded to questions from group members. The group made no attempt to reach a consensus and did not formulate any recommendations on tariff policy. The author bears sole responsibility for opinions and judgments expressed in this book, in which individual members may or may not concur.

Liberal use was made of reports of the Tariff Commission, Department of Commerce and other government agencies, daily newspapers and trade journals. Printed sources were not adequate, however, for the kind of book I wanted to write. Hence, I relied heavily on interviews. Businessmen, economists and technical experts, both in government and private employment, supplied useful information and new insights. Visits to factories gave first-hand acquaintance with products and processes. Conversations with corporation exec-

---

[1] The Council's guests at the meetings of the study group are listed in the Appendix.

utives, factory managers, importers, buyers for department
stores, wholesalers and dealers afforded opportunities to dis-
cuss the tariff in its relation to the operations of individual
firms. The names of these helpful persons, which constitute
a sort of bibliography, will be found in the Appendix. I want
to acknowledge my indebtedness to them and to thank them
most sincerely for their generous assistance.

I am indebted particularly to Eleanor S. Cavanaugh, librarian of Standard & Poor's, and Ruth Jackendoff, Director
of Economics and Statistics of the Wool Bureau, Inc. They
helped to identify sources of information and permitted me
to use their valuable collections. Maps were drawn by Gustav
Schweizer (p. 134) and Christopher Williams (p. 14). Mr.
Williams and William D. Schlutow prepared the charts.

Thanks are due to William Diebold, Jr., the Council's
Director of Economic Studies, for help in planning the project
and advice at all stages of the work, and to Ruth Savord, the
Council's librarian, Donald Wasson, assistant librarian, Janet
Rigney and other members of the library staff for their
efficient attention to my many inquiries. Bernice Tell and
Cecile Censor deserve credit for deciphering and typing my
manuscript.

Helena Stalson, economist, a member of the Council's research staff, was associated with me in this enterprise. The
book owes a great deal to her intelligent and loyal collaboration.

New York   PERCY W. BIDWELL
May 15, 1956

CONTENTS

TABLES

Chapter 1

THE TARIFF AS A LOCAL ISSUE

"THE TARIFF is a local issue" is a familiar saying. It implies that the votes of Congressmen and Senators on tariff matters are more likely to be influenced by the presence, or absence, in their constituencies of protected industries than by considerations of national interest. The predominance of local interests can easily be understood, for the federal legislator has a legitimate concern for the welfare of his constituents. Moreover, he may believe that raising or lowering a tariff rate involves no real conflict between local and national interests.

A legislator wants to know the facts in the cases presented for his consideration, but how can he discover them in the welter of conflicting testimony? He learns from a manufacturer in his district that competitive imports are increasing and that his business is on the down grade. The manufacturer claims that foreign competition is responsible for his difficulties and he asks for increased tariffs or, perhaps, for quota restrictions on imports. To support his position, he may assert that his products are essential to national defense.

But among the Congressman's constituents there may also be firms which sell a substantial part of their products abroad. They point out that increased imports make more dollars available to foreigners and hence stimulate American exporting industries. They warn against exaggerating the damaging effects of imports. They suggest that the alleged injury to the domestic firm arises from causes which have nothing to do with increased competition from abroad. Or they assert that, if the complainant would cut his costs, or diversify his product, or explore his markets more thoroughly, he would be able to cope successfully with foreign competition. The defense argument, they imply, is a red herring.

What is the truth in these matters? What are the indications that a firm has actually suffered injury from imports? How can this factor be distinguished from disturbances arising from other causes? If foreign competition turns out to be the real threat, does that mean that increased tariffs are the only, or the best, remedy? What are the possibilities that "injured" firms can introduce more efficient methods in production or in marketing, or otherwise revise their operations so as to meet effectively competition from abroad? What responsibility, if any, should the federal government assume in assisting firms actually injured by tariff reduction? What is the meaning of "defense essentiality"? Questions like these arise in public hearings before Congressional committees and in their closed sessions. Legislators, before casting their votes, want to know who gets hurt and how badly.

In a democracy one expects that the electorate will be educated by frequent exposure to discussion of questions of public policy. But in this respect a century and a half of tariff controversy has proved sterile, for each of the opposing sides has failed to meet squarely the issues raised by the other. Advocates of lower tariffs have stressed the benefits which the nation as a whole would derive from more effective use of our labor, capital and natural resources. Protectionists have stressed the damage which increased foreign competition would inflict on vulnerable American industries. Thus the discussion has proceeded on parallel tracks without either side subjecting the arguments of the other to rigorous examination. It is one of the purposes of this book to bring about a head-on collision on the "local interest" track.

What the Tariff Means to American Industries may seem an ambitious title. But "industries," for the purposes of this book, means only manufactures. Products of agriculture, the fisheries, mining and lumbering play an important role in present-day tariff controversy. To have included them in the present project, however, would have made it unmanageable. The book concentrates on a few branches of manufacturing which present differing situations of import competition. Each of the eight case studies presents information necessary to understand the situation of a single industry vis-à-vis its foreign competition. Scrutiny and analysis of this information have led to conclusions regarding the industry's need for continued tariff protection.

The eight industries selected as case studies are:

household chinaware	woolens and worsteds
watches	hand-fashioned glassware
bicycles	synthetic organic chemicals
iron and steel	electrical manufactures

Some of these industries, glassware particularly, are concentrated geographically; others, chemicals and electrical manufactures, for example, are widely dispersed. Woolens and worsteds are old industries, tracing their origins back to colonial days. Synthetic chemicals and electrical manufacturing are new, the products of the technological advances of the past 50 or 60 years. Chemicals, iron and steel and electrical manufacturing are characterized by large-scale operations and by heavy investments of capital in proportion to the numbers of workers employed. At the other end of the scale is hand-fashioned glassware which is still made by skilled workers using rather primitive tools; capital investment is small, and labor makes up a large part of manufacturing costs. Between the extremes are found bicycles, watches, woolens and worsteds, produced in fully mechanized factories operated typically by firms of medium size. All eight industries have felt the impact of imports in varying degrees, and each has responded differently.

Sample industries can never be altogether typical; inevitably they will overemphasize certain characteristics of American manufacturing while neglecting others. Hence, the reader should exercise caution in applying conclusions drawn from these studies to the tariff problems of American industry in general.

The eight chapters devoted to separate industries show how each has been affected by tariff reduction and what adjustments each has made to the new situation. Adjustment may be described as the process of avoiding injury. It comprehends all the methods of self-help, including the introduction of new cost-reducing techniques in production and in marketing, whereby progressive American firms are constantly endeavoring to maintain their share of the market, or to improve their position vis-à-vis their domestic as well as their foreign competitors. But what will happen to firms which are not able through their own efforts to cope with increased competition from imports? What help may they expect from state development commissions and from local bodies, private and public? Should the federal government assume responsibility for assisting business firms injured by tariff reduction? If so, how can it best discharge this responsibility? These matters are treated in the chapter, "Injury and Adjustment." The final chapter considers the tariff needs of defense industries and ends with some general conclusions drawn from the case studies.

Many writers have dealt competently with the broad aspects of American tariff policy. They have discussed the effects of import duties on the allocation of our national resources, on real incomes and on our standard of living. They have commented on the impact of changes in our policy on economic conditions in foreign countries and on political relations with our allies in the free world. But they have given much less attention to the effects at home on the industries and branches of industry which may have been injured or benefited. On this somewhat neglected aspect of tariff policy this book focuses its attention. It deals with the particular rather than with the general, with special rather than with national interests. Thus it is designed to supplement studies with a wider perspective.

Chapter 2

WHAT THE TARIFF MEANS TO THE GLASSWARE INDUSTRY

A TECHNOLOGICAL revolution in the past 50 years has transformed glassmaking in the United States from "the almost exclusive domain of the skilled craftsman" to one of the country's most highly mechanized industries. The impact of this revolution, however, has not affected all sections of the industry equally. In the production of window glass, plate glass, standardized glass containers and most of what is known as pressed and blown glassware, semiautomatic and fully automatic machinery has reduced costs and made possible great expansion in output. In these lines American firms, making full use of mass-production techniques, have successfully met foreign competition in both domestic and export markets. They have largely outgrown the need for tariff protection.

There remains, however, a small group of firms which have been untouched by mechanization. These are the producers of hand-fashioned glassware, principally tableware and ornamental objects. With handicraft methods and simple hand tools, which have changed little in the course of centuries, they are turning out goblets, wineglasses and other "stemware," and a miscellaneous assortment of art objects. In this business they are meeting increasingly active competition from German, Swedish, French and Japanese goods produced at lower labor costs. For American manufacturers in this group, import duties have long been a matter of real concern.

Many factors have contributed to the development of the American glassware industry in the past 50 or 60 years. Of great importance after 1880 was the development of large supplies of natural gas, a cheap fuel ideally adapted for glassmaking. In addition to major labor-saving inventions, improvement in the design of furnaces and many minor changes contributed to the reduction of costs and better quality of the

5

product. All these changes depended on the rapid progress which was being made in the chemistry of glassware, whereby new types of glass were developed which were susceptible of manipulation by mechanical means.

Perhaps the most basic factor contributing to continued growth in glass usage is the ever-expanding versatility of the material itself. One leading glass manufacturer is said to have developed 50,000 formulas for the making of glass, which comprise combinations of practically all of the earth's 99 elements. From these formulas, it is possible to make glass products that are "lighter than cork or almost as heavy as iron, as strong as steel or as fragile as an eggshell, as soft as cotton, or hard as precious stones." Glass products can also be made to resist corrosive acids, exceptional heat, and violent, sudden changes in temperature; to transmit or absorb infrared, ultraviolet or X-ray bands of the spectrum and to conduct or stop electricity.[1]

Inventions and discoveries, however, only partly explain the surprising developments in the glass industry in the past half century. The general rise in economic activity in the United States and the expansion of its great internal market were fundamental conditions for the successful exploitation of the new technology.

The American Glassware Industry—Its Dimensions

Table 1 shows the dimensions of the principal branches of the industry and the position of each in relation to import and export trade.

Glass containers. Firms engaged in the manufacture of glass containers have little reason to be concerned with tariff problems. Automatic machinery has entirely displaced hand methods in making the standardized utility items which constitute the bulk of domestic production. The business is in the hands of a few large companies. Their shipments rose in value from $165 million in 1937 to $577 million in 1953. Imports, valued at a few hundred thousand dollars yearly, consist principally of specialized items such as perfume bottles and jars for toilet preparations. Tariff duties do not seem to be a factor in maintaining the prosperity of this branch of the glassware industry.

[1] Clyde Williams, "Glass Processing Forges Ahead," *Monthly Business Review*, Federal Reserve Bank of Cleveland (October 1, 1953), p. 15.

The ability of the American firms to meet foreign competition is demonstrated by exports of over $20 million annually.

Flat glass. With the aid of only moderately protective duties, American manufacturers of window glass and plate glass achieved in the early years of the present century practical control of their domestic market. Thorough mechanization had kept their costs low in relation to those of foreign manufacturers. In addition, transportation costs on their bulky commodity, particularly on rail shipments to interior points, afforded a considerable measure of "natural protection."

Table 1

THE AMERICAN GLASSWARE INDUSTRY, 1953

(in thousands of dollars)

Product	Domestic Shipments	Imports	Exports
Glass containers	577,000	413	22,455
Flat glass	500,000	19,608	13,317
Pressed and blown glassware[a]	367,865	9,440	28,732
All other	175,000	781	1,477
Total	1,619,865	30,243	65,981

[a] Including both hand-fashioned and machine-made.
Source: U. S. Bureau of the Census

In the early 1920's, when domestic firms were unable to supply the unprecedented demand from the automobile and building industries, imports filled the gap. In the peak year 1923, imports of plate glass were 27 percent of domestic production. Falling rapidly thereafter, they were less than one percent in 1935 and disappeared entirely during World War II.

Although largely unnecessary after 1900, import duties were maintained and even increased. In the early 1930's the duties collected on imports of plate glass were 96 percent of the foreign values. But as the result of reductions in trade agreements, combined with rising prices, the average rate collected in 1953 was only 16.5 percent. Window glass duties followed a parallel downward course. In 1953 the duties were

17.4 percent of the foreign value. Twenty years earlier the percentage had been almost 70.

At present the production of plate glass and window glass is very largely in the hands of two companies, Pittsburgh Plate Glass and Libbey-Owens-Ford. Economies of large-scale production and management, made possible by mechanization, have been principally responsible for this concentration. But the restriction of foreign competition by the tariff has been a contributing factor.[2]

During World War II and in the early postwar years, when imports of window glass and plate glass were negligible, the tariff cuts were painless, but in 1953 and 1954 complaints of injury were heard. Increasing imports were cited in June 1954 as the cause for the closing of several factories in West Virginia and for the laying off in others of several hundred workers.[3] Viewing this situation, one manufacturer predicted that the effect of future lowering of import duties would be "little short of cataclysmic." [4] But the 1953-54 depression in the flat glass industry proved to be a short-run affair resulting from domestic factors, stagnation in building activity and declining sales of new automobiles, rather than from increased imports. With the upturn in domestic business, the two leading domestic producers made a rapid recovery. Within a 12-month period all their facilities were again in operation. Other companies which had been slow in adapting new processes were reported to be doing less well.

Pressed and blown glassware. The manufacture of hand-fashioned glass tableware, the product with which we are chiefly concerned in this chapter, is considered for statistical purposes a subdivision of pressed and blown glassware, a broad category comprising thousands of different items in three main groups: (1) tableware, kitchen utensils, and art objects;

---

[2] George W. Stocking and Myron W. Watkins, *Monopoly and Free Enterprise* (New York: Twentieth Century Fund, 1951), pp. 124-126, 475; Pearce Davis, *The Development of the American Glass Industry* (Cambridge: Harvard University Press, 1949), pp. 203, 268.

[3] See remarks of the Hon. Robert C. Byrd of West Virginia, in *Congressional Record*, 83rd Cong., 2d sess. (June 8, 1954), p. A4244. (Daily edition.)

[4] Mr. W. A. Gordon, Pittsburgh Plate Glass Company, in *National Glass Budget* (January 8, 1955), p. 17.

(2) illuminating and electronic ware; (3) technical, scientific and other pressed and blown ware.

The first steps in the use of machinery in making pressed glass were taken very early, before 1860. But really significant developments in mechanization did not come until the years 1890-1930. After 1930 rapid progress was made in the use of fully automatic machines in blowing glass for the manufacture of light bulbs, illuminating glass, glass tubing, and tableware and art objects. Thus progressively, as mechanization reduced costs and prices, import competition declined and the bulk of the American market in pressed and blown ware was taken over by domestic firms. But machines never completely displaced hand processes in this branch of glassmaking. The production of hand-fashioned tableware and art objects remained a vulnerable spot. The moderate reduction in import duties on these products, brought about in trade agreements, was followed in postwar years by a substantial increase in imports. These years have also witnessed declining domestic production and falling off in employment. Profits have been unsatisfactory, and some firms have gone out of business.

How Glass Tableware Is Made

The production of table glassware and art objects is carried on in the United States both by machine operations and by hand methods. The two types of production divide the industry into two separate and distinct branches. Attempts to combine machine production and hand operations in a single plant or even under a common management have uniformly proved unsuccessful.

The feature which is generally regarded as distinguishing "hand" from "machine" production of glassware is in the method by which the molten glass is taken from the pot or tank in which the glass has been melted for shaping into the final article (by blowing or pressing). In hand production a hand operator dips a pipe or rod into the molten glass and collects (gathers) the proper amount for the item to be made. In machine production the molten glass is fed automatically to the machines by which the articles are shaped. . . .

Use of equipment for the continuous feeding of the hot glass to machines requires a very substantial investment in equipment for the handling of raw material, the installation of a continuous tank for melting the glass, the use of a number of costly feeding and forming machines, a heavy investment in molds, extensive warehouses, and a sales force adapted to selling large quantities of ware.

On the other hand, most hand plants have simple equipment for the mixing of raw material and even the largest hand plants handle only a small fraction of the material that a machine plant requires. Most of the hand plants use individual pots or day tanks for melting the glass, which must be recharged with raw material periodically. No equipment other than a simple iron rod or pipe is used for feeding, and little forming equipment other than molds with simple devices for opening and closing them are required in the hand operation. . . .

In all these essentials the differences between hand plants and machine plants are numerous, chiefly because of the very great difference in rates of output and type of ware produced. A small machine plant would produce nearly 10 times the volume of ware that even the largest hand plants produce.

The difference in the rates of output between a hand plant and a machine plant also has an effect on the types of ware produced. In the automatic machine production of glassware it is not economical to keep changing the articles made. Thus the operator of a machine plant must be assured of a large market for each size, shape, and kind of article he produces. The minimum production per machine for a run on a single article would range from 10,000 to 30,000 pieces. In hand operation several dozen pieces of each article can be made reasonably efficiently.[5] With such limitations on the range of articles he can produce, a machine-plant operator is forced to make articles the demand for which is dependent on the use rather than on the style or design of the ware. The investment required in designs, molds, and sales promotion to produce a new item is considerable, more than a machine manufacturer usually desires to hazard unless assured of a mass market. On the other hand, production by hand methods is very flexible, and thousands of different shapes, styles, and kinds of glassware are

[5] These figures require qualification. For the machine plants a minimum run of a standard item might be as low as 10,000 *pieces*, but for a new article the minimum quantity requirement might be 10,000 *dozen*. Likewise in the hand plants, although occasionally a small manufacturer of high-grade stemware might accept an order for a few dozen pieces, the usual minimum requirement would be the amount a "shop" would produce in a four-hour turn, 350 to 400 pieces. (P. W. B.)

made in order to achieve consumer preference in the market for fancy glassware.[6]

The Mechanized Branch of the Industry

The plants of the 10 or 12 firms which use automatic machinery in making tableware and artware are mostly situated in the triangular area where the states of West Virginia, Pennsylvania and Ohio come together. Most of the factories are large, employing several thousand persons each. Several are owned by firms whose principal business is the manufacture of glass containers.

In contrast to the static condition of the hand-fashioned branch of the industry, production by machine operations has expanded considerably. (See Chart A.) Shipments of machine-made ware, which in prewar years were valued at about $31-$33 million annually, rose to $66 million in 1946 and to $82 million in 1953.[7] During World War II a considerable export trade was built up in machine-made ware so that by the years 1950-1953 about 10 percent of all shipments from domestic factories was sold abroad. Imports are negligible.

Handicraft Production

Hand-fashioned tableware and artware[8] are the principal products of 35 or 40 American factories, of which about 20 are concentrated within a radius of 75 miles of Wheeling, West Virginia. (See map.) Cheap fuel—first coal and, after

[6] U. S. Tariff Commission, *Hand-Blown Glassware*, Report to the President on Investigation No. 22 (Washington: Author, 1953), pp. 20-22.

[7] These and later figures in this section refer to tableware, artware and, in addition, small amounts of kitchenware which cannot be segregated. Cooking ware (heat-resistant) is excluded. No cooking ware is made by hand processes, nor is any imported; hence it does not meet competition in any of the areas under discussion. Dollar values do not include "value added by cutters and decorators"; much of this work is done by separate firms.

[8] Hand-fashioned glassware may be either blown or pressed. Blown ware, such as tumblers and other drinking glasses, bottles, vases and bowls, is formed by forcing air into a molten blob of glass which is then expanded into the desired shape, usually with the help of a mold. Pressed ware is formed by pushing a plunger into a mold partly filled with molten glass which is thus given the desired form. Cups and saucers, plates and other flatware, as well as many ornamental objects, are usually pressed. Hand-fashioned tumblers and stemware are also made by this process; their heavy, massive character distinguishes them from the lighter, thinner blown ware.

CHART A

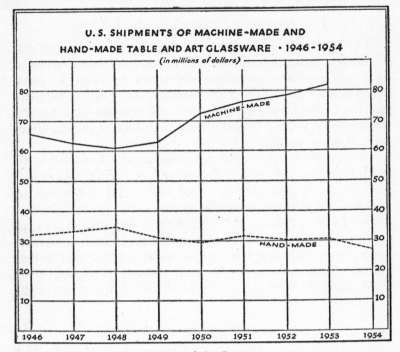

U. S. SHIPMENTS OF MACHINE-MADE AND
HAND-MADE TABLE AND ART GLASSWARE · 1946-1954
(in millions of dollars)

Source: Table 2 and U. S. Bureau of the Census

1880, natural gas—attracted glass factories to this area. Good sand was also easily available. In 1955, 16 factories were in operation in West Virginia and 10 in nearby areas of Ohio and Pennsylvania. Almost all of them are situated in communities of less than 25,000 population where they supply most of the employment. In some cases they are the only industrial enterprises.

The making of glass articles by hand is a small-scale business. Some of the factories employ less than 50 persons each; a few have 500 to 700 workers. Representative firms employ between 100 and 350 persons. Altogether, the firms in the West Virginia area which are making hand-fashioned glassware have about 8,000 workers. The Tariff Commission estimated in 1952 that about 3,500 were engaged in making hand-blown tableware and ornamental objects.

The equipment of a typical factory consists principally of one or two furnaces, usually gas-fired, for melting the batch, and a number of hand-operated molds and presses. Some machinery has been introduced, particularly for decorating,[9] in the processes which follow the initial shaping of the articles. But the glassmaker still fashions his product with a few simple tools, of wood and steel, which resemble closely those in use in European glass works 400 or more years ago.

Investment in the smallest plants producing hand-blown ware, those that employ 25 to 50 workers each, probably does not exceed $500 or $600 per employee. In the largest factories per capita investment might be as high as $3,000 but even so would be much lower than in most American manufacturing industries. Hence fixed costs tend to be low. Raw materials also are cheap. In consequence, labor cost of hand-fashioned glassware is high, making up about 65 percent of the factory selling price. By contrast, the labor costs in the automatic machine plants range from 20 to 25 percent of their selling price.

In the hand plants such as we have described above there is little opportunity for the cost-reducing, large-scale operations which have characterized other branches of the glass industry. No tendency is apparent toward concentration of ownership or control; very rarely does a single firm operate more than one plant. Two attempts at mergers proved unsuccessful. The United States Glass Company, a combination of 15 firms organized in 1891, now operates only two factories. The National Glass Company, which brought together 19 firms in 1899, lasted only a few years.[10]

The group of firms which make glass tableware and art objects by hand furnishes a significant example of the persistence of small-scale business in the United States. As a rule these firms have no connection, financial or otherwise, with

[9] Some factories decorate their own ware by etching, enameling, or by other processes. But decorating is also an ancillary industry which is carried on by some 25 widely scattered firms, many of them in the larger Eastern cities. They purchase blanks from importers as well as from domestic manufacturers; in fact, some of the decorating shops are owned and operated by importers.

[10] See Warren C. Scoville, *Revolution in Glassmaking* (Cambridge: Harvard University Press, 1948), pp. 236-238.

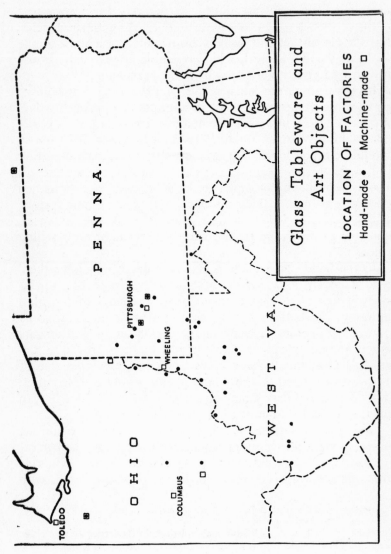

Source: *Glass Factory Yearbook and Directory, 1954*, published by American Glass Review

the large-scale enterprises which make flat glass, glass containers and other products. The Steuben Glass Center, a division of the Corning Glass Works, appears to be the only important exception to this rule. Ownership and management are often in the hands of members of a single family. In postwar years an increased proportion of the hand-blown ware has come from small, nonunion plants situated in isolated communities where wages and living costs are lower than in the larger centers. A few of the smaller firms have been set up on a cooperative basis by groups of skilled workmen.

Postwar Depression

There is plenty of evidence that in this country the making of hand-fashioned glassware, taken as a whole, is not a prosperous industry. In postwar years the shipments from domestic factories, whether measured in dozens or in dollars, have declined steadily. Employment has fallen, some firms have failed, and the average level of profits for those which have remained in business has been low. As we shall see later, the decline in the industry was evident even before World War II, but comparable statistics are lacking for that period, and the war period, of course, was abnormal. So for the moment we shall confine our attention to postwar developments.

Imports had disappeared during the war and in the early postwar years. To fill this gap domestic shipments[11] of hand-fashioned tumblers and stemware rose to a peak of 6.4 million dozen pieces, valued at $15.4 million, in 1946. In succeeding years shipments fell to 2.4 million dozen in 1953, valued at $12.4 million. Including ornamental ware, for which quantity figures are not available, the sales value of all shipments from domestic factories declined from $32 million in 1946 to $27 million in 1954. (See Table 2 and Chart A.)

Roughly parallel with the decline in production, employment fell off. In the plants making hand-blown glassware there were 4,750 workers in 1946 and only 3,500 six years later. Total employment in 1953, including workers making pressed glass, also a hand operation, was about 8,000.

[11] The U. S. Bureau of the Census does not report production of glassware, but only shipments. In this case the Tariff Commission has estimated that shipments differ from production by less than 5 percent.

Table 2

U. S. SHIPMENTS OF HAND-MADE GLASS TABLEWARE
AND ARTWARE, 1946-1954

(in thousands of dollars)

| Year | Tumblers, goblets and other stemware | | | All shipments (including artware) |
	Pressed	Blown	Total	
1946	3,203	12,175	15,378	32,003
1947	2,738	14,806	17,544	33,106
1948	2,595	14,134	16,729	34,640
1949	2,024	12,700	14,724	30,737
1950	1,825	11,901	13,726	29,510
1951	1,758	11,779	13,537	31,590
1952	1,726	10,712	12,438	30,113
1953	2,025	10,350	12,375	30,335
1954	n.a.	n.a.	n.a.	27,090

Source: U. S. Bureau of the Census

Because some of the factories went on part time during
this period, the decline in man-hours was even greater. The
displacement of glass workers has aggravated, in a number of
communities, an already bad labor situation. Nineteen of the
factories covered in this study are situated in IV-A areas, with
6-12 percent unemployment, and 6 in IV-B areas, where unemployment was over 12 percent in early 1955.[12]

Manufacturers have repeatedly stated to Congressional committees and to government agencies that their industry has
not been prospering. They have complained that many factories have operated at a loss and that only a few have been
breaking even. A 1953 report of the Tariff Commission confirmed their statements, showing that the profits earned in the
production of pressed and blown glass in postwar years were
lower than the average of all manufacturing industries and
that several firms had gone bankrupt or discontinued operations.[13]

But the depression in the industry has not affected all firms
with equal force. Some plants have shut down temporarily or

[12] U. S. Department of Labor, Bimonthly Summary of Labor Market Developments in Major Areas (March 1955).
[13] U. S. Tariff Commission, Hand-Blown Glassware, cited, pp. 30, 67-68.

have cut down their working force. A few have gone bankrupt or have sold out and dismissed their workers. The causes
of distress or business failure are varied. For example, the
deaths of the principal owners of three glass companies were
largely responsible for their going into bankruptcy and for
the closing of four plants which they had operated. Labor
troubles have hit some firms harder than others. Some have
suffered losses from fires or from floods. But, in addition, a
number of well-established firms have suffered declining
profits in postwar years, and even losses, which seem attributable to market conditions rather than to random factors.

Among the firms which report profitable operations there
is considerable diversity. A number of small plants in isolated
communities have managed to keep going by hiring nonunion
labor and by reducing overhead costs to a bare minimum.
Even so, strict accounting practices might show that some
of them were "selling bricks and mortar" as well as glassware.
Low labor costs are found in a number of small factories
organized on a cooperative, or semicooperative, basis. Among
the moving spirits are skilled glass workers displaced from
their jobs by the failure of the firm which formerly employed
them. Some of these enterprises have been fairly successful.
More often, however, the cooperators, although competent
craftsmen, lack the necessary training and experience in business management.

Among the 20-odd firms for which reliable information is
available, there are five or six substantial concerns which, by
the exercise of exceptionally good business management, have
been able to maintain profitable operations. They have introduced economies in production and have built up a market for
unique products and designs.

The Reduction in Import Duties, 1935-1955

Manufacturers find the explanation of the depressed state
of their business in tariff reduction and in the ensuing postwar
increase in imports. The Tariff Act of 1930, which represented
the peak of a long upward trend in import duties, taxed
foreign glassware in paragraph 218(f) at a flat rate of 60
percent. The beautiful simplicity of this paragraph was destroyed in a series of trade agreements, beginning in 1935,
which complicated the business of importing without effect-

Table 3

U. S. RATES OF DUTY ON HAND-MADE GLASSWARE

(percent ad valorem; cents per unit)

	Tariff Act of 1930	Effective January 1 1945	1955 rate[a]
Par. 218(f)			
Table and kitchen articles and utensils, and all articles of every description, n.s.p.f. (exc. Christmas tree ornaments), composed wholly or in chief value of glass, blown or partly blown from molten glass gathered by hand:			
Articles primarily designed for ornamental purposes, decorated chiefly by engraving and valued at not less than $8 each..................	60%	30%	15%
Articles and utensils commercially known as bubble glass:			
Cut or engraved and valued—			
$1 or more, but under $3, each................	60%	45%	50¢[b]
$3 or more each.........	60%	45%	22½%
Other...................	60%	30%	30%
Other articles and utensils:			
Cut or engraved and valued—			
$1 or more, but under $3, each................	60%	45%	50¢[b]
$3 or more each.........	60%	45%	22½%
Other...................	60%	60%	50¢[c]

[a] Not applicable to Communist-dominated countries or areas, which pay 60%.
[b] Minimum, 30% ad valorem.
[c] Minimum, 30% ad valorem; maximum, 50% ad valorem. In the 1955 trade agreement with Japan this rate was reduced to 30% ad valorem on articles other than tableware and artware. These articles include wind chimes, miniature glass figures and artificial gem stones, of which domestic production is negligible.

ing any serious reduction in the protection afforded to American manufacturers. This was accomplished by the introduction of "value brackets" (subclassifications) in the agreements with Sweden in 1935 and the United Kingdom in 1939, which restricted the benefits of the lowered duties to the medium- and high-priced articles imported principally from those countries. These agreements and later multilateral bargaining reduced the rate on ornamental objects valued at $8 a piece and over to 15 percent; other rates were cut to 30 percent. But the bulk of the imports, plain undecorated ware valued at less than $1 each and imported principally from Japan, fell only to 50 percent. (See Table 3.) The 1955 trade agreement with Japan made no concessions on imports of hand-fashioned glass tableware and artware.

The Postwar Boom in Imports

The rapid rise after the close of World War II in imports[14]

[14] In the use of official statistics of imports of glassware, as reported by the Bureau of the Census, two difficulties arise: (1) The Bureau does not distinguish between hand-made and machine-made products nor, in all cases, between pressed and blown ware. The Tariff Commission, however, in examining foreign invoices for selected years, has found that almost all imported glassware is hand-made, and more than 90 percent of it is blown ware. (2) The imports of glassware, as reported by the Census Bureau, include not only tableware and artware but also certain glass articles, such as colored glass stones and mosaics, glass eyes and glass wind chimes, which are not germane to this study since they are not produced by any of the American firms which make hand-fashioned glass tableware. The Tariff Commission has estimated that in the years 1947-1952 the extraneous items made up 19 to 27 percent of all the glassware imports which we are here considering. The reader should therefore keep in mind that the import values used in this chapter overstate the impact of foreign tableware and artware on the domestic market.

Statistics of the Census Bureau have been used in this study since they are available for 1953 and 1954. The following table indicates the disparity between these data and the more refined statistics of the Tariff Commission.

	Census Bureau All glass imports under par. 218(f)ᵃ	Tariff Commission Imports of glass table and artware
	(foreign value, in thousands of dollars)	
1950	3,321	2,427
1951	4,469	3,504
1952	4,533	3,655

ᵃ Except Christmas tree ornaments.

CHART B

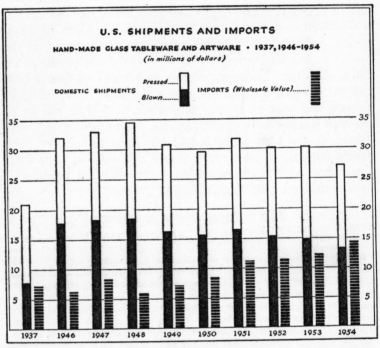

Source: Tables 4 and 5 and U. S. Bureau of the Census

of hand-pressed and hand-blown glassware contrasts with the decline in domestic production. (See Table 4 and Chart B.) The estimated U. S. wholesale value of foreign glassware brought into this country in 1946 was $6.1 million; eight years later the corresponding figure was $14.4 million. In 1954 the foreign-made glassware supplied 35 percent of apparent consumption, i.e., of all purchases in the American market; in 1946 the percentage had been only 17.

The impact of imports in the American market may in fact be greater than is indicated in Tables 4 and 5. Imports consist almost entirely of hand-blown ware, whereas American factories make both pressed and blown ware. A calculation based on the assumption that 90 percent of the imports are hand-blown ware indicates that the foreign products in 1954 supplied nearly 50 percent of the domestic market for that type

Table 4

U. S. IMPORTS OF HAND-MADE GLASS TABLEWARE
AND ARTWARE, 1936-38, 1946-1954

(in thousands of dollars)

Year	Foreign value	Estimated wholesale value[a]
1936–38 average	2,358	5,895
1946	2,437	6,092
1947	3,307	8,268
1948	2,322	5,805
1949	2,866	7,165
1950	3,321	8,303
1951	4,469	11,172
1952	4,533	11,333
1953	4,950	12,375
1954	5,756	14,390

[a] Wholesale values in the United States have been estimated by the U. S. Tariff Commission at 175 percent of duty-paid foreign value, equivalent to 250 percent of foreign invoice value (Investigation No. 22, pp. 48, 49). By substituting wholesale values in the U. S. market for foreign invoice values, the impact of imports can be more accurately measured since both foreign and domestic goods are thus brought into a common market.
Source: U. S. Bureau of the Census

of table and ornamental ware, as compared with about 30 percent in 1947.

Analysis of the sources of the imports in Table 6 shows that the gains were made principally by the reviving glassware industries of Japan, West Germany and Austria. The increase of imports from these countries in the years 1947 to 1953 amounted to $2 million, which was about $350,000 more than the total increase in imports in these years. This apparent paradox was explained by the virtual disappearance of imports from Czechoslovakia.

Why Czech Glassware Disappeared from U. S. Markets

In prewar years most of the imported tableware and artware came from Czechoslovakia. Political rather than economic factors explain the relative unimportance of that source at present. The 1938 trade agreement reduced import duties on Czech glassware. But in April 1939, after Hitler's invasion,

Table 5

HAND-MADE GLASS TABLEWARE AND ART OBJECTS:
DOMESTIC SHIPMENTS, EXPORTS, IMPORTS AND
APPARENT CONSUMPTION, 1937, 1946-1954

Year	Domestic shipments	Exports	Imports[a]	Apparent consumption	Ratio of imports to consumption (percent)
		(in thousands of dollars)			
1937	21,000	1,750[b]	7,315	26,565	27.5
1946	32,003	1,493	6,092	36,602	16.6
1947	33,106	1,108	8,268	40,266	20.5
1948	34,640	408	5,805	40,037	14.5
1949	30,737	347	7,165	37,555	19.1
1950	29,510	333	8,303	37,480	22.2
1951	31,590	430	11,172	42,332	26.4
1952	30,113	313	11,333	41,133	27.6
1953	30,335	321	12,375	42,389	29.2
1954	27,090	222	14,390	41,258	34.9

[a] Wholesale value; includes a small amount of machine-made ware.
[b] Includes a small amount of machine-made ware.
Source: U. S. Bureau of the Census

the United States denied Czechoslovakia most-favored-nation treatment and again imposed the 1930 rate of 60 percent on imports from that country. World War II cut off all imports from enemy and occupied countries, and, after the war, the recovery of the Czech glassware industry was hindered by the loss of many of its best workers through the expulsion of the Sudeten Germans.

Czechoslovakia, having been a party to the Geneva agreement (effective January 1, 1948), benefited for a few years from the American concessions on glassware. But on November 1, 1951, the United States, in accordance with Section 5 of the Trade Agreements Extension Act of 1951, withdrew all trade agreement concessions from the U.S.S.R. and the Iron Curtain countries. This action was only nominal, for the State Department, a month earlier, had already imposed what amounted to an embargo on all imports from Czechoslovakia. Actually, the Department had announced that there

Table 6

U. S. IMPORTS OF HAND-MADE GLASS TABLEWARE AND ARTWARE, BY COUNTRIES, 1936-37, 1947-54

(foreign value, in thousands of dollars)

	1936-37 (average)	1947	1948	1949	1950	1951	1952	1953	1954[a]
Total	2,533	3,307	2,322	2,866	3,321	4,469	4,533	4,950	5,756[a]
West Germany	367	4	115	113	303	720	915	1,042	1,123
Sweden	109	598	351	258	266	558	670	675	620
Japan	468	1	60	185	320	510	549	617	608
Austria	29	56	3	33	73	238	267	403	436
Italy	89	232	123	184	274	520	673	515	399
France	96	172	122	180	254	346	353	360	391
United Kingdom	93	313	403	401	396	461	415	449	309
Czechoslovakia	999	1,248	527	468	455	456	12	36	154
Belgium	137	191	199	214	259	276	147	137	128
Hungary	43	20	41	91	74	18	75	62	54

[a] The total value of imports for 1954 includes $1,030,000 of glassware which, owing to a change in the method of recording imports, cannot be distributed by countries. Consequently, the 1954 imports ascribed to each country understate, in most cases if not in all, the value of glassware received from that country.
Source: U. S. Bureau of the Census

would be an indefinite delay in certifying invoices on exports of Czech goods to the United States. This action was part of a program of economic pressure designed to secure the release of William Oatis.[15] Oatis was released on May 15, 1953, and shortly thereafter invoices were again certified. Meanwhile, imports of Czech glassware dropped from $456,400 in 1951, to $11,700 in 1952 and $35,600 in 1953. Imports recovered to somewhat over $154,000 in 1954 but are still limited by the unfavorable attitude of American dealers and consumers which amounts to an informal boycott of glassware from Iron Curtain countries.

Consumers' Preferences

Comparison of statistics of imports with production affords an imperfect and sometimes misleading view of what the invasion of his home market may mean to the American manufacturer. The kind and quality of the imports must also be considered, their prices, how they are marketed and other factors which may be described as "conditions of competition."

Americans buy imported glassware, as they do many other foreign-made products, not so much because it is cheaper than the domestic product as because it is different. Consequently, importers and buyers for department stores are always on the lookout for unusual designs and combinations of colors. Some of the imported tableware can be identified at once as a kind not made in the United States and hence not directly competitive with a product of any American factory. Such noncompetitive imports include secondhand ware (semiantique), cut cased glassware, bubble glass and enameled lusters. Certain foreign firms, moreover, have established a reputation for distinctive products, the like of which could not be made in this country except at prohibitive costs; for example, the deeply cut English Waterford glass, the Swedish Orrefors, the Belgian Val St. Lambert, the French Baccarat and the Italian Murano. The proportion of noncompetitive goods was estimated by the Republican members of the Tariff Commission

[15] Oatis, an American newspaper correspondent, had been convicted of espionage and sentenced (July 4, 1951) to 10 years' imprisonment.

at 29 percent of total imports, and by the Democratic members at about half.

English, Swedish, Italian and other foreign glassware enjoys a certain market preference over the products of most American factories, especially among the more well-informed and discriminating buyers. The imported stemware and art objects, because of their prestige value, will often sell at prices higher than those of the most nearly comparable domestic ware. Importers have testified at a Tariff Commission hearing that some of the American factories sell their finest lead crystal, duplicates of foreign designs, at lower prices than the originals.[16]

Glassware from some foreign countries, however, meets "consumer resistance." Prejudice against German goods, although rapidly disappearing, is still noticeable in some cities. Unwillingness of almost all importing firms to have anything to do with the U.S.S.R. or its satellites is a major handicap in selling glassware made in Czechoslovakia, Poland and Hungary. Fear of unfavorable customer reaction helps to explain why some department stores, jewelry stores and gift shops refuse to handle Japanese glassware, although low price and inferior quality are perhaps more often responsible. It is significant that in advertisements the Japanese ware is almost never referred to as "Japanese" but usually as "imported."

In general, both the imported and the domestic glassware reaches the consumer through the same retail outlets. The higher-priced ware is sold in department stores, jewelry stores and gift shops. In chain stores imports from Japan meet the cheapest grades of domestic hand-made glass, and also the machine-made product. The big mail order houses in their catalogues display both imported and domestic stemware. The institutional trade, i.e., sales to bars, restaurants, hotels, hospitals, etc.—which takes 10 to 15 percent of all domestic shipments of hand-blown ware—seems not to have been invaded by the foreign manufacturers. But in this market, which ab-

---

[16] *Hearing on Hand-Blown Glassware*, before the U. S. Tariff Commission, on Investigation No. 22 under Section 7 of the Trade Agreements Extension Act of 1951 (Washington, March 2, 1953), pp. 28, 32, 71. (Stenographic transcript.)

sorbs large quantities of standardized goblets and other stem-ware, the hand-fashioned glass meets strong competition from domestic machine-made products.

Prices

For a comparison of prices, the Tariff Commission has grouped the imported and the domestic ware into three broad categories: (1) low-priced ware selling at under $12 a dozen wholesale, (2) medium-priced ware selling from $12 to $24 a dozen, and (3) high-priced ware selling at $24 a dozen and over. The following table shows the proportion of imported and domestic ware which in 1951 sold in each of these categories:

Wholesale price (per dozen)	Approximate retail price (per piece)	Percent of total sales	
		Domestic	Imported
Under $12	Under $2	60.3	39.3
$12-24	$2-4	27.1	20.0
$24 and over	$4 and over	12.6	40.7

Source: U. S. Tariff Commission, *Hand-Blown Glassware*, cited, p. 86. Computed from data supplied to the Commission by domestic producers and importers.

The bulk of the domestic product, these figures indicate, was in the lowest price range, and about 40 percent of the imports, largely Japanese goods, fell into this category. In the highest price bracket the imported ware dominated the market. A 1955 survey by the *Retailing Daily*,[17] covering 125 stores in 30 cities across the country, gave the following results:

Retail price per piece	Percent of total sales	
	Domestic	Imported
Under $1	30	57
$1 to $2	21	23
$2 to $3	45	9
Over $3	4	11

The most popular price for imported stemware, according to this survey, was 59 cents each; for domestic stemware, $1.50 to $2.25. The price range for the best selling items was: imported, 50 cents to $7.00; domestic, 40 cents to $3.50. The

[17] *Retailing Daily*, June 6, 1955, p. 42.

Retailing Daily found that 80 percent of the imported glass-ware sold at less than $2 per piece. Four years earlier the Tariff Commission had found that only 39 percent sold in this price range. This discrepancy may be explained by the exceptionally large increase in imports from Japan in the intervening four years.

Wages and Labor Conditions

High, and rapidly rising, wages, according to American manufacturers, constitute a major handicap in competing with foreign producers of glassware. Wages in the glassware industries of the United States and of the principal competing countries, as reported recently by the Department of Labor, were as follows:

	U. S. currency
United States (January 1955)	
Average for pressed and blown, both automatic and hand plants	$1.83
Glass containers	1.85
Flat glass	2.58
Sweden (average 1953)	.69
United Kingdom (April 1954)	.35-.60
West Germany (May 1954)	.24-.48
Belgium (December 1953)	.25-.46
Japan (average 1953)	.23

In the United States, although the conditions of employment and the nature of the work are not strictly comparable, the wages paid in the machine plants set a standard to which the hand plants in general must conform.

The large investment of capital equipment in the automatic machine plants reduces labor costs to only 20 to 25 percent of factory price. These plants meet no foreign competition in their home market and are able to export about 10 percent of their products. The production of hand-fashioned glass, on the other hand, is a labor-intensive operation. This branch of the industry affords little opportunity, as we have pointed out earlier, for reducing labor costs by introducing mass-production techniques. Under these conditions, low foreign wages constitute a real competitive advantage. This advantage is accentuated by the higher rate of output per worker in some foreign countries. American manufacturers and importers who in 1954 visited factories in West Germany found productivity abroad considerably above that at home. The substitution of machines for hand labor in some processes was largely responsible. Moreover, the output of foreign workers is not limited by the restrictions on production which are imposed, or sanctioned, by American trade unions.

About 85 percent of the workers in the hand plants, according to union estimates, are members of the American Flint Glassworkers Union, one of the oldest and strongest organizations in the American Federation of Labor. For many years union membership was limited to only the skilled glassmakers, but recently the unskilled or "miscellaneous" workers, who make up 75 to 80 percent of the total labor force, have been brought in.

After World War I the union abandoned formal restrictions on production and other types of featherbedding. In many unionized shops, however, workers limit production by indirect methods, for example, by setting the "turn" (the normal production for four hours) at a low figure, by demanding excessive rest periods, or by insisting on the hiring of unneeded workers. A few employers, however, deny the existence of restrictions of any kind in their factories.

In postwar years, according to the Tariff Commission, domestic manufacturers have been able to raise their selling prices by about 60 percent. This, they say, has not been enough to compensate them for higher costs, particularly labor costs. The records of one of the larger manufacturers show that in the period from 1946-1953 his average hourly wages increased by 89 percent, from 97 cents to $1.83. In the same period the average selling price of his product per dozen rose 69 percent, from $7.78 to $13.18.

Are Imports Responsible for the Decline in Hand-fashioned Glassware?

There seems to be plenty of evidence that the production of hand-fashioned tableware and artware in recent years has not shared in the prosperity enjoyed by other branches of the glass industry or by manufacturing in general. In fact, there seems to be some justification for referring to it as a declining industry. For this situation there are three principal causes: (1) the increased competition from the reviving glass-exporting industries of Western Europe and Japan; (2) the competition of domestic machine-made stemware; and (3) the contraction in the market for stemware as the result of changed habits of living and entertaining.

Manufacturers find the source of their difficulties in the increased postwar competition from imports. Between 1947 and 1954, the wholesale value of imports increased from $8.3 million to $14.4 million, and they now supply more than one-third of the domestic market. In these years domestic production declined. But a glance at the history of the domestic hand-fashioned glassware industry shows that its decline did not date from 1947 when the postwar import competition first became severe. Even in prewar years the industry appears to have been in a more or less chronically insecure position. An investigation of representative firms made in 1941 by the U. S. Department of Commerce[18] showed that half of them lost money in the years 1937 to 1940; in those years the average rate of net profit on sales for the group was about 2 percent. Employment was irregular and uncertain. During World War II, it is true, the interruption of imports and the inflation of prices and incomes brought increased sales and high profits. But this prosperity was only a brief interruption in a long-term downward trend.

In September 1952 the domestic producers appealed to the Tariff Commission for relief, alleging that imports of foreign-made glass tableware and artware were causing injury.[19] After investigation by its experts and a public hearing, the Commission rendered a split decision. Three Republican members

[18] The sample used by the Commerce Department accounted for the bulk of the industry's production. See U. S. Department of Commerce, *Economic Survey of the Hand-made Table Glassware Industry* (Washington: Author, 1942), Table 2.
[19] Under the "escape clause" which has been a standard feature of all trade agreements since 1948. This clause reserves for the United States the right to withdraw a tariff concession on any article which is being imported in such increased quantities as to cause or threaten serious injury to domestic producers of like or directly competing products. (See Executive Order 9832, February 25, 1947.) Neither the Executive Order nor subsequent legislation provided a definition of what constitutes injury. Actually, in interpreting the clause the Tariff Commission has used as criteria trends in domestic production, employment and profits of domestic firms.

found evidence of injury and recommended to the President that he raise import duties substantially.[20] Three Democratic members denied that increased imports of glass tableware and art objects had caused or threatened to cause serious injury to the domestic industry producing similar items. They recognized the deterioration in the domestic industry but ascribed it to other causes, viz., (1) the competition of machine-made glassware of American make, and (2) the shrinkage in the domestic market for stemware, the principal product of the American plants utilizing hand processes. President Eisenhower accepted the view of the Democratic members and refused to raise the import duties.

The Competition of Machine-made Glassware

The President wrote: "After the closest possible study of the situation on the basis of the data available, I believe that the fundamental cause of the difficulties of this industry lies in competition offered by machine-made glassware to both imported and domestic hand-made ware." [21] Taking a long-run view, the President pointed out that between 1937 and 1952 total consumption of hand-blown tumblers and stemware had fallen from 7.2 million dozen pieces to 3 million. This decline occurred at a time when population and national income were rapidly rising, and in this same period consumption of machine-made tumblers and stemware rose from 40 million dozen to 65 million. The result was that, whereas in 1937 the consumption of hand-blown glassware had been more than one-fifth of the machine-made product (tumblers and stemware combined), 15 years later the ratio was less than one-twentieth.[22]

The President also pointed out that imports, measured in

[20] They suggested the following rates as necessary to prevent the continuance of injury:

Cut or engraved articles and utensils valued at less than
$3 each but not less than $1 each .... 67½% ad valorem
Other articles and utensils, valued at less than $3
each .... 90% ad valorem

[21] In identical letters to Chairman Millikin of the Senate Finance Committee and Chairman Reed of the House Committee on Ways and Means. Press release of September 9, 1954.

[22] Consumption of hand-blown ware in 1937 was abnormally large; if an average of 1936-1937 had been used the apparent rate of decline would have been somewhat less but not enough to invalidate the comparison.

dozens, in spite of the steady increase after 1946, had not in 1952 come close to regaining their prewar volume. On a quantity basis, the imports supplied about the same proportion of the domestic market in 1952 as in 1937.

Reporting in 1948, the U. S. Tariff Commission had found that the invasion of the domestic market by machine-produced glassware had caused the decline, between 1929 and 1935, in the sales of hand-blown glass.[23] About 1925, the Libbey Glass Company, at one time one of the largest producers of hand-fashioned ware, devised a machine for making thin, blown tumblers. Within a few years the rapid expansion of low-cost machine production took away almost all the tumbler business from the factories making glassware by hand, including Libbey's own factory in Toledo, Ohio. A few years later, in 1935, new machines were devised, again by Libbey, for producing "sham" tumblers, i.e., those with heavy bottoms, by machine. Thus the handicraft branch of the industry lost another slice of the American market.

The stemware field, the last refuge of the hand plants, was not invaded by machine-made products until after World War II when the Libbey company began mass production by newly perfected machines. At present practically all the stemware used in bars, restaurants and hotels, except in a few of the more exclusive, is machine-made. Thus, over a period of some 20 years the manufacturers of hand-fashioned glassware suffered progressively the loss of markets for items which formerly had made up a large part of their total output. During World War II competition from the machine product was less noticeable, for the manufacturers received large orders for hand-fashioned ware for use in laboratories and hospitals and for specific military purposes, as in radar equipment. To produce these articles by machine processes was impracticable.

Manufacturers who fashion stemware and art objects by hand do not regard the competition of machine-made ware as a major source of their difficulties, and they deny that it is comparable with their products. Machine-made ware, they assert, because of its uniformity lacks the artistic qualities of hand-made glassware. The machine-made product, they point out, is sold principally in chain stores and hardware stores, by

[23] U. S. Tariff Commission, *Summaries of Tariff Information*, v. 2, pt. 2 (Washington: GPO, 1948), p. 46.

mail order houses and, in smaller cities, by department stores. Jewelry stores, gift shops and the more exclusive department stores in the larger cities usually handle only hand-fashioned glassware.

Nevertheless, it seems that the markets for the hand-made and the machine-made products do overlap. The cheapest grades of hand-blown glassware, retailing from 29 to 49 cents each, are displayed in chain stores side by side with machine-made ware in much the same price range. Also, machine-made tumblers and stemware, when decorated by gray cutting or polished cutting, are sold in some of the better shops in competition with similarly decorated hand-fashioned ware.

The small plants producing stemware which sells in the same price range as the machine-made product keep in business principally because of their superior flexibility. They can afford to take orders for 25 or 30 dozen of a single item; the machine plant would probably not want to handle an order for less than a day's run, which might be as high as 6,000 dozen. A small plant will sometimes take a large order from a department store or mail order house which would be turned down by a larger factory for fear of tying up too large a part of its facilities.

The Declining Market for Stemware

If the market for hand-fashioned glassware were expanding, the American manufacturers might be able to take the competition from imports and from automatic machine plants in their stride. Unfortunately for them, however, the long-term trend of consumption, including both domestic and imported products, is not up but down. Total sales in the American market of all hand-blown tableware and artware (including imports as well as domestic production) were as follows:

1937	7,240,000 dozen
1946	5,996,000 "
1947	4,162,000 "
1950	3,580,000 "
1951	3,596,000 "
1952	3,461,000 "
1953	3,860,000 "

Calculated on a per capita basis, taking into account the growth of population, the 1937 sales of glassware were 67 pieces per 100 persons; in 1947, 35 pieces, and in 1953, 30 pieces.

The dollar values of sales of hand-blown and pressed ware have risen. In 1937 they were $26.6 million; in 1947, $40.3 million; and in 1954, $41.3 million. But this increase resulted from (1) the intervening rise in the price level, and (2) the upgrading of the domestic product. Reduced in terms of purchasing power (1947-49 = 100), the sales would be approximately as follows:

1937	$47.4 million
1947	41.8 "
1954	37.4 "

Stemware, particularly in the lower price range, is being displaced by tumblers, a manifestation of the trend toward more informal ways of living which has also affected the consumption of woolens and worsteds and fine chinaware. Small, modern, suburban houses and city apartments lack the space to store the dozens of goblets, wineglasses and other stemware which graced the tables of an earlier generation. Servants are lacking to care for the glassware, and many housewives hesitate to entrust their more valuable and fragile pieces to modern dishwashing machines. The present generation drinks little wine. It serves cocktails in stemware, usually machine-made, and old-fashioneds and highballs, as well as soft drinks, in machine-made tumblers. In short, stemware is less and less consistent with the pattern of living in America.

Tumblers are marketed in increasing quantities and in a bewildering array of shapes and decorations. But this type of drinking utensil, although it may be decorated by hand, is made almost exclusively by automatic machines. Consequently, any expansion of the market in this direction does not help the firms using hand processes. The hard fact seems to be that the total market for stemware, the principal hand-fashioned product, is contracting. This shrinkage of the market has affected importers as well as domestic manufacturers.

Adjustment to New Conditions

Among the causes for the decline in the hand-fashioned

glassware industry, changes in technology and in consumers' preferences, I believe, are fundamental, and increased imports only contributory. Had imports remained constant at the 1947 level, the domestic industry might have fared somewhat better, but it could not have profited by an expanding market. Its sales would still have been limited by the competitive machine product and by the shift in consumers' tastes. Thus, even with stable or even declining competition from foreign glassware, the domestic producers would have been confronted with a serious problem of adjustment to new conditions in their domestic market. Increased imports, from one point of view, may have made adjustment more difficult, but they did not prevent it from taking place. In fact, it is probably true that the pressure of foreign competition has been responsible in a number of cases for accelerating the process.

Over-all statistics of production, employment and profits indicate that the manufacture of glass tableware and artware by hand processes is a declining industry. But examination of the operations of individual firms reveals significant variations which are concealed by data referring to the industry as a whole. Some firms, undoubtedly, are in a bad way, but others show a good deal of vitality. They have displayed ingenuity and enterprise in adapting their operations to the new conditions of competition. Adjustment, it should be remarked, has been a *general* remedy for declining sales and profits, no matter whether the injury has come from abroad or from changes in the domestic market. For the most part, the new business policies and procedures have not been specifically designed to meet, or to evade, competition from imports. Two general methods of adjustment have been (1) cutting costs by introducing economies in production and in marketing, and (2) diversification of products. Another type of adjustment, designed specifically to meet increased competition from abroad, has been the combination of importing with manufacturing.

Cost-reducing Techniques

Manufacturers of hand-blown tableware and artware cannot revive their declining industry by mechanizing it. Two firms which experimented with making tableware by automatic machines found the venture unprofitable. Their labor force, they found, was not readily transferable from one type of production to the other, and the marketing problems were entirely different. Salesmen needed retraining so that they could think in hundreds, not dozens. This meant finding a new set of customers.

The manufacture of hand-fashioned glassware is, and must remain, typically a handicraft industry. From the moment the hot metal is taken from the pot or from the furnace, hand-fashioned glassware has to be made by hand. For some items 15 to 30 separate operations are involved before they leave the factory. The ability of the manufacturers to successfully market their products depends upon qualities of elegance and originality of design, and perfection of workmanship, characteristics which distinguish hand-fashioned glassware from machine-made products. Hence, mechanization on any extended scale seems out of the question. A further limitation on the introduction of cost-reducing techniques is found in some factories in the opposition of strongly entrenched trade union organizations.

In some plants continuous tank furnaces have been substituted for pot furnaces, thus reducing fuel and labor costs. Firms that operate their own decorating departments have uniformly adopted simple, power-driven machinery for cutting and grinding, but these operations still involve rather high labor costs. Recently, however, one of the largest and most progressive firms, the Fostoria Glass Company, installed specially designed machinery for etching glassware which does away with the work of 18 employees. The best possibility for a reduction in manufacturing costs seems to lie, not in a substitution of machines for hand operations, but in making those operations less costly through the introduction of time and motion studies. By careful analysis of these operations, one firm has been able to simplify them, thus achieving a considerable reduction in its labor costs. It seems probable that similar results might be obtained by other manufacturers if they were able to overcome trade union opposition. Now that the acceptance of unskilled workers has brought a new and perhaps more progressive element into the unions, their leaders may prove less obstructive.

Specialization and Diversification

The salvation of the hand-fashioned glass industry, it seems, lies in maintaining a high degree of flexibility in output and exploiting that advantage to the maximum. For even with maximum use of labor-saving devices and with ideal labor-management relations, production costs for *identical items* of tableware or artware will almost certainly remain substantially higher in this country than in Western Europe and, particularly, in Japan. The cost differences will probably be greater than could be offset by the present import duties, or by any future duties which are within the range of reasonable expectation. If these premises are correct, it seems that the sensible course for American manufacturers is not to make what the foreigner is making, not to try to beat him at his own game, but to offer the American housewife something new and different.

In their search for types of glassware which are not sensitive to import competition and which cannot be economically made by automatic machines, a few manufacturers have specialized in pressed glass. In this product the American industry has long maintained a dominant position. Articles of pressed glass are heavier than comparable blown ware items; hence transport costs afford a greater measure of natural protection. Furthermore, pressed glass seems less in favor abroad, and consequently foreign glass factories have practically no home market for this product. For these reasons imports into the United States have remained negligible. Recently, however, exports by American machinery manufacturers of hand-pressing equipment have raised fears that this situation may not long continue.

In any case, it would not be feasible for all firms in the industry to switch to pressed glass. For many, the additional capital expense, particularly for molds, would be too great.[24] Some skilled workers would have to relearn their trade. Furthermore, any large-scale transfer of resources to this line would soon swamp the limited market.

[24] For example, a mold for pressed glass plates might run to over $250; for a goblet, nearly $500; for a pitcher, over $600.

In blown glassware, indications of product differentiation are found at both ends of the price range. One firm is doing a thriving business in "juice sets" of colored glass and in other kinds of fancy and special products. A substantial part of the business of another firm is in monogrammed stemware for clubs, steamship lines and hotels. In the highest price range, a few firms are successfully maintaining a limited market for lead crystal ware of high artistic merit.[25] Conversely, firms which are suffering most from the competition of imports are those whose products have shown the least variation from standard patterns.

Investment in products outside the field of tableware and artware has been tried by a few manufacturers as a means of utilizing unoccupied plant facilities and supplementing their principal product. Several firms are now making illuminating ware (shades, bowls, etc., for lighting fixtures) as well as tableware. One company is devoting a part of its factory to the manufacture of fiber glass. The addition of a new product of this kind, which although made of glass requires an entirely different kind of technical skill and knowledge of unrelated markets, involves many risks.

The combination of importing with manufacturing is still another method of adaptation, not yet introduced but possibly in the offing. In order to offer a full tableware line to their customers, certain of the larger firms, now manufacturing only pressed ware in their own factories, obtain blown ware from smaller firms specializing in that product. It may be that they could more profitably get the blown ware from abroad. This method of joining foreign competitors whom you cannot beat has already become standard practice in the watch industry; importing has been taken up by manufacturers of woolens and worsteds, bicycles, dyes and chinaware. Obviously, it is an incomplete remedy for injury from foreign competition. It may protect the management from loss of income, but it is no help to the workers whose jobs have been lost or are endangered.

---

[25] The high reputation established by Steuben lifts it out of competition with imports. Other U. S. firms which have specialized in the highest grade of ware have been less successful.

Can the Market for Stemware Be Expanded?

The declining over-all sales of stemware in the American market, including foreign as well as domestic, emphasizes the impact of foreign competition. Both importers and domestic producers would like to know how the trend could be reversed so that the total sales curve would rise again. On the face of things the prospects for such a change do not seem too bright. There seems to be no indication at present that the next generation of young married couples will revert to the formal ways of living and entertaining practiced by their grandparents. Their houses will probably remain small, and the great majority will do their own housework. In the higher income brackets, however, there still remains a market for stemware of the best quality. Through skillful and persistent advertising some of the larger manufacturers are endeavoring to build up this market. Their aim is to educate the taste of American housewives so that they will appreciate the beauty of fine glassware. With only limited budgets for advertising, the results have not been outstanding. Several years ago a number of firms cooperated in institutional advertising, the promotion of table glassware as such, without mention of individual firms or brands; the project was later abandoned because of lack of support by some of the smaller firms.

Chapter 3

THE CHINAWARE INDUSTRY
AND THE TARIFF

LIKE HAND-FASHIONED GLASS, the manufacture of china tableware, especially china for household use and art objects of china, retains some of the characteristics of a handicraft. Its products are distinguished by excellence of designs executed by the painstaking labor of skilled craftsmen. Mechanical processes are much less utilized than in typical American industries, and labor therefore makes up a higher percentage of total manufacturing costs. On this account, principally, American producers have felt the competition of imports from Japan where wages are about one-tenth those paid in this country, as well as imports from England, Germany and other countries of Western Europe where wages are much lower than in American potteries.

Until World War II, imported chinaware for household use, in spite of high tariff duties, supplied practically the entire American market. Wartime conditions, operating as an almost complete embargo on shipments from abroad, were responsible for a sudden spurt in the output of American factories, which, continuing after the armistice, carried production to a peak in 1949. Meanwhile English and Japanese china had reappeared in the U. S. market in substantial amounts. Until 1950, however, the imports supplied no more than the accumulated deficiency in domestic consumption. Since that year they have been a source of mounting anxiety to American manufacturers. Some have suffered declining sales and falling profits. The foreign ware, nevertheless, is still far from regaining the dominant position in the American market which it held 20 years ago.

Ascribing their troubles to increased imports, certain American firms on three separate occasions appealed to the Tariff

39

Commission for increased tariff protection. But on each occasion the Commission rejected their plea. In the following pages we will examine the reasons for the Commission's action and will attempt to estimate the significance of tariff protection for the future of the American chinaware industry. First, a brief description of how chinaware is made and a sketch of the development of the industry in the United States may prove helpful.

How Chinaware Is Made

In its basic processes, and in the materials used, the manufacture of china has not greatly changed from what it was centuries ago. Clay and other materials mixed with water are shaped into the required forms, baked at high temperatures and then given a variety of finishes and decorations.

The materials used in the American factories are now all of domestic origin; kaolin or china clay, ball clay, pulverized quartz and feldspar. After careful weighing on "blind" scales according to a formula which each manufacturer, often unsuccessfully, tries to keep secret, the materials are mixed with an equal weight of water. The mixture (clip) is passed over magnets to remove iron particles and then strained through fine metal sieves (lawns). After excess moisture has been removed in filter presses, the clay is passed through pug mills which remove air and turn out a clay paste in cylindrical form ready for the ware maker.

Up to this point the processes are fully mechanized, but now hand operations predominate. The ancient potter's wheel has been transformed into a semiautomatic jigger, but still each plate, cup or other item must be shaped by skilled craftsmen on, or in, a plaster of Paris mold. Each item has to be handled separately, often by several persons in succession. Overhead conveyors and conveyor belts are in general use for moving the ware from one stage of production to the next, but much hand labor is still necessary.

Various operations require skilled labor, for example, the shaping of flat ware on the potter's wheel, the forming of hollow ware in molds, fixing handles to cups and pitchers, loading ware in saggers for firing. "Selecting," i.e., inspecting, the finished ware is highly skilled work, and decorating is an art as well. To become fully competent in some of these operations requires eight to ten years of training and experience.

Firing takes place in tunnel kilns through which the ware moves in continuous progress. All chinaware requires at least two firings. In the first (the bisque kiln) vitrification is accomplished at a temperature of about 2250 degrees F. After firing comes the application of decalcomania decorations, again a labor-expensive operation. The ware is then coated with a glaze by hand dipping, or by mechanical spraying, and is placed in a special kiln for glost firing. The decoration of some ware, especially the more expensive grades of household china, involves hand painting over the glaze. Such overglaze decoration requires a third firing.

For both household china and hotel ware the materials used are identical, and the same kilns and other equipment may be employed. A considerable part of the labor force employed on hotel china could be shifted to household china without difficulty; some workers, however, would require retraining. The heavier hotel ware, with a more dense and durable body, is less liable to breakage than dinnerware. On this account it can sometimes be handled by machinery in the process of manufacture when the more fragile dinnerware would require hand operations. Moreover, hotel ware, being simpler in shape and less elaborate in decoration than household china, is a more standardized product. It is produced on a larger scale; hence the use of special machinery, for example, in spraying glaze, becomes economical. Being a cheaper product, less rigorous standards of selections are applied, and the percentage of "rejects" is lower.

The similarity of processes, materials and equipment used in making both hotel ware and household chinaware makes it possible to combine both operations in a single plant. A plant specializing in hotel ware usually requires larger investment in fixed capital, but one company, which usually makes the two products in separate factories, transfers a part of its hotel ware production at times to the dinnerware plant. It should be observed, however, that the market outlets for the two products are separate, and the marketing processes are dissimilar.

History of the American Industry

The manufacture of chinaware is one of the newer American industries. Other types of pottery, stoneware and earthenware,[1] had been produced since early colonial days, but it was not until the last decade of the 19th century that vitrified china was first made commercially in this country. Syracuse, New York and Trenton, New Jersey soon became centers of the American industry. Its principal market was originally found in the institutional field. Hotels and restaurants, clubs and railway dining cars demanded a strong and durable ware that would stand hard usage without chipping or breaking. In this respect vitrified china proved far superior to the earthenware previously used. In 1929 practically the entire production of the 18 American chinaware factories (eight million dozen pieces) was hotel ware. At that time they supplied nearly 100 percent of American consumption. Pioneers in making vitrified, translucent china for household use were the Onondaga company in Syracuse and Lenox in Trenton. For many years, however, their products supplied only a minute portion of the domestic market. The china plates, cups and saucers with which most American housewives set their tables —their "best china"—were almost exclusively of English, French or German manufacture.

During the 1930's American producers maintained their dominant position in the supply of hotel ware, although with a lower volume of business. Sales of imported household china suffered a severe decline. Domestic production also fell somewhat during the depression, and at the beginning of World War II it still supplied less than five percent (by quantity) of total domestic consumption.

World War II, by cutting off all imports of two of the principal suppliers of foreign china, Germany and Japan, and by reducing imports from England, created a gap in the sup-

[1] China has a vitrified, impermeable body which is often translucent. Earthenware is distinguishable by its absorbent, opaque body. The American earthenware industry, much larger than the china industry, consists of a group of twenty-five to thirty firms whose annual sales were estimated by the Tariff Commission in 1950 at about $78 million. In that year imports were less than $5 million. Production techniques are simpler than in chinaware and labor costs are lower.

ply of household china. At the same time many new purchasers with increased incomes came into the market. To supply the enlarged demand, firms already established expanded their operations, and three new companies began production. Six firms which had been making hotel chinaware and also earthenware added lines of household china. Manufacturers increased their production facilities by about one-third and introduced labor-saving techniques. The result was that sales of domestic household china, which had never equalled 200,000 dozen a year before World War II, rose to 560,000 dozen in 1946. (See Table 7.)

Table 7

U. S. PRODUCTION OF HOUSEHOLD CHINAWARE,
1929, 1937, 1939, 1946-1953

Year	Quantity (in 1000 dozens)	Total value (in 1000 dollars)	Value per dozen
1929	160	1,200	$7.50
1937	140	930	6.64
1939	170	1,200	7.06
1946	560	5,400	9.64
1947	728	7,958	10.93
1948	874	10,606	12.14
1949	908	11,875	13.08
1950	857	12,542	14.63
1951	808	13,036	16.13
1952	814	15,621	19.19
1953	800 [a]	14,000 [a]	17.50 [a]

[a] Estimated.
Source: U. S. Tariff Commission, U. S. Bureau of the Census

Responding to the continued active demand for household tableware, domestic manufacturers raised their production year by year until in 1949 it was slightly over 900,000 dozen. A decline began the following year, and in 1951-1953 production leveled off at somewhat over 800,000 dozen. (Later figures are not available.) The value of the annual output, however, continued to rise with the increase in factory prices.

If one compares the course of production of household tableware with hotel ware some interesting facts emerge. Production of hotel ware reached its postwar peak in 1947; after that date, owing to the shrinkage of orders for the armed services, the decline was continuous until 1950. During these years a shift was taking place within the industry. Factories producing both kinds of ware were transferring facilities and personnel into household china for which the demand was still strong.

The Present Situation

In the United States at present some 30 firms make tableware of vitrified china, both hotel ware and household tableware. Most of the productive capacity is found in the states of New York, Pennsylvania, West Virginia and Ohio. Chinaware is also made in New Jersey, Missouri, Arkansas and California. The dominant position of hotel ware in the industry in 1952 is shown in the following tabulation:[2]

Total number of chinaware firms	30
Specializing in hotel ware	20
Producing both hotel ware and household ware	5
Producing household china and miscellaneous products	2
Producing only household china	3

Ten firms made all the household china of domestic origin. It is significant that five of these firms, which accounted for two-thirds of the total output, were principally interested in making hotel ware. Sales of hotel ware in the 1930's were seven to ten times those of household china; at present the ratio is about two to one. Since 1948 tariff legislation has dealt with the two products separately, presumably because foreign competition has affected only the household ware. But, when we examine the technology and the economics of the industry, this separation seems artificial. In fact the production of household china and hotel ware are so intimately related as to constitute for practical purposes two branches of a single industry.

Manufacturers of household china have based their pleas for higher protection on unsatisfactory conditions in the industry, dating from 1950, which they assert are evidence that they are

[2] U. S. Tariff Commission, *Household China Tableware*, Report No. 186, Second Series (Washington: GPO, 1953), p. 7. Two of the firms which produced both household ware and hotel china have since gone out of business.

being injured by increased imports. The dollar value of their sales has risen year by year, but not enough, they say, to off-set rising costs. Moreover, sales of household china have not kept pace with the growth in the sales of consumers' goods in general or with disposable consumers' income.

For employment only scattered data are available. They show that the chinaware industry had about 800 workers in 1939, 2,700 in 1949 and 2,100 in 1952. Comparison of these data with the quantities produced indicate increasing output per employee, as follows:

Year	Dozens per employee
1939	212
1949	336
1952	388

No satisfactory information is available regarding the prof-its currently earned in the manufacture of household china. When the Tariff Commission, in 1953, invited ten firms to supply financial data, only two submitted the requested infor-mation, and one of them did not segregate profits on house-hold ware from profits earned in other operations. The Com-mission, making use of fragmentary data, concluded that earnings varied widely among the various firms in the indus-try. Some had earned profits in the same years that others suffered losses. The profits of four firms in 1949-51 "enabled the companies to improve their financial position through re-tention of earnings. Working capital, earned surplus, and net worth were generally at higher levels in 1951 than in 1949." The Commission found no evidence that five of the ten firms had had "unsatisfactory profit experience" in the postwar period. "On the contrary," the Commission reported, "such evidence as is available indicates that at least 2 of these con-cerns have made substantial profits in all postwar years, and that 2 others began production of household china tableware only within the last 2 years." [3]

Some manufacturers still insist, however, that the industry is in a bad condition. Their spokesman told the Senate Finance Committee, in March 1955, that firms which made 60 percent

[3] U. S. Tariff Commission, *Household China Tableware* (1953), cited. p. 8.

of the 1954 output of household chinaware suffered losses, before taxes, equal to 1.47 percent of their combined sales. (In 1948 these firms had earned 13.79 percent before taxes.) Since June 1950, the informant stated, four producers, three of whom had been in the business for a total of 184 years, had been forced to quit.[4] In some of the cases, however, it seems doubtful whether increased imports were responsible. One factory, closed in 1951, was known to have antiquated equipment. Another which began making dinnerware during World War II had experienced several changes in ownership and for several years had been hovering on the margin between success and failure. It seems unlikely, also, that the disappearance of the four firms will mean a decline in total production, for two of the more successful companies have recently built new factories to take care of expanding sales.

Competition from Abroad

The accumulated backlog of unsatisfied wartime demand for household china and other house furnishings stimulated imports as well as domestic production. With the revival of the pottery industries of the United Kingdom, Germany and Japan and the resumption of trade with the former enemy countries, their shipments of chinaware to the United States rapidly expanded. Imports rose from 202,000 dozen in 1946 to almost 5,000,000 dozen in 1953.[5] (See Table 8.) The share of the market supplied by foreign china rose from one-quarter to over four-fifths.

If only the postwar period is considered, it seems that the

[4] U. S. Senate, Committee on Finance, *Trade Agreements Extension*, Hearings, 84th Cong., 1st sess., on H. R. 1 (Washington: GPO, 1955), pp. 941-942.

[5] In addition to imports officially recorded, substantial quantities of foreign chinaware were brought in free of duty by returning American tourists. At present a tourist who has spent 24 hours in a contiguous foreign country, or 48 hours in a noncontiguous country, may bring in $200 of foreign goods without payment of duty. If he has been absent 12 days, the exemption is $500, and it may be claimed twice a year.

Most of the chinaware which thus by-passed the tariff was English ware entered over the Canadian border. A spokesman for the domestic manufacturers estimated that the informal imports of English ware amounted each year to one-third to one-half of those officially recorded. (See U. S. Tariff Commission, *Hearing on Chinaware* [Washington, June 23, 1952], p. 44. [Stenographic transcript.]) The *Economist* (April 19, 1952) estimated the value of British pottery—earthenware and china—reexported from Canada in this fashion in 1951 at £700,000 ($1,960,000).

imports were ruining the American industry. But a longer perspective shows that the foreign suppliers, notwithstanding their rapid gains and the declining tendency in domestic production, had still not regained in 1953 the dominant position in the American market which they had occupied 15 years earlier. (See Chart C, p. 48.) These comparisons are based on the *quantities* of chinaware produced and imported. If we look at the *value* figures, the situation appears even less favorable to the importers. Reckoned in dollars the foreign ware now supplies a considerably smaller proportion of the domestic market than it did before the war. (See Table 9.)

The imports are not homogeneous. British ware is unlike that imported from Germany, and both may be distinguished by even a moderately discriminating purchaser from most Japanese chinaware. Imports of Japanese ware, which in 1937 and 1939 had averaged over 4,000,000 dozen, vanished during World War II. After 1946 they came back strongly, reaching the 4,000,000 dozen level again in 1951. By 1953 they supplied 68 percent of the American market, but in prewar years Japan's share had been nearly 85 percent.

The concern with which American manufacturers now view Japanese competition is based, not so much on the increased quantity of goods received, as on the low prices at which they enter the American market. The average 1953 foreign values of British, German and Japanese china are shown below, together with estimated average wholesale prices in the New York market.

	Average foreign value	Estimated average wholesale price[a]
	(per dozen)	
Chinaware imported from:		
United Kingdom	$7.01	$14.72
Germany	5.34	11.21
Japan	1.31	3.41

[a] The foreign values represent wholesale prices in the countries of origin. To make them comparable to the factory prices of the domestic chinaware, ocean freight and other transportation costs must be added and also customs duty and an allowance for importers' profits. This has been accomplished by multiplying the values of English and German ware (dutiable, for the most part, at 35 percent) by a coefficient of 2.1, and the Japanese (dutiable at 70 percent) by 2.6.

CHART C

U. S. CONSUMPTION OF HOUSEHOLD CHINAWARE,
1929, 1937, 1939, 1946-1953

(in millions of dozens)

IMPORTS

DOMESTIC
PRODUCTION

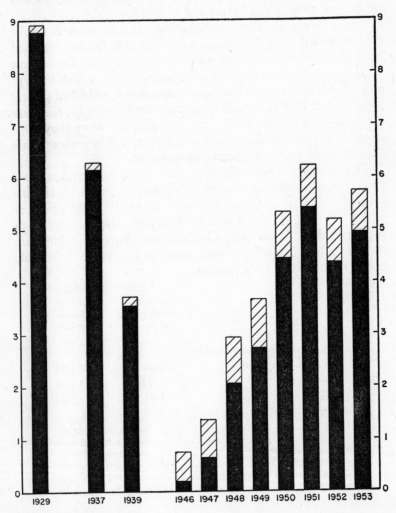

Source: Table 9

Table 8

U. S. IMPORTS OF HOUSEHOLD CHINAWARE, BY COUNTRIES, 1929, 1937, 1939, 1946-1954

Year	Japan	Germany	United Kingdom	All other	Total
			Quantity (in 1000 dozens)		
1929	5,627	2,101	96	931	8,755
1937	5,379	317	43	408	6,147
1939	3,121	163	73	209	3,566
1946	a	a	162	40	202
1947	205	118	188	144	655
1948	1,125	487	292	166	2,070
1949	1,847	411	357	163	2,778
1950	3,375	350	535	200	4,460
1951	4,171	462	623	136	5,392
1952	3,282	427	555	83	4,347
1953	3,911	529	436	55	4,931
1954 c	4,924	526	423	477	6,350
			Foreign value (in 1000 dollars)		
1929	3,576	2,617	820	1,564	8,577
1937	2,796	534	407	502	4,239
1939	1,682	269	398	249	2,598
1946	b	6	1,388	215	1,609
1947	414	371	1,604	701	3,090
1948	2,064	1,862	2,459	739	7,124
1949	2,564	1,890	2,777	730	7,961
1950	3,915	1,566	3,141	719	9,341
1951	5,785	2,428	3,943	752	12,908
1952	4,751	2,294	4,061	696	11,802
1953	5,139	2,827	3,056	528	11,550
1954 c	6,670	2,699	2,911	1,468	13,748

a Less than 500 dozen.
b Less than $500.
c The total value of 1954 imports includes an estimated $937,000 (representing approximately 400 thousand dozen) which, owing to a change in the method of recording imports, cannot be distributed by countries. Consequently the 1954 imports ascribed to each country understate, in most cases if not in all, the value and quantity of chinaware received from that country and overstate the amounts attributed to "all other."
Source: U. S. Tariff Commission, U. S. Bureau of the Census

The 1953 average factory price of American china, a roughly comparable figure, was $17.50 per dozen. Because of differences in price and quality, Japanese china is sold principally to purchasers in the lower income groups (see pp. 62-63).

Table 9

HOUSEHOLD CHINAWARE: APPARENT CONSUMPTION IN THE UNITED STATES, 1929, 1937, 1939, 1946-1953

Year	Quantity 1,000 dozen	Percent supplied by imports	Value 1,000 dollars	Percent supplied by imports
1929	8,915	98.2	22,643	94.7
1937	6,287	97.8	11,528	91.9
1939	3,736	95.4	7,695	84.4
1946	762	26.5	9,423	42.7
1947	1,383	47.4	15,683	49.3
1948	2,944	70.3	28,416	62.7
1949	3,686	75.4	31,778	62.6
1950	5,317	83.9	35,895	65.1
1951	6,200	87.0	45,306	71.2
1952	5,161	84.2	45,126	65.4
1953	5,731[a]	86.1	42,875[a]	67.3

[a] Estimated.
Note: Apparent consumption has been arrived at by adding imports and domestic production. Exports are negligible; the quantities and values entered in official export statistics can be disregarded since they are the result of misclassification.
   The value figures for imports have been made more nearly comparable to those for domestic production by substituting wholesale prices for foreign invoice values of the imports; these wholesale prices have been estimated as equivalent to 250 percent of foreign invoice values.
Source: U. S. Tariff Commission, U. S. Bureau of the Census

Imports from the United Kingdom and from Germany have increased substantially in postwar years. In supplying the American market, moreover, their gains, when compared with prewar figures, far exceed those made by Japan. The United Kingdom supplies bone china of excellent quality produced by firms whose names, Wedgwood, Minton, Spode and others, carry great prestige in the American market. This English ware and some of the fine porcelain supplied by long-established, well-known firms in West Germany (Rosenthal) and France (Haviland) are competitive with only the best products of one or two American factories.[6] Purchasers of these high-priced wares are usually knowledgeable and discriminating. Often, when entering a retail salesroom, they ask for English bone china, or Limoges ware, or some brand of Bavarian china. Or they may ask for the product of some well-known American firm. For this group of purchasers price is a secondary consideration.

High Tariffs Fail to Protect

The history of the tariff on household china might be called the story of the child that never grew up. The beginnings of commercial production of chinaware in the United States go back over 70 years. During this entire period the industry, thanks to the persistent activities of its representatives in Washington,[7] has been the object of tariff protection, usually at high rates of duty. As early as 1883, decorated ware was dutiable at 60 percent of foreign value,[8] and this rate became standard for the next generation. The Wilson-Gorman Act (1894) made a dent in the tariff wall by dropping the rate to 35 percent, but this was soon repaired in the Dingley Act of 1897. Even the Underwood Act (1913), supposedly a free-trade measure, provided a rate of 55 percent.

World War I shut off chinaware imports and stimulated domestic production. But in 1922, to protect their position against the anticipated flood of postwar imports, manufactur-

[6] The chinaware made in continental Europe is known to ceramic experts as "porcelain." Unlike the American vitrified china, porcelain is given its first firing at a relatively low temperature. The glaze, when it is applied, permeates the body of the ware and is fused with it in the second high temperature firing. This procedure gives porcelain a higher translucency but a more fragile structure than the American product.

[7] William F. Burgess, a manufacturer, gave up his business in 1904 to become a "career lobbyist" devoting his whole time to promoting tariff legislation in the interests of the pottery industry. He was vice president of the United States Potters Association from 1904 until 1929, except for four years when he served on the U. S. Tariff Commission. After leaving the Commission he returned to the Association. See E. E. Schattschneider, *Politics, Pressures and the Tariff* (New York: Prentice-Hall, 1935), p. 186.

[8] Plain ware carried a rate of 55 percent. Only small amounts of undecorated ware have been imported; hence the rates quoted in this section refer only to the decorated china.

ers obtained a 70 percent duty in the Fordney-McCumber Act. The Hawley-Smoot Act in 1930 capped the climax by adding a specific duty of 10 cents per dozen pieces. This gadget proved an effective supplement to the ad valorem rate in the business depression of the 1930's when prices were falling. The compound duty was responsible for the fact that chinaware imported in the years 1931 to 1938 paid average rates ranging from 82 to 94 percent of foreign value.[9] (See Table 10.)

During the years of high protection, import duties seem to have had little effect in restricting the entry of foreign chinaware into the American market, and they were equally ineffective in stimulating the growth of the American industry. The infant did not grow up; until World War II the output of the American factories producing vitrified china for household use never exceeded 200,000 dozen pieces a year. Imports, rising and falling with the tides of American prosperity, never supplied less than 95 percent (by quantity) of the domestic market.

Trade Agreements Lower Import Duties, except on Japanese Chinaware

Paradoxically, the long-awaited growth of American production came after the peak of tariff protection had passed, under a regime of lowered import duties. Here again it was not the tariff rate but an extraneous factor that was responsible, viz., the interruption of imports during World War II. The first break in the long upward trend in chinaware duties came in the 1939 trade agreement with the United Kingdom which revived a separate classification for bone china and reduced the rate to 45 percent.[10] By this device the benefit of the tariff concession was confined to the English manufactur-

---

[9] The specific rate served a second purpose also. It was a means of making low-priced ware pay a higher rate than the more valuable china. Thus, on items valued at $1 a dozen, a 70 percent rate plus 10 cents works out at 80 percent ad valorem; on ware valued at 50 cents the equivalent ad valorem would be 90 percent.

[10] In order to comply with the provisions of the 1934 Trade Agreements Act, which limited reductions in duty to 50 percent of the 1930 rates, the proviso was added "but not less than 5 cents plus 30 percent" on plain ware and 5 cents plus 35 percent on decorated. A similar proviso was retained in later agreements.

Table 10

U. S. RATES OF DUTY ON HOUSEHOLD CHINAWARE

(percent ad valorem; cents per dozen pieces)

	1930 rate	*1955 rate*
Par. 212 China, porcelain and other vitrified table and kitchen articles and utensils Containing 25% or more of calcined bone: Plain white	60% + 10¢	30% but not less than 5¢ + 25%
Decorated	70% + 10¢	35% but not less than 5¢ + 30%
Containing less than 25% of calcined bone: Plain white or decorated— Plates, not over 6⅝ inches in diameter, valued over $.90, not over $2.55 per dozen, or over 6⅝ inches, not over 7⅛ inches in diameter, valued over $1.35, not over $3.45 per dozen, or over 7⅛ inches, not over 9⅛ inches in diameter, valued over $1.80, not over $5 per dozen, or over 9⅛ inches in diameter, valued over $2.70, not over $6 per dozen; cups, valued over $1.35, not over $4.45 per dozen; saucers, valued over $.90, not over $1.90 per dozen; articles, not plates, cups or saucers, valued over $4.50, not over $11.50 per dozen.	60% + 10¢ª 70% + 10¢ᵇ	60% + 10¢ᶜ
Plates of diameters specified above, cups, saucers and other table and kitchen articles; each of the foregoing valued over the *maximum* value specified above for a like article.	60% + 10¢ª 70% + 10¢ᵇ	35% + 10¢
Plates of diameters specified above, cups, saucers and other table and kitchen articles; each of the foregoing valued at not more than the *minimum* value specified above for a like article.	60% + 10¢ª 70% + 10¢ᵇ	45% + 10¢ᶜ

ª Applicable to plain white.
ᵇ Applicable to decorated.
ᶜ Effective September 10, 1955, on admission of Japan to GATT.

ers who were practically the sole exporters of chinaware containing calcined bone. Feldspar china, imported from Japan and continental Europe, remained dutiable at the 1930 rates.

The geographic area to which tariff reductions applied was somewhat widened by the Geneva agreement (1948). It further reduced the 1939 rate on bone china and also for the first time cut the rate on feldspar china. This action encouraged imports from Germany and other continental countries. To make assurance against Japanese competition doubly sure, the 1948 agreement introduced "value brackets" into the provisions of paragraph 212. Thus, the negotiators provided a means of discrimination which was familiar to all practitioners of tariff bargaining. The reduced rates were made applicable only to plates, cups, saucers and other items *valued at more than specified amounts*. The minimum values were so fixed as to admit at the lower rates practically all china imported from the United Kingdom and continental Europe while depriving the bulk of the imports from Japan of the benefit of the change.

Formally, the United States, like most modern nations, is committed to a tariff policy which treats all countries equally. Except in unusual cases, all nations are entitled to as liberal treatment as that given to the most favored nation. Value brackets, however, afford an opportunity to circumvent this pledge without formally violating it. It should be added that the United States is not the only, or perhaps the most ingenious, practitioner of this device.

Since 1948 the upward trend of chinaware prices has lifted a portion of imports from Japan into the preferred category, thus weakening the force of the discriminatory action. At Torquay (1951) minor reductions were made on the higher grades of feldspar china.

Twelve years of tariff bargaining, 1939 to 1951, cut about in half the rates of duty on bone china from England and on high-priced ware from other suppliers, but did not affect Japanese ware. The rate of 70 percent on china from that country, which supplied the bulk of the imports, was the bastion of tariff protection on chinaware. But the bastion was not impregnable. Even the 70 percent duty proved inadequate to check the continued inflow of Japanese china into the American market. The domestic industry wanted more protection, but the usual remedy, action under the escape clause, was not available, for Japan had not benefited from any of the trade agreement concessions. Since Japanese chinaware was still paying the 70 percent rate of the Hawley-Smoot tariff, it was obviously impossible to satisfy the legal requirements for escape clause action, namely, to show that the domestic industry was seriously injured, or was threatened with such injury, *as a result of a tariff concession.*

Tariff Commission Rejects Manufacturers' Pleas

A possible remedy specifically applicable against Japanese chinaware, however, was discovered in an obsolete provision of the Act of 1922, reenacted as Section 336 of Title III of the Act of 1930. This section authorized the President to raise, or to lower, any import duty by an amount up to 50 percent of the 1930 rate. The change in the rates was limited to the amount necessary to compensate for differences between foreign and domestic costs of production. Cost differences were to be ascertained by the Tariff Commission. This cumbersome procedure, misnamed "the flexible provision," almost inevitably resulted in boosting tariff rates. Its use was abandoned after the Trade Agreements Act of 1934 came into force, but the paragraph was not repealed.

The Tariff Commission at first (on October 23, 1951) rejected the manufacturers' plea for a cost-of-production investigation. Some of the Commissioners may have recalled the Commission's previous investigation of costs in the chinaware industry which ended in a complete fiasco.[11] But they were forced to undertake the unwelcome task by a Senate resolution of May 12, 1952. The result, however, was not what the domestic industry had hoped for. The Commission, after considerable delay, on June 24, 1954 threw the case out of court on the grounds that Section 336 was not applicable. A ma-

[11] In studies extending over more than two years, 1925-1927, the Commission's experts obtained a mass of cost data from 13 chinaware manufacturers in the United States, 14 in Germany, and 11 in England. But, because of variations in quality, in designs and decoration between the imported and the American products, the Commission found it impossible to determine a rate of duty which would be equal to the difference between foreign and domestic costs. See *Annual Reports* of the U. S. Tariff Commission, 1925, 1927, 1928. See also *Hearings* before the Senate Select Committee on Investigation of the Tariff Commission, 69th Cong. (Washington: GPO, 1928).

jority of the Commission found that the imports from the principal competing country, namely, the cheaper grades of feldspar ware imported from Japan, were not "like or similar to domestic chinaware" and that therefore no basis existed for determining differences in cost of production. In support of this view the Commissioners cited the wide gap between the prices of domestic and Japanese ware. The two kinds of chinaware, they found, were usually sold in different markets and to different classes of consumers.[12]

Two members of the Commission disagreed. They insisted that Japanese and American ware, being made of approximately the same materials and adapted to substantially the same uses, were commercially interchangeable and, hence, like or similar within the meaning of the law, irrespective of differences of price and quality.

The dispute over comparability goes to the heart of tariff administration. For many years it has figured prominently in the decisions of customs courts. A broad interpretation of "like or similar" would lead to a rigorous application of protectionism over a wide area of import trade. A narrow interpretation, on the other hand, would mean the liberal treatment of many foreign goods on the grounds that they were noncompetitive. The two members who took the broad view recommended the application of a 49 percent duty *based on American selling price* as necessary to equalize cost differences.[13]

While the Tariff Commission was dealing with the application to raise duties on Japanese china, the Vitrified China Association, on behalf of two of the firms then manufacturing household china, set in motion an action looking toward the restoration of the 1930 rates on the higher grades of china, imported principally from the United Kingdom and from Germany. In this application, made under the escape clause pro-

---

[12] U. S. Tariff Commission, *Household China Tableware*, Report to the President on Investigation under Section 336 of the Tariff Act of 1930 (Washington: Author, 1954), pp. 7-9.

[13] Actually, the Commission's investigation showed that the rate of duty necessary to equalize costs, if based on foreign value, would be 284 percent plus 15 cents per dozen pieces. But this amount of change exceeded the President's authority; hence, the shift to American selling price, a procedure authorized in the statute.

visions of the Trade Agreements Act of 1951, the National Brotherhood of Operative Potters also joined. But once again the embattled manufacturers failed to obtain the relief they desired, for on February 6, 1953 the Tariff Commission, in a unanimous decision, reported to the President that it found no evidence that imports of household china, of the kind on which tariff reductions had been made, were causing or threatening to cause serious injury to domestic firms. (The Commission's decision left wide open the question whether imports from Japan were causing injury.)

The applicants had based their case on the rapid increase in imports *in postwar years*, contrasted with falling domestic shipments. The Commission, however, insisted on viewing the competition between foreign and domestic chinaware over a longer term. Its report contained this statement:

> In view of the great expansion of output—since prewar years —by the domestic industry producing household china tableware (whether calculated in absolute or relative terms), an expansion which reached its peak in 1949, the absolute and relative decline in the domestic industry's output from such peak production is not considered as being per se a cause or threat of serious injury to that industry. The domestic industry could hardly expect to continue to supply virtually the whole of the United States market as it did during the war. A revival of imports was to be expected when the end of war conditions enabled the foreign producers to reenter this market.[14]

This unanimous pronouncement, if adhered to in other cases, could have great significance in the administration of the escape clause.

Manufacturers Demand Quotas

Because of the failure of import duties to stem the flow of chinaware from abroad, American manufacturers have urged the application of import quotas.[15] From the point of view of the domestic industry, quotas would have two advantages: they would restrict the imports in a given period to a fixed amount or to a specified percentage of domestic consumption.

[14] *Household China Tableware* (1953), cited, p. 6.
[15] Not to be confused with tariff quotas which fix only the amounts which can be imported at a given rate of duty.

For example, a representative of the manufacturers has suggested [16] that the importers' share should be fixed at 36.8 percent, which he calculated represented the division of the market in the years 1948 and 1949. Obviously, such a rule would freeze the competitive situation at a point far more favorable to the domestic industry than that of prewar years.

Quotas, also, afford a means of discriminating among foreign suppliers. This is often the compelling reason for advocating their use. The secretary of the U. S. Potters Association has said: "Obviously the quota is a fair thing. It is not right that the same tariff should apply to Japan and England where England is paying four times as much wages as Japan." [17]

The 1955 Trade Agreement with Japan

After their unsuccessful attempts to restrict imports from Japan by higher duties and quotas, American manufacturers naturally fought hard against any reductions in duties on chinaware in the 1955 bilateral trade agreement with Japan. Their opposition was only partially successful. The rates on the imports of the cheapest decorated ware were reduced from 70 percent to 45 percent and on the slightly more expensive ware from 70 to 60 percent. In addition, the duty on hotel ware, supplied by Japan in only negligible amounts, was cut from 70 percent to 45 percent. The specific rate of 10 cents a dozen, a significant addition to the rates on the low-priced ware, was retained on all imports from Japan. To reassure domestic producers, the State Department announced that about half of the imports which would be affected by the tariff reductions consisted of types of ware not produced in the United States.

Future Competition from Abroad:
State of the English Industry

Repeatedly, in the last half-century, manufacturers of china tableware have warned their Congressmen and the negotiators of trade agreements that their industry was vitally dependent

[16] By Robert F. Martin in *Hearing on Chinaware* (1952), cited, p. 63.
[17] Testimony of Joseph M. Wells, in Senate Finance Committee hearings on extension of the Trade Agreements Act (1955), cited, p. 937.

on the continuance of tariff protection at a high level. Since 1939 their warnings have been disregarded. Trade agreements have reduced duties on china of the highest quality from England and medium-grade china from Germany and other Western European countries. Limited reductions were made in the 1955 trade agreement on imports from Japan. It seems improbable that the trend will soon be reversed so that import duties will again be raised to their former height, or that quotas or other restrictive measures will be adopted.

Under these conditions, what may we expect will be the future of the chinaware industry in the United States? With respect to imports of English and German ware, the predominant consideration, I believe, is the level of income in the United States. A prosperous American market exerts a powerful, attractive force on foreign goods, especially those of the luxury type. As long as national income in this country continues its upward course, with a gradual increase in the level of prices, or at least with no sharp decline, we may expect a continued rise in imports of chinaware from Western Europe. A business recession, on the other hand, would check imports of chinaware more effectively than higher import duties.

The chinaware industries of Germany and England are organized for export trade and are strongly oriented toward the United States market. In England, in the vicinity of Stoke-on-Trent in Staffordshire (the Five Towns of Arnold Bennett's tales), over a third of the working population is employed in the potteries, and a large proportion of the remainder in allied industries. The British industry during the past 20 years has undergone a minor technical revolution. From the end of the war to the beginning of 1950, the Staffordshire potteries invested more than £4,000,000 in a modernization program. Continuous tunnel ovens fired by gas have replaced batch firing in the old-style, upright kilns that used coal as fuel. Other improvements designed to raise output per man include improved factory layouts and the introduction of semiautomatic and fully automatic machinery. The chinaware produced in British potteries in 1954 had a value of £8,874,000, about $25,000,000. The dollar value was three times that of 1935 and 50 percent greater than in 1947.

Exports of English chinaware go principally to the United

States and Canada. On this account, in 1947 the English government, faced with a critical shortage of dollars, ordered
that all decorated pottery be reserved for export. At the end
of 1952 these restrictions were removed, and in 1954 exports
were valued at £5 million ($14 million), making 56 percent
of the domestic output.[18]

In view of the renewed export ability of the British potteries, we may expect growing imports from that country,
but the British ware still continues to sell in a restricted, high-
quality market. In this market, moreover, a few American
firms which make chinaware of excellent design and workmanship are successfully meeting foreign competition.

Condition of the Japanese Industry

At the opposite end of the scale we find the imports from
Japan. The "invasion" of the market by Japanese chinaware
is not a new experience for the American producers. Since
the early 1930's, when the devaluation of the yen gave a boost
to all exports, Japan has supplied, except during the war years,
the bulk of the chinaware bought in the United States. Low
wages, probably not more than one-tenth those paid in American potteries, are primarily responsible, but credit must also
be given to the skill of the Japanese workers and to the business abilities of merchants and manufacturers.

In Japan the damage to the potteries inflicted by the war
has now been entirely repaired and the working force reas-
sembled, thanks to the assistance of the U. S. military authorities. In 1953 total production was estimated at 15 to 20
percent below that of 1938, but the output of dinnerware was
about 50 percent larger. Most of the potteries are small household enterprises producing the kinds of earthenware and
chinaware which the Japanese use in their own homes. Some
of their output is exported, however, and about one-half of
the Japanese chinaware imported into the United States is the
product of the household industry.

Before World War II dinnerware in shapes and designs

[18] Information on British chinaware is taken from a report of the United
Kingdom, Central Office of Information, *Some Manufacturing Industries in
the United Kingdom* (November 30, 1954). See also the *Economist* (January 7, 1950, August 9, 1952, April 18, December 5, 1953).

suitable for the markets of Western Europe and North America was made in only two large factories and three smaller concerns. Their total monthly capacity amounted to 15,000 to 20,000 sets of 93 pieces each. Now 25 to 30 factories with a monthly capacity of 26,000 sets are making dinnerware, but the bulk of the business is done by eight firms. In technical equipment, the Japanese factories do not measure up to the American. Under the pressure of rising labor costs, however, they are making considerable progress. Before the war only two Japanese firms had tunnel kilns; now five of the largest have them. "Everyone is working to develop improved methods of firing, training of workers, better filters and other equipment. . . ." [19]

Will Japanese Manufacturers Restrict Exports?

In studies of international trade, as in all economic studies, one should beware of the dangers of extrapolation. The fact that the quantity of chinaware imported from Japan increased by more than 300 percent in the years 1948 to 1954 does not indicate that the years 1954-1960 will show a corresponding gain. Japanese firms making dinnerware for export are now said to working at or near capacity. They have practically no home market for chinaware of the kind which they export to the United States. Under these conditions exports may show considerable inelasticity. Moreover, the Japanese manufacturers, even if they were able economically to "flood" the American market, might decide against this course. They might take a leaf out of the textile industry's book and choose to restrict their chinaware exports rather than run the risk that the United States Congress might impose import quotas. Leading firms in the industry have already agreed on a policy of limiting their shipments of low-priced dinnerware sets, retailing at about $60 in the United States, to 20 percent of all dinnerware exports. [20]

[19] *Retailing Daily*, April 20, 1953, p. 43. My information on the Japanese industry has been taken in large part from the report in this periodical of a survey conducted by the Fairchild News Service in the spring of 1953. See also *Trade and Industry of Japan* (June 1953 and January 1954), published by the Japanese Ministry of International Trade and Industry.

[20] *Retailing Daily*, April 20, 1953. It would be ironic if antimonopoly laws, introduced at the suggestion of U. S. occupation authorities, should render this attempted control of exports ineffective.

Is Japanese Ware "Like or Similar"?

But even if imports of Japanese ware should continue to increase at the 1948-1954 rate, how much injury would they cause? Does the Japanese ware actually compete with the American or is it only supplementary? This raises again the question of comparability to which we have already referred. According to the Tariff Commission, the ware produced by the *household* industry of Japan consists principally of tea ware or short-line tableware.[21] This ware, which is frequently defective in construction and finish and decorated in traditional Japanese style, is marketed in the United States through variety stores of the 5-and-10-cent type "at prices which are only minor fractions of the prices of domestic chinaware articles of similar sizes and shapes. These imports compete more with the cheapest classes of domestic and imported earthenware and glass tableware than with chinaware domestically produced or imported from European countries."[22]

The full-line dinnerware produced in Japanese factories more nearly approaches the quality of domestic chinaware and is frequently sold in the same retail stores. But the prices of this higher-quality Japanese ware also are much lower than those of domestic china. The Commission's experts found that over 95 percent of all the Japanese dinnerware imported in 1952 was sold at wholesale at $2.73 per five-piece table setting or less. None of the domestic chinaware was offered at this price, and 99 percent of it was offered at more than $3.23. Retail prices show a corresponding divergency. An American retailer testified that the price range on Japanese starter sets was from $3.99 to $5 or $6. In domestic sets the range was from $7 to $20 or $21. A 93-piece Japanese dinner set retails at $60 to $100. A corresponding set of American china would bring several hundred dollars.[23] The lower prices reflect the

[21] Tea ware, or short-line tableware, includes only cups and saucers or breakfast sets, tea sets, coffee sets, or salt and pepper shakers; it does not include the larger plates and some other articles which are used in complete dinner services. Dinnerware consists of lines in which all the articles used in a complete table setting are produced in each pattern of decoration.
[22] U. S. Tariff Commission, *Household China Tableware* (1954), cited, p. 6.
[23] Statement by Ernest E. Eckerson before the U. S. Tariff Commission, *Hearing on Specified Household China Tableware, Kitchenware, and Table and Kitchen Utensils* (Washington, December 16, 1953), p. 230. (Stenographic transcript.)

lower quality of workmanship, obvious only to the more discriminating buyer, and also another closely associated factor, prejudice against Japanese goods of any kind.

Having in mind these and other facts, the majority of the Commission concluded that "imported Japanese chinaware, by reason of its availability at prices greatly lower than the prices of domestic chinaware, reaches a class of consumers who generally would not buy chinaware if Japanese ware were not available." [24] The strong implication here, perhaps not fully warranted, is that the producers of domestic earthenware and glass and plastic ware, not the chinaware factories, bear the brunt of Japanese competition.

Direct Competition—Measures of Adjustment

The remainder of the imports, feldspar china from Germany and the higher-quality Japanese ware, fall into the medium-priced category. This category also includes more than half the domestic product. Here is the principal area of direct competition. How successful will American firms be in meeting it at the reduced tariff rates?

There seems little prospect that they will be able to overcome the handicap of higher wages by substantially raising their output per man-hour. The process of mechanization seems to have advanced about as far as is practicable if the industry is to retain the distinguishing features of a handicraft.

American china manufacturers have been criticized for lack of originality in their designs, a defect which has handicapped them in competition with foreign china. Some time ago an expert remarked that American china, although satisfactory in quality and workmanship, lacked beauty and distinction and the "intangible quality which comes from the hand of a skilled creator. . . ." [25] This is a defect which American manufacturers themselves have recognized. Recently, several of them in an effort to meet foreign competition have made heavy investments in new designs.

Domestic manufacturers are handicapped by high costs of marketing. Most American ware is sold, either in dinner sets or in starter sets, from open stock. This means a heavy cost for

[24] U. S. Tariff Commission, *Household China Tableware* (1954), cited, p. 8.
[25] *Encyclopaedia Britannica*, v. 18 (Chicago: 1945), p. 373B.

inventories which uniformly must be carried by the manufacturer. It explains a reluctance to add new designs. One manufacturer attempted to deal with this difficulty by discontinuing all patterns whose sales in any year fell below a stipulated minimum. By this method he has already cut down the number of patterns in open stock from 400 to 100.

Door-to-door selling has been adopted with some success by a few domestic concerns as a means of marketing a part or all of their household china. By effective salesmanship, coupled with the customer's privilege of paying on installments, they have had some success in opening a new market among middle and lower income families. But door-to-door selling is an expensive method of merchandising. Probably on this account it has not yet been adopted by importers who operate with smaller capital investment than manufacturers.

In his efforts to cut his marketing costs and expand his sales the American manufacturer is faced with what appears to be a long-term downward trend in consumption in the United States. The economic depression of the 1930's gave chinaware sales a body blow from which they have never recovered. In 1929 the American market took about 9 million dozen pieces, almost exclusively of foreign make. Ten years later consumption was only 3.7 million dozen, of which 95 percent was imported china. During World War II domestic production expanded somewhat but not nearly enough to make up for the disappearance of imports. The backlog of demand explains the rapid postwar recovery in chinaware purchases. But still in the peak year, 1951, only 6.2 million dozen were bought, almost 50 percent less than in 1929. Because of the intervening growth of population the per capita decline is even more striking. Consumption in 1929 was 88 pieces per 100 persons; in 1937, 59 pieces; and in 1953, 43.

The explanation is found, as in the case of hand-fashioned glassware, in changes in the ways of living and entertaining of the American people. The recent great increases in national income have gone principally to low-income groups who have not been in the habit of using fine china and who prefer to spend their money in other ways. Families in the higher-income brackets have had to reduce the number of their domestic servants. They give fewer large dinner parties and use a smaller number of pieces of chinaware at each meal. Families living on salaries, professional earnings and fixed incomes have found that on account of rising prices their real incomes have been so reduced that they can no longer afford dinner sets of chinaware. With the shift from large houses to small houses and apartments, 100-piece dinner sets have become an encumbrance. Young people setting up housekeeping now buy five-piece place settings for four, six or at most eight persons, amounting in all to only 20 to 40 pieces of china.

The trend toward informal living has resulted also in a shift from chinaware to earthenware, both domestic and imported. A few of the more progressive earthenware producers have recently introduced new styles for table use. With their smartly designed and colorfully decorated wares they have broken down in the minds of many purchasers the traditional distinction between "fine china" and "everyday earthenware." They have created a new market for high-priced earthenware, to some extent at the expense of chinaware sales.

What the Tariff Means to the American Industry

In the history of the American chinaware industry, shifts from prosperity to depression, changes in American ways of living and entertaining, and a world war have played a much larger role than tariff policies. Before World War II, 50 years of high import duties had failed to build up an American industry which could supply as much as five percent of the domestic market. For a few years the war seemed to have succeeded where the tariff had failed. It shut off imports and at the same time raised consumers' incomes. Profiting by this situation the two firms which up to then had constituted the American industry enlarged their operations, manufacturers of hotel ware added lines of dinnerware, and new firms entered the business.

The boom in chinaware lasted for only a few years after the war. Then imports reappeared, the backlog of unsatisfied demand was whittled away and the market proved not sufficiently elastic to absorb both the imports and the output of the expanded domestic industry.

American manufacturers blamed their troubles on reductions in tariff duties made under trade agreements. But the

Tariff Commission found no evidence of injury, saying in effect that it was not the purpose of the tariff to guarantee to any group of producers the share of the domestic market which they had been able to obtain under abnormal wartime conditions. The Commissioners might have added as *obiter dicta* that in any case the remedy which the applicants sought would not have accomplished the desired result. If after a half-century of high tariff protection the domestic industry had not been able to compete successfully with foreign producers, what reason was there to believe that now it would be more successful?

In an industry like chinaware, which retains many of the characteristics of a handicraft, American firms because of higher labor costs will always be handicapped in competition with low-wage countries. Only the application of a quota would effectively restrict imports from Japan, and even then the benefits would go principally to the makers of earthenware. Doubling the import duties on the high-quality English and continental ware, which sells largely on a prestige and quality basis in a market of its own, would probably not greatly help American manufacturers.

Somewhat later than most American manufacturers, the chinaware firms have had to face problems of postwar readjustment. Those problems were made more difficult of solution by the long-term downward trend in the American market for fine china. Diversification of products seems to offer little hope. Nor is there much to be gained from a shift to the related hotel ware and earthenware industries, both of which are undergoing contraction.

A gradual reduction of import duties might cause some firms producing low- and medium-priced china to shrink their output and discharge some of their employees, but there seems no good reason for assuming that the American chinaware industry would disappear. Firms which over the course of 60 or 70 years, by virtue of good management and the excellence of their products, have been able to survive would still survive. Hence, from the point of view of public policy the question is not, shall the chinaware industry live or die, but instead "how large a chinaware industry do we want?" On economic grounds there would seem to be no reason for preserving the less efficient firms. No one has seriously argued that a large chinaware industry is essential to national defense. It has been argued that there are cultural values connected with the making of tableware and art objects of china which should be preserved. But it is doubtful whether these values can be fostered by import duties which restrict the entry of foreign china. The reverse is more apt to be true. The makers of really beautiful objects will always find patrons and purchasers. They will be stimulated rather than discouraged by competition from artists in other lands.

Chapter 4

BICYCLES

AMERICAN PARENTS in 1955 bought their children over a million imported bicycles. Until a few years ago foreign-made bicycles were a novelty in the American market; in 1949 imports had been one percent of total domestic sales. At that time few American boys and girls had ever seen an "English bike"; five years later millions were demanding them for Christmas presents, and many got them.

. The American manufacturers in 1951 appealed to the Tariff Commission to protect their market, by raising tariff duties and by imposing an absolute quota on imports of foreign bicycles. This request the Commission denied in 1952, having found no evidence of injury. But when bicycles continued to arrive from England, Germany and other countries in rapidly increasing numbers, the industry filed another application. After a second investigation the Commission recommended to President Eisenhower, in March 1955, an increase of 200 percent in duties on lightweight bicycles (under 36 pounds) and 50 percent on other models.

The President on August 18 proclaimed higher rates of duty, but the increases were less than the Commission had recommended. The letter in which the President explained the reasons for his action was an unusual document. It clearly presented a number of cogent reasons for not raising the duty, viz., the need of strengthening valued allies in the free world; the building of markets abroad for American exports; obligations which the United States had incurred in trade agreements not to raise import duties without compensation to other contracting parties; and, finally, the protection of the American consumer "against unnecessary and unjustified price increases." These were all "fundamental questions bearing on the security and well-being of 165,000,000 Americans," which the President recognized he should take into account. Nevertheless, he evidently decided that they were less important than safeguarding the domestic bicycle manufacturers against injury.

It will be the purpose of this chapter to analyze the characteristics of the American bicycle industry and to examine its present condition, as affected by imports and other factors, in order to lay a basis for judging how far the industry is dependent on tariff protection for its survival.

The American Industry

Bicycles are made in the United States by some 15 firms. The 10 members of the American Bicycle Manufacturers Association produce full lines of machines; the remaining nonmember firms specialize in only a few models and operate on a smaller scale. The members of the Association—designated in what follows as "the industry"—employed in 1952-1954 about 6,000 persons. Of these, 3,400 were working on bicycles and parts[1] and the remainder on a variety of other products, including power lawn mowers, baby strollers, heating and ventilating units, etc. Sales of 1.6 million bicycles in 1954 accounted for $51.4 million out of their total sales of $100 million.

Bicycle manufacturing typically is a small-scale business. The smallest firms employ 200 to 300 workers; only a few have as many as 500 or 600 workers. The largest firm, Arnold Schwinn & Company (established in 1894), normally employs in its Chicago plant somewhat over 1,000 people, most of whom are engaged in making bicycles. Smaller, but equally well known, is the Westfield Manufacturing Company at Westfield, Massachusetts, established in 1877 as the Pope Manufacturing Company. Since 1933 it has been operated as a wholly owned subsidiary of the Torrington Company, a manufacturer of industrial needles, bearings and bicycle parts. Westfield's annual sales have recently been estimated at approximately $7 million, 90 to 95 percent bicycles. Other companies making bicycles as a major product include the

[1] U. S. Tariff Commission, *Bicycles*, Report to the President on Escape-Clause Investigation No. 37 (Washington: Author, 1955), Statistical Appendix, Table 4. These figures refer to production workers only. The secretary of the Bicycle Institute of America in May 1956 estimated that total employment on bicycles varied from 4,000 to 6,000 according to the season.

Cleveland Welding Company, one of the 15 subsidiaries of the American Machine and Foundry Company, Monark Silver King of Chicago, and H. P. Snyder Manufacturing Company of Little Falls, New York. The latter owns the Excelsior Manufacturing Company which makes bicycles in a small factory in Michigan City, Indiana.

About half of the business of the Murray Ohio Manufacturing Company of Cleveland is in bicycles. The company also manufactures toy airplanes, trucks and wagons; total employment is approximately 1,500. The Huffman Manufacturing Company of Dayton, Ohio employs about 500 persons in the manufacture of bicycles, lawnmowers and service station equipment. Sales of bicycles make up only a minor part of the total business of the Evans Products Company of Plymouth, Michigan; other products are loading and safety devices, plywood, and heating and air conditioning units.

Bicycle manufacturing is not an integrated industry. Most of the factories are actually assembly plants. They manufacture frames and forks and some other parts for the machines. They purchase from 80 or more independent suppliers the rims, spokes and hubs for the wheels, chains, sprockets, pedals, handlebars, saddles, lights and horns. Thus the capital investment needed to equip a bicycle factory is a rather low figure when related to numbers of employees or to volume of sales. Labor costs are apparently a small proportion of total factory costs. But there is a large element of labor in the purchased parts.

The characteristic feature of the American bicycle industry is its limited market. Since adults in the United States no longer use bicycles as a means of transportation or for recreation, American machines for the past 25 years have been sold almost exclusively to boys and girls between the ages of 5 and 14. Some 15-year-olds continue to ride, but social custom, especially strong among adolescents, taboos the bicycle after its user becomes eligible, usually at 16 years of age, for an automobile driver's license. On this account, principally, bicycle manufacturing has never attained the status of a large-scale industry.

The Postwar Depression

The American bicycle industry in 1954, according to the secretary of its trade association, found itself faced with the "stark possibility of extinction" owing to a "ruthless flood of imports." The statement exaggerated the danger, but nevertheless the facts disclosed by a Tariff Commission report[2] gave grounds for pessimism. The report showed a sharp decline in postwar shipments of bicycles from domestic factories, and an even sharper upward trend in imports in the same period. (See Table 11 and Chart D.) Domestic factories produced[3]

Table 11

U. S. PRODUCTION AND IMPORTS OF BICYCLES, 1937, 1939, 1946-1955

Year	Domestic production		Imports	
	Quantity (1000 units)	Value (1000 $)	Quantity (1000 units)	Foreign Value (1000 $)
1937	1,068	21,696	16	n.a.
1939	1,253	22,467	12	185
1946	1,653	n.a.	47	1,488
1947	2,802	80,996	20	632
1948	2,795	84,338	17	562
1949	1,483	44,229	16	483
1950	1,964	60,414	68	1,592
1951	1,919	64,423	177	4,026
1952	1,930	64,785	246	6,057
1953	2,083	73,066	593	13,983
1954	1,554	51,406	964	21,037
1955	1,729	n.a.	1,224	25,252

Source: U. S. Tariff Commission, U. S. Bureau of the Census

2.8 million bicycles in 1947 and sold them for $81 million; seven years later they sold only 1.6 million, for which they received $51.4 million.

Meanwhile imports rose from 20 thousand machines in

[2] *Bicycles*, Report to the President on Escape-Clause Investigation No. 37, cited.
[3] Production and shipments are practically the same since the manufacturers carry only small inventories.

CHART D

U. S. SHIPMENTS AND IMPORTS OF BICYCLES, 1937, 1939, 1946-1955

(in millions of units)

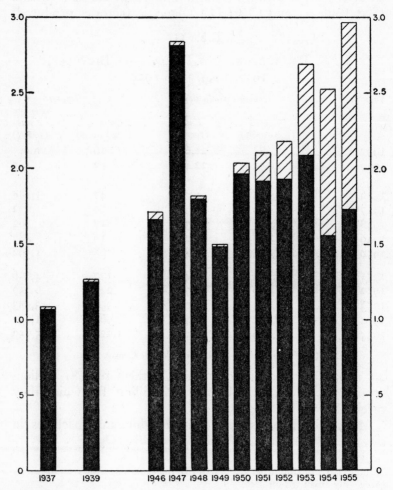

Source: Table 11

1947 to almost 1 million in 1954, and their share of the market grew from less than 1 to 38 percent. (See Table 12.) With the decline in domestic production, employment also fell. In 1947, 10 factories employed 5,270 production workers on bicycles; in 1954, 9 factories employed only 2,901. The manufacturers reported that their profits on bicycle operations

Table 12

THE AMERICAN MARKET FOR BICYCLES,
1937, 1939, 1946-1955

Year	Domestic production	Imports	Total supply on market[a]	Share of domestic production	Share of imports
	(in thousands of units)			(in percent)	
1937	1,068	16	1,084	98.5	1.5
1939	1,253	12	1,265	99.0	1.0
1946	1,653	47	1,700	97.2	2.8
1947	2,802	20	2,822	99.3	.7
1948	2,795	17	2,812	99.4	.6
1949	1,483	16	1,499	99.0	1.0
1950	1,964	68	2,032	96.6	3.4
1951	1,919	177	2,096	91.5	8.5
1952	1,930	246	2,176	88.9	11.1
1953	2,083	593	2,676	78.0	22.0
1954	1,554	964	2,518	62.0	38.0
1955	1,729	1,224	2,953	58.6	41.4

[a] Domestic production plus imports. Exports have been negligible; they reached 100,000 units in only one year, 1948, and since 1951 they have been less than 20,000 annually.
Source: U. S. Tariff Commission, U. S. Bureau of the Census

had been $7.4 million in 1947, but in 1954 their combined income accounts showed a net loss of half a million dollars.

The increase in the tariff proclaimed by the President in August 1955 failed to give any immediate relief. Imports in 1955 were 1,223,990, a gain of 27 percent over the previous year. Domestic production recovered but at a slower rate.

The Causes of Previous Disturbances

Wide fluctuations in production, resulting from changing methods of transportation and changes in general business conditions, have characterized the American bicycle business throughout its history. It suffered a sharp contraction at the beginning of the present century when the electric street cars supplied a new means of local transportation. Before the industry had recovered, the invention of the automobile put a stop to bicycle riding by adults for pleasure. The depression of the early 1930's also was responsible for declining sales of bicycles.

In spite of these discouragements a few firms continued in the business, but it was not until 1937 that bicycle production regained the level which had been attained 40 years previously. During World War II, when nearly all of the facilities of the industry were converted to defense work, bicycle production practically disappeared. Two firms were permitted to make a total of 144,000 units yearly of a simplified "victory" model.

In 1946 all the plants went back to making bicycles. Production in 1947 and 1948 averaged 2.8 million units. By 1950 it had fallen to about 2 million and remained close to that amount until 1954. In these years important changes in ownership took place. The Cleveland Welding Company in 1952 acquired the Shelby Bicycle Company. Two years later the Evans Products Company bought the bicycle division of the Colson Corporation. Diversification and the need to substitute civilian products for vanishing defense orders were the purposes of these investments.

The sharp decline in bicycle production which took place in 1954 is explainable partly by an inventory situation. Because of a slump in business activity, jobbers and retailers ended 1953 with heavy stocks, about 300,000 bicycles. These acted as a damper on their 1954 purchases. But even basing our comparison on the average of the three years 1953-1955, we find the level of production has fallen more than a third since 1947.

The longer-range view is hardly less discouraging. The output of American factories is still 50 percent greater than in prewar years, but meanwhile the domestic market has increased by almost 200 percent. Whereas in 1937 and 1939 the American-made bicycles supplied about 99 percent of the market, their present share has been reduced to less than 60 percent.

Some Firms Have Prospered

"What has happened to the bicycle industry?" may be a misleading question. In this study we are not so much concerned with statistical aggregates as with the operations of individual bicycle manufacturers. Their experience in postwar years has not been at all uniform. For example, the Tariff Commission, in its study of profits, found that one company reported losses in 1952, two in 1953 and four in 1954. But in 1954, the worst year in the recent history of the industry, five firms were operating profitably. Two showed a ratio of net profits to sales of 7.7 and 7.8 percent, respectively. "These two manufacturers," said Commissioner Sutton in his minority report, "are among the smaller of the bicycle-producing concerns, but there is no indication that they operate under especially favorable circumstances. There is no reason to believe, therefore, that the domestic industry as a whole, if organized and operated as efficiently as those concerns, could not operate just as profitably." [4]

In the 1953-1954 recession, before the President raised import duties, two, at least, of the bicycle manufacturers viewed the future optimistically. Monark Silver King invested substantial sums in new manufacturing facilities, and the American Machine and Foundry Company announced plans for building a $1,250,000 factory at Little Rock, Arkansas; equipment from the Cleveland Welding Company has been transferred to this factory. In 1955 the Huffman company built a new plant in Celina, Ohio.

Imports Supply Enlarged Demand

Between 1950 when imports first became significant and 1955, total sales of bicycles in the American market showed a gain of over 900,000 units. The enlarged demand was more than supplied by foreign-made machines which came mainly from two sources, the United Kingdom and West Germany. British manufacturers, who even before World War II had

[4] U. S. Tariff Commission, *Bicycles,* cited, p. 38.

been selling small quantities of lightweight bicycles in American markets, principally on the Atlantic seaboard, began to expand their shipments in 1950. At that time they were 58,-480 units; by 1955 they had risen to 532,632. Imports from Germany showed even more surprising growth. In 1950 they were only 6,446 and five years later 427,743. (See Table 13.)

Table 13

U. S. Imports of Bicycles, by Country of Origin, 1939, 1946-1955

(in units)

Year	United Kingdom	West Germany[a]	France	Austria	Nether-lands	All other	Total
1939	9,131	970	1,751	—	40	322	12,214
1946	44,429	—	1,657	—	1	753	46,840
1947	18,552	6	737	4	12	447	19,758
1948	15,057	—	215	1	17	1,484	16,774
1949	14,537	42	65	4	28	1,259	15,935
1950	58,480	6,446	277	21	18	2,547	67,789
1951	123,202	48,755	684	152	1,523	2,328	176,644
1952	191,762	39,326	7,850	16	4,272	2,537	245,763
1953	407,727	110,984	41,344	10,060	16,335	6,549	592,999
1954	530,230	262,276	88,331	35,493	33,191	14,146	963,667
1955	532,632	427,743	110,564	91,307	35,063	26,681	1,223,990

[a] Includes Austria, West Germany and East Germany in 1939; West Germany and East Germany in 1946-1951; West Germany in 1952-1955.
Source: U. S. Tariff Commission, U. S. Bureau of the Census

Imports of English Bicycles

President Eisenhower said that the development of the present American market for imported, large-wheel lightweights was "attributable almost entirely to the ingenuity and resourceful efforts of foreign producers and American importers." [5] American manufacturers would not agree. They attribute the sudden growth of imports to the fall in the prices of the foreign, particularly the English, machines. Neither of these explanations taken alone is adequate. Each is a necessary supplement to the other.

The purpose of reducing tariff duties on bicycles in the multilateral trade agreement signed at Geneva in 1947 was to

[5] In his letter accompanying the proclamation of August 18, 1955.

facilitate the sales of foreign-made, especially English, bicycles in the United States. In fact, the lower rates (see Table 14), together with the 1949 currency devaluation, made it possible for importers to bring in the machines at substantially lower prices than heretofore. The American manufacturers, in the brief they presented to the Tariff Commission, found in the

Table 14

U. S. RATES OF DUTY ON BICYCLES

(percent ad valorem; dollars and cents per unit)

	Act of 1930	Rate effective before proclamation of August 18, 1955	Rate effective after proclamation of August 18, 1955
Par. 371			
Bicycles, with or without tires, having wheels in diameter (measured to the outer circumference of the tire)			
Over 25 inches:			
If weighing less than 36 pounds complete without accessories and not designed for use with tires having a cross-sectional diameter exceeding 1⅝ inches	30%	$1.25 each, but not less than 7½% nor more than 15%	$1.875 each, but not less than 11¼% nor more than 22½%
Other..................	30%	$2.50 each, but not less than 15% nor more than 30%	$3.75 each, but not less than 22½% nor more than 30%
Over 19 but not over 25 inches	30%	$2.00 each, but not less than 15% nor more than 30%	$3.00 each, but not less than 22½% nor more than 30%
Not over 19 inches........	30%	$1.25 each, but not less than 15% nor more than 30%	$1.875 each, but not less than 22½% nor more than 30%

falling prices of the foreign machines a completely satisfactory explanation of the increased imports. They denied that the importers had created a new market for their product. A bike is a bike, they asserted, "notwithstanding the many variations in form, type, style, weight, accessories and appearance. . . . *All are sold interchangeably in a single market.*" Later the brief stated: "There is only one major difference between the bikes made in America and those coming in from any foreign source. *That single difference is price.*"[6]

Common observation throws considerable doubt on the accuracy of this statement. Practically every American boy or girl above the age of 10 years knows the difference between an English bicycle, the typical import from the United Kingdom, and the balloon-tire models which make up the bulk of the product of American factories.[7] The English bike is a light machine weighing 30 to 35 pounds, with clean lines not obscured by gadgets and accessories. Distinguishing features are the narrow tires that reduce road friction, caliper brakes attached to the handlebars and operating on the rims of both front and rear wheels, and a three-speed gear built into the rear hub.

The typical American machine, on the other hand, has balloon tires, $2\frac{1}{8}$ inches in diameter, and weighs about 45 pounds. Its rear wheel has a single-speed, coaster-brake hub. Designers of the American balloon-tire bicycle have adorned it, in imitation of the motorcycle, with a variety of brightly colored or chromium-plated fittings and accessories, including false gasoline tanks, as well as horns, lights, carriers, etc.

It is apparent that American juveniles have demanded the English bicycles principally because they are different, because they offer certain novel features which make them more desirable than the American product, *when offered at a comparable price.* Hence it was the ability of the importers after

---

[6] *Brief of the Applicants, American Manufacturers* before the U. S. Tariff Commission, Investigation No. 37 (Washington, November 26, 1954), pp. 8, 13. (Italics in original.)

[7] In 1954, 91 percent of American machines were balloon-tire models. The proportion fell to 67 percent in the early months of 1955 owing to the introduction of the new middleweight models (see p. 83.) About 742,000 lightweight bicycles were imported in 1954, 78 percent of total imports; of these lightweights, nearly three-fourths were made in the United Kingdom.

1948 to offer lightweight English bicycles to American buyers at a "comparable price" which gave them the entering wedge.

Actually, the lightweight bicycle was not entirely unfamiliar to bicycle riders in the United States. As early as 1917 domestic manufacturers had put out a machine of this type, with a three-speed gear as optional equipment. But it had never amounted to more than a small percentage of total American output. Manufacturers found that the higher production costs of lightweights, principally because of the three-speed gear, made it necessary to price them higher than the standard balloon-tire model. The Tariff Commission's 1954 investigation showed that in 1954 the average factory price of the American bicycles was $32.63 for balloon-tire models, while lightweights averaged $41.91. At retail the spread was, of course, considerably greater, and the American public was not willing to pay the difference.

But beginning in 1949 and 1950 the British importers, whose machines had also been selling at a premium over the balloon-tire model, were able to reduce their prices.[8] Now for the first time American parents were able to buy lightweight machines for their children for approximately the same prices as a standard balloon-tire model, and in some cases for less. At once the mounting sales of the imported lightweights indicated a strong shift in demand. Buyers recognized that at a comparable price the lightweight was a better bargain. The secretary of the Bicycle Institute of America phrased it in this way: "If a customer examines an imported lightweight and a domestic balloon tire bicycle of about the same price

[8] Average foreign invoice prices (unit values) of British lightweight bicycles are shown below:

Year	Unit value	Year	Unit value
1949	$29.63	1952	$24.79
1950	23.58	1953	25.57
1951	25.42	1954	24.53

These figures refer to bicycles of standard size (with 26-inch wheels) weighing less than 36 pounds.

The average cost of importing a bicycle, including ocean freight, insurance and the expense of entering the merchandise and delivering it to the importers' warehouses, according to data supplied to the Tariff Commission, amounted in 1954 to $4.44 per unit. If we add these costs to the foreign invoice value, plus the duties at the rate of 7½ percent, we get an average landed cost, duty paid, of $30.80.

he should invariably choose the former because it is a better dollar for dollar value." [9]

The British manufacturers and their American representatives, grasping their opportunity, persuaded mail order houses, department stores, automobile supply houses and other mass distributors to place large orders abroad. Many new "fly-by-night" importers offered second-grade English bicycles at exceptionally low prices. Americans, returning GI's and tourists, who had seen and ridden the lightweights when abroad, began to buy English bicycles for their children. Once introduced into a community, English bikes became a fad (Johnny wanted what Jimmy had, down the street), and sales increased at a rate which surprised both the importers and American producers. In some sections of the country the lightweights outsold the domestic balloon-tire models by a wide margin.

After waiting hopefully a few years for the craze to disappear, some American firms stepped up their production of lightweights in 1953. But when they could not meet foreign, particularly British, competition they discontinued these models. Instead, leading American manufacturers, following the pattern of adjustment developed on a large scale by the watch factories,[10] began importing many, in some cases all, of their lightweight machines from abroad.

Imports from Germany

For several reasons the imports of bicycles from West Germany, although still fewer in number than the English, have been more disturbing to American manufacturers. (See Table 15.) The English bicycles are different, and a considerable proportion sell for a higher price than the bulk of the American product. Hence it can be argued that to some extent they are supplementary rather than competitive. But the German bicycles are balloon-tire models which resemble very closely the typical American product. They do not have the prestige appeal of the English lightweights; on the contrary, they are usually regarded as somewhat inferior

[9] *Statement* submitted to the U. S. Tariff Commission, Escape-Clause Investigation No. 37 (Washington, June 20, 1955), p. 25. (Mimeographed.) This statement was repeated in somewhat different language on page 26.
[10] See p. 116.

Table 15

U. S. IMPORTS OF BICYCLES, BY TYPE, 1939, 1946-1955

Year	Light-weight	Balloon-tire (in units)	Total	Light-weight (percent)	Balloon-tire (percent)
1939	10,716		10,716	100	0
1946	43,956		43,956	100	0
1947	18,018		18,018	100	0
1948	16,108		16,108	100	0
1949	15,053		15,053	100	0
1950	59,019	6,210	65,229	90	10
1951	121,627	44,591	166,218	73	27
1952	211,328	32,380	243,708	87	13
1953	522,599	68,858	591,457	88	12
1954	742,146	208,382	950,528	78	22
1955	851,500	360,000	1,211,500	70	30

Note: This table does not include small bicycles, classified in the tariff schedule as having wheels with a diameter of not over 19 inches. Imports in this category have never exceeded 15,000 machines annually.

Official statistics do not distinguish between lightweight and balloon-tire imports. The breakdown in this table has been made on the assumption, employed by the Tariff Commission in its 1952 investigation, "that all imports prior to 1950 were lightweight types, and that all imports of balloon-tire types in 1950 and later periods have comprised only those imports from Germany with wheels over 19 inches but not over 25 inches and those from that country with wheels over 25 inches in diameter but weighing not less than 36 pounds." See U. S. Tariff Commission, *Bicycles and Parts* (Washington: Author, 1952), p. 19. This assumption probably results in an understatement of the ratio of balloon-tire to lightweight imports.
Source: U. S. Tariff Commission, U. S. Bureau of the Census

to American makes. Importers say that the German machines are actually as well made as the American but that, because of a negative prestige factor, they have to sell at a lower price.

The Possibilities of Adjustment

Bicycles, it appears, are a product well suited to American methods of manufacture. Unlike chinaware and hand-fashioned glassware, they do not require for their production rare artistic talents or extraordinary manual skills. Unlike watches, they are not precision products; their working parts,

except for the variable-speed gear, do not have to be machined
with great accuracy.

American manufacturers have certain "natural" advantages.
Nearness to the major population centers means lower transportation costs, except in sales to the Pacific coast. (Bicycles
can be shipped more cheaply from England to Los Angeles
by water than from eastern factories by rail.) Domestic factories can make more rapid deliveries. One American manufacturer claims that he can ship his bicycles within five days
from the receipt of the customer's order; an importer estimates his delivery time at six weeks. Importers can supply
spare parts in the larger distributing centers, but in smaller
localities boys and girls may find difficulty in obtaining
prompt repair service on the foreign machines.

Lower wages constitute a decisive advantage for both English and German suppliers. In English bicycle factories, according to the *Wall Street Journal* (March 21, 1956), the
average hourly wage in 1955 was 79½ cents per hour and in
the American, $2.00. These figures reflect in general the wide
differential between the wages paid by American bicycle
manufacturers and their principal foreign competitors. Even
if American labor is somewhat more productive—evidence on
this point is lacking—the greater output per hour or per day
is not sufficient to offset the differences in wages.

In the United States a bicycle is a toy, or a convenience, for
children of school age; the market is highly seasonal—more
than 60 percent of all bicycles are sold for Christmas gifts.
In England, Germany and elsewhere in Europe the bicycle is
an essential means of transportation for a substantial part of
the adult population. To supply this all-year-round market,
English manufacturers make every year 3,500,000 machines,
almost all of them lightweights. The largest manufacturing
plant is that of Raleigh Industries which, with over 9,000
workers, turns out about 1.3 million bicycles annually,[11]
practically all of the type exported to the United States. By
contrast the total output of *10 American factories* in the years
1950-1954 averaged something less than 2 million bicycles.

---

[11] The number of workers includes those employed on parts, such as three-
speed gears, which the company sells to other manufacturers, including the
American.

If we consider only the output of American lightweights which compete directly with the English bicycles, the disparity in scale of operations is even more striking. The largest number of bicycles of this type produced in all American factories in postwar years was 152,000 in 1953.

American producers have been criticized for failing to meet the British competition on its own ground by making more lightweight machines. But their hesitation to do so is understandable. To change over from the balloon-tire bicycle to the lightweight would have meant abandoning a fairly stable market, long safe from foreign competition, for one, already dominated by foreign producers, whose size and characteristics were unpredictable. And, after all, the change might perhaps have proved unnecessary, for there was always the chance that the popularity of the English-type bicycle might prove only a passing fad. Moreover, they saw no possibility of getting their costs on these machines down to a level where they could compete with those made abroad. Mr. N. A. Clarke (Westfield) has written: "My reason for not making more lightweights is that my customers have not ordered more lightweights. The reason they haven't ordered more lightweights is that they can buy much cheaper models that appear to be —and in most cases are—of an equal quality level with our own. These, of course, came from abroad. . . ." For these reasons, although a few firms produced lightweights on a small scale, none of them diverted a substantial proportion of productive facilities to the new type.

The middleweight bicycle, first introduced by an American manufacturer in 1954, represents an attempt to recapture a share of the market which had been lost to foreign competition. The new machine is in several ways a compromise between the typical English and American types. It has tires 1.75 inches in diameter ("the only true lightweight with the low-pressure tire ride") and the same type of frame and coaster brake as the balloon-tire bicycles. Soon after the introduction of the first middleweight, other bicycle manufacturers followed with their own models, and in 1955 every firm was advertising at least one middleweight.

In the first five months of 1955, before the tariff increase, twice as many middleweights were produced as in the entire year 1954. In early 1955 they accounted for 30 percent of the domestic output. But West Germany's manufacturers have already copied the middleweight, as they have the balloon-tire model. Thus the American manufacturers may find that their attempt to evade foreign competition by diversification of their product has been unsuccessful.

Effects of Increased Tariff Rates

The American bicycle industry experienced a series of unfavorable events in postwar years: (1) the decline after 1948 in both home and export markets; (2) tariff reduction; (3) devaluation of sterling; (4) large imports after 1950 of British lightweights; (5) increasing imports from West Germany and other European countries of the balloon-tire bicycles, long an exclusive American product.

The relief sought by the American manufacturers was an "absolute import quota" on foreign bicycles. The restoration of the 1930 rates of 30 percent, they asserted, would not be sufficient to remedy the serious injury they had already sustained or avert the threat of further injury. The President, however, did not impose a quota.[12] Instead, in August 1955 he raised the tariff duties, but by only 50 percent of the existing rates so that, even after the increase, the duties afforded no more than moderate protection, at a level considerably below that provided by the Act of 1930.

The tariff increase on the lightweight machines was too small, from $7\frac{1}{2}$ to $11\frac{1}{4}$ percent (amounting to about $1.00 on bicycles retailing at $50 to $65 each) to have any perceptible effect on imports. Nor did the rise from 15 to $22\frac{1}{2}$ percent on balloon-tire models hold these imports in check. Actually they have increased faster than the higher-priced lightweights. Imports of all types of bicycles in 1955 were 1,223,520 units, 27 percent over the record imports of the previous year. It is true that part of this gain can be explained by increased receipts in the first half of 1955, in anticipation of the higher rates, but even after the new rates had become

---

[12] Authority to impose quotas was given in the 1951 extension of the Trade Agreements Act. The 1955 act enlarged this power with respect to imports which "threaten to impair the national security."

effective imports of foreign machines continued to exceed all previous records.

Since the tariff increases went into effect the American bicycle industry has shown some evidence of recovery. Although in the summer of 1955 two plants were shut down by strikes, factory shipments for the year (1,729,000 units) were 11 percent larger than in 1954. It would be a mistake, however, to attribute much of this improvement to the rise in import duties. Even before the President announced his decision, domestic firms, responding to better business conditions, were stepping up production; their shipments for the first five months of 1955 were 37 percent greater than in the same months of the preceding year.

Prospects of the Domestic Market

Judging from present indications, the American industry would be foolish to pin its hopes for salvation on tariff protection, either at the present level or at any level attainable in the near future. What, then, are the prospects that the industry might survive and prosper, relying on its own resources?

Some ground for optimism is to be found in the expansion of the domestic market for bicycles. After the boom years, 1947 and 1948, and the consequent reaction in 1949, the annual sales of bicycles (domestic production plus imports) in the next three years settled down to about 2 million machines a year. This was more or less accepted as a norm fixed by the number of children of bicycle-riding age. But in both 1953 and 1954 the American market took more than 2.5 million bicycles, counting both foreign and domestic makes, and in 1955 close to 3.0 million.

The "baby boom" which developed after 1945 is the basis for estimating the future size of the bicycle market. Live births in the United States averaged 2.9 million annually in the five years 1941-1945, at the rate of 21.4 per 1,000 population. In 1946 the birth rate jumped to 24.1, and in 1947 to 26.6. The number of live births in these years exceeded the 1941-1945 average by 500,000 and 900,000, respectively, which means that after a lag of six or seven years approximately the same number would be added to the potential purchasers of bicycles. After 1947 the number of live births fell off somewhat, but the increase began again in 1951 and continued through 1954. In that year the baby crop was 4.0 million. Using these figures, Professor Emile Despres estimated [13] that in the years 1954-1959 about 900,000 new bicycles would be required annually to meet the demand generated by population growth. In addition, the normal replacement of the 21 million bicycles now in use will require 2.1 million annually. Fluctuations in consumers' incomes may affect the sales in any individual year, but it seems reasonable to expect that in the years 1956-1959 sales will average 3 million units annually. Longer-range estimates, based on similar data, show that sales of 3.5 million might be reached by 1965.

These estimates are conservative; they take no account of the possible increase in the proportion of bicycle owners among children 5 to 14 years of age.[14] It has been estimated that about 75 percent of the children in this age group have bicycles; an increase in living standards would raise this percentage somewhat. The figures we have cited, moreover, do not allow for a possible increase in cycling as an adult sport or recreation.

The Vital Question

The vital question for the American manufacturer is "How will the 3-million, or 3.5-million, bicycle market be split?" It is possible that American adolescents will lose their interest in the English lightweight machines. Also the expansion of exports may cause increases in British costs. In 1955 there were already indications that the imports from the United Kingdom might be approaching their maximum.[15] But this is not true of imports of the cheaper balloon-tire models from Germany which may for some years furnish formidable competition to American firms.

[13] See the *Brief for Certain Importers of British Bicycles* before the U. S. Tariff Commission, Investigation No. 37 (Washington, November 26, 1954), pp. 104-110.
[14] An analysis of the market for bicycles prepared by the New Departure Division of General Motors fixed the limits of the bicycle-riding group at 5-14 years of age.
[15] But a large producer was reported, in March 1956, to be expanding his plant so as to be able to supply increasing demand from foreign countries, including the United States.

If imports should continue at a rate of not much more than a million bicycles per year, the remaining two-thirds of the market would keep the American industry occupied at the 1950-1954 level of production, but it would afford no opportunity for growth. Gaining a larger share of the expanded market, or perhaps even maintaining production of 2 million bicycles a year, will pose a challenge to American ingenuity and initiative in both production and marketing. More investment in engineering research will be required and greater sensitivity to changes in consumers' preferences. Manufacturers may make a practice of importing certain models to supplement their own lines of bicycles. It is possible, however, that none of these methods of adjustment will be successful. The continuing pressure of foreign competition, if we assume that no further tariff increases are granted and no quotas applied, may force a reorganization of the industry. It seems inevitable that marginal firms will be eliminated and that bicycle production, perhaps somewhat reduced in volume, will be concentrated in the best-equipped and best-managed plants.

Chapter 5

WATCHES AND DEFENSE

On July 27, 1954, President Eisenhower raised import duties on watches and watch movements. By this action he decided in favor of the domestic manufacturers in their eight-year struggle to restrict imports of Swiss watch movements. No other tariff question involving a single commodity had attracted as much attention in postwar years as the watch case. For several years both importers and manufacturers had bombarded the country with vigorous propaganda campaigns in newspapers and magazines and on the radio. Both sides had brought strong pressure to bear on the White House through Senators and Congressmen.

The economic interests involved in the United States were small in comparison with the sum total of the national economy. The watch and clock factories employed 21,500 workers; total sales of all products amounted to about $300 million; practically all of the manufacturing business was in the hands of eight companies. Importing, also, was concentrated; most of the business was done by a half dozen large firms.

To the Swiss, the ability to sell 10 to 13 million watch movements each year in the United States was a serious matter. Their watch industry exported 95 percent of its output and nearly one-third of that to the American market.

Apart from economics, the watch case had strong political implications. Watches were the first major manufactured product to come before President Eisenhower for a tariff decision. Repeatedly, during his election campaign and during the first 18 months of his administration, he had asserted his belief in freer international trade. How then was the action on watches to be interpreted? Did it mean a change in basic economic philosophy, or only a temporary shift in position under overwhelming pressure? In his press conference, on the day following his proclamation, he reaffirmed his belief in the desirability of freer world trade but said that watches represented a special case. He indicated that his decision had been strongly influenced by considerations of national security.

The watch case came before the President on an escape clause application. American watchmaking firms had petitioned for the maximum possible restriction on imports of Swiss watch movements. With the Swiss supplying 80 percent of the domestic market, the American manufacturers complained that they were suffering serious injury. As evidence they cited the postwar decline in production and employment. Four of the Tariff Commissioners agreed with the manufacturers, but two, who had before them the same set of facts, found no evidence of injury. Instead, they were impressed by the prosperous condition of the domestic industry.

The President's Decision

The President is not obliged to accept the Commission's reports; on several occasions he had rejected them. As Chief Executive, he is the guardian of the public interest and, at his discretion, can take account of matters lying outside the Tariff Commission's terms of reference. The impact of the higher duties on trade relations with Switzerland was one of these matters. Switzerland had been buying about $150 million of American exports yearly, somewhat more than she sold to this country. Watches made up between one-third and one-half of Swiss sales to the United States. Hence the President had to consider the possibility that the Swiss would retaliate.

Political repercussions abroad also had to be taken into account. Watches had become symbolic. The President knew that other Western European countries might interpret his decision on Swiss watches as an indication of the tariff treatment which they, under similar circumstances, might expect. The prospect, perhaps, might dampen their enthusiasm for an American alliance.

Finally, there was the issue of national security. It lay outside the purview of the Tariff Commission, but the President could take it into account. Workmen in watch factories, the complainants asserted, constitute a reservoir of skills essential to the production of timing devices and other complex items for military use. Unless Swiss competition were restricted by higher tariff rates, domestic production would no longer furnish an adequate "mobilization base." The labor force in watch factories would be dispersed and its skills dissipated.

On this point the President had before him contradictory evidence presented by the importers' association which said that watchmaking firms had no monopoly of highly skilled workers. In World War II, other industries had demonstrated their ability to successfully produce military items requiring the greatest precision. Hoping to resolve the conflict, the President sought the advice of the Department of Defense and the Office of Defense Mobilization. His decision seems to have been influenced largely by their opinions.

Reactions at Home and Abroad

The American Tariff League hailed the President's proclamation as "an historic turning point" in the policy of safeguarding domestic industries against injury from low-wage imports. But this was a minority opinion. Leading magazines with nation-wide circulation were practically unanimous in denouncing the tariff increase. They reasoned that it would damage U. S. prestige abroad and set back progress toward freer international trade.

A country-wide survey of editorial opinion, financed by the importers' association, showed that 79 percent of the U. S. daily newspapers which commented on the watch decision were opposed to it. In the South and Southwest, editorial comment revealed fears that Swiss retaliation might take the form of diminished purchases of American tobacco and other farm products. Middle West editors were concerned with exports of both farm products and automobiles and machinery. In these areas 90 percent of the commenting newspapers were against the increase. In three leading Eastern industrial states, New York, New Jersey and Pennsylvania, the opposition fell to 80 percent. In New England and on the West Coast editorial opinion was evenly divided. Both the American Farm Bureau Federation and the Congress of Industrial Organizations urged the President not to raise the duties on watches. After the proclamation Walter Reuther, president of the CIO, said: "Creation of this barrier to international trade is certain to create hostility in those very countries whose friendship we seek, want and need in these trying times. The President's decision is more than unfortunate. It is tragic." [1]

The Swiss government promptly protested against the tariff increase on watches which it characterized as "a serious blow not only to existing good relations between Switzerland and the United States but also to the very principle of freedom of trade." [2] In Swiss cities indignation meetings petitioned their federal government to take reprisals. There was much talk of boycotting American cigarettes, motor cars and other exports, but this proposal, lacking official support, was soon abandoned.

In summarizing the European as well as the Swiss reaction, Michael L. Hoffman, *New York Times* correspondent in Geneva, wrote: "With one blow the President proved, to the satisfaction of everyone in Europe who cares about such things, that all that the Socialists, Communists, neutralists and home-grown anti-Americans say about United States trade policy is right, and that everything Mr. Eisenhower, the Randall Commission, the Chamber of Commerce of the United States and every U. S. Ambassador in Europe says about it is wrong." The decision, he said, added "another stone to the pile that is weighing down United States prestige and influence in Europe." [3]

* * *

In this chapter we shall consider:

(1) The various factors entering into the competitive struggle between American manufacturers, on the one hand, and the Swiss producers and the importer-assemblers, on the other.

(2) The attempts, largely unsuccessful, to check imports through tariff restrictions.

(3) The various phases of the process of adjustment by which American manufacturers have been able to maintain a profitable business.

(4) The claims of the manufacturers that their industry is

[1] *Journal of Commerce*, July 28, 1954.
[2] *New York Times*, July 28, 1954.
[3] Same, August 1, 1954.

essential to national defense and on that account deserves tariff protection.

Finally, we shall attempt to formulate an appropriate government policy.

The Domestic Industry

The American watch industry is composed of four groups of business firms:

(1) The manufacturers of jeweled-lever watches.[4]

(2) The manufacturers of pin-lever watches.

(3) The importer-assemblers who bring in some complete watches but many more watch movements which they put in American-made cases, add bracelets, straps, etc., and otherwise prepare for sale.

(4) The manufacturers of watch cases. Most watch cases are made better and cheaper in the United States than in Switzerland or elsewhere in the world. Hence no significant tariff problem arises in this business.

Four companies, Waltham, Elgin, Hamilton and Bulova, make jeweled-lever watches in the United States.[5] The first three have been in the business for 105, 90 and 62 years, respectively. The fourth, Bulova, began manufacturing watch parts in the United States in 1930 and by 1942 was making in its Long Island factory all parts for jeweled-lever watches, except mainsprings and hairsprings. But the principal business of this company remains the importing and assembling[6] of watch movements made in Switzerland, where it owns and operates several plants.

---

[4] The terms "jeweled-lever" and "pin-lever" apply to the escapement, the mechanism in a watch which controls the rate at which it runs. All high-grade watches contain jeweled-lever escapements, but some cheap movements with this type of escapement are of poorer quality than the better pin-lever watches.

Pin-lever watches ordinarily have no jewels, but some have as many as 17. The number of jewels, however, is not a dependable basis for judging the quality of the watch.

[5] Gruen, an importing firm which makes a small number of watches in the United States, using some imported parts, should perhaps be added.

[6] The operations of the "assemblers" should not be confused with the assembling of watch movements from watch parts, a much more elaborate process carried on in American and Swiss factories.

Pin-Lever Watches

Pin-lever watches in general are less expensive, less accurate and less durable than the jeweled-lever variety. The domestic firms now supply a smaller proportion of the domestic market for inexpensive timepieces than in prewar years. In 1936-1940 their share was 97 percent (89 percent if only wrist watches are considered). In 1953 they supplied 65 percent (50 percent of wrist watches).[7] The change is closely related to the declining popularity of the pocket watch. In prewar years manufacturers sold 7 million of the "dollar watches" a year, 70 percent of the total output. In 1953 only 2.7 million of this variety were sold. The decline of 4.3 million watches of this type is considerably greater than the loss in total output, 3.8 million units.

Until recently the pin-lever branch of the industry, which also makes clocks, has been less vulnerable to foreign competition, and less concerned with tariff matters, than the jeweled-lever watch manufacturers. The pin-lever watch firms did not join the firms making jeweled-lever watches in their applications for escape clause relief.[8] However, the Tariff Commission's two investigations and the President's proclamation covered all types of watches.

Jeweled-Lever Watches

In this study we shall give attention principally to the segment of the industry which produces watches with jeweled-lever escapements. This is the area in which the critical problems of national policy arise, both economic and strategic. Unless otherwise specified, "watches" and "the watch industry" will refer only to the jeweled-lever variety.

The domestic output of jeweled-lever watches over the period 1929-1953 showed only a moderate rate of growth.

---

[7] There is no way of determining exactly how many pin-lever movements are imported. The Tariff Commission considers that all imports of watch movements with less than 2 jewels and about 10 percent of those with 2 or more jewels are competitive with the American pin-lever watches. The figures quoted in this section are based on the Commission's estimates.

[8] In January 1956, however, manufacturers of pin-lever watches asked the Office of Defense Mobilization to recommend a quota limitation on competing imports.

Table 16

Jeweled-Lever Watches: U. S. Production,
Competitive Imports and Estimated Consumption,
1929-1955

(in thousands of units)

Year	Production	Competitive imports[a]	Estimated consumption[b]
1929	1,737	4,688	6,376
1930	1,330	2,530	3,812
1931	612	774	1,379
1932	488	401	887
1933	463	409	870
1934	950	799	1,748
1935	1,393	1,080	2,472
1936	1,702	2,027	3,706
1937	2,111	2,809	4,882
1938	1,042	2,028	3,054
1939	1,624	2,565	4,164
1940	1,912	3,103	4,986
1941	2,510	3,944	6,409
1942	2,070	4,980	6,978
1943	1,313	7,420	8,604
1944	1,014	6,588	7,461
1945	1,103	8,487	9,566
1946	1,720	7,969	9,605
1947	2,364	6,617	8,813
1948	3,018	6,696	9,515
1949	2,793	5,904	8,352
1950	2,480	6,915	9,232
1951	3,162	7,953	10,977
1952	2,433	7,877	10,069
1953	2,365	9,030	11,173
1954	1,716	6,573	7,823
1955	1,926	6,300[c]	8,000[c]

[a] Imports which compete principally with domestic jeweled-lever watches. For method of calculation, see note on p. 93.
[b] Small quantities, representing exports of domestic watches and reexports of watches containing imported movements, have been deducted in order to arrive at estimated consumption.
[c] Preliminary.
Source: Computed from official statistics of the U. S. Tariff Commission and the U. S. Bureau of the Census.

In the same period, however, the total sales of watches of this type in the American market increased by 75 percent, the increase having been supplied principally by imports. The sharp decline in 1954, in both domestic production and in competitive imports,[9] appears to be the result of unusual market conditions (particularly the accumulation of inventories in the previous year). Table 16 shows the variations in production, competitive imports and annual consumption of watches in this period. (See also Chart E.) Both imports and production declined in the depression of the 1930's. Both also increased with the upturn in the business cycle. In each phase imports were more flexible; they fell off more rapidly in depression years and picked up faster when general business recovered.

World War II witnessed a great expansion in the demand for watches, both for civilian and for military use. This increase was supplied principally by imports, for during the war domestic manufacturing facilities were shifted to the production of fuses, fire-control devices and other military items. After civilian production was resumed, it climbed in 1948 to 3.0 million movements, a figure about 1.4 million in excess of the 1935-1939 level. With rising national income the postwar market for jeweled-lever watches continued to expand, but again the increase was supplied entirely by imported watches. After 1948 (except for 1951 when the Korean affair led to new government purchases) domestic production declined steadily through 1954. The year 1955 brought only a slight increase.

Employment has fallen. The decline in the average number of employees (as reported by the Tariff Commission) in plants making jeweled-lever watches is shown in Table 17 (p. 97).

It is significant that the loss since 1946 of 4,000 workers in watchmaking personnel has been more than offset by the gain of 5,000 workers in departments making other products, so

[9] U. S. customs schedules do not distinguish between imports of jeweled-lever and pin-lever watches, but the Tariff Commission has made a calculation of "imports" which compete principally with domestic jeweled-lever watches," as follows: From the total number of imports containing 2 or more jewels (excluding small clocks), it subtracts 5 percent for the period 1931-1940; 2½ percent for 1941-1945; 5 percent for 1946-1947; and 10 percent thereafter. See U. S. Tariff Commission, *Watches, Movements, and Parts* (Washington: Author, 1954), Table 11.

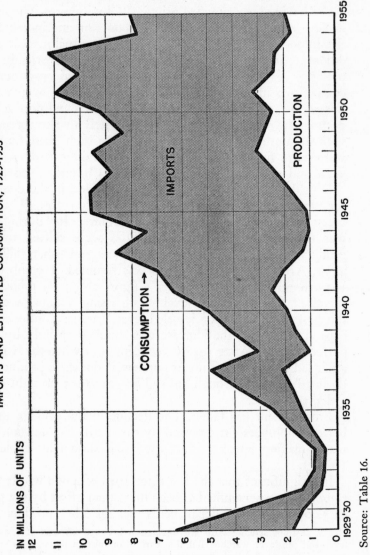

CHART E

JEWELED-LEVER WATCH MOVEMENTS: U. S. PRODUCTION, COMPETITIVE
IMPORTS AND ESTIMATED CONSUMPTION, 1929-1955

Source: Table 16.

Table 17

EMPLOYMENT IN THE U. S. JEWELED-LEVER WATCH
INDUSTRY, 1934-1954

Years	Employed on watches, service and parts	Employed on other products	Total
		(average number of employees)	
Average:			
1934-1935	5,595	285	5,880
1936-1940	6,473	176	6,649
1941-1945	7,572	2,427	9,999
1946-1950	9,318	188	9,506
Annual:			
1946	8,565	351	8,916
1948	10,349	99	10,448
1950	7,761	50	7,811
1952	7,147	2,808	9,955
1954 (April)	4,242	5,512	9,754

Source: U. S. Tariff Commission, *Watches, Movements, and Parts* (Washington: Author, 1954), Table 15

that the total working force was somewhat larger in 1954 than in the first postwar year, and 50 percent larger than in the prewar period 1936-1940. (See Chart F.)

The decline in employment in watchmaking in postwar years is not to be attributed solely to declining production. Output per employee has probably increased, although this would be hard to demonstrate statistically.

The Importer-Assemblers

A few complete watches are brought into the United States from abroad, mostly of the self-winding variety, but the imports consist almost entirely of movements to be "assembled" in this country, i.e., installed in American-made cases, fitted with bracelets (also made in this country), and packed in boxes ready for delivery to the retailers. Most of the importer-assemblers[10] operate in small factories and shops, but the bulk of the business in jeweled-lever watches is done by four large

[10] The total number of firms engaged in this business fluctuates widely. During the war it rose to about 500, but the number now is considerably less.

CHART F

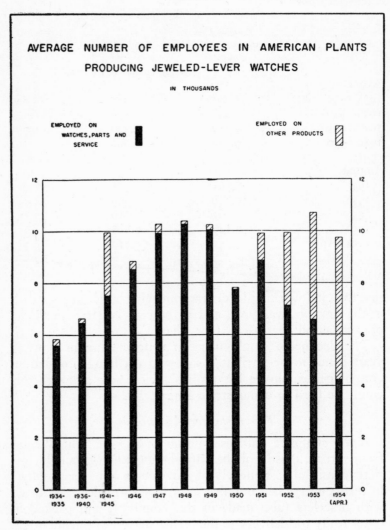

Source: Table 17

firms—Bulova, Gruen, Benrus and Longines-Wittnauer. They
are publicly owned American companies with thousands
of stockholders. The importer-assemblers in 1950 employed
directly between 4,000 and 4,500 persons in this country.
Each of the largest firms owns and operates plants in Switzerland which produce watch movements.

The Strength of Import Competition

The ability of the Swiss manufacturers to gain a predominant position in the American market for jeweled-lever
watches, and to make substantial gains in supplying pin-lever
watches, rests partly on economic factors and partly on the
tight control of production and exports exercised by a gov-
ernment-sponsored cartel. The watch industry of Switzerland
is the largest in the world; it quite overshadows that of the
United States, the second in size. The Swiss in 1953 made 35
million movements, four times the American output of both
jeweled-lever and pin-lever watches. In Switzerland production is dispersed among about 1,000 separate establishments.
Less than 100 are integrated factories that make complete
watches; the balance includes small and middle-size shops
that make parts (mainsprings and hairsprings, dials, jewels,
cases, etc.). Some parts are made by workers in their own
homes. Several hundred firms are engaged in assembling
watches from purchased parts.

Although production units in Switzerland are many and
widely dispersed, their operations are subject to strict control
by trade associations, holding companies and by a semiofficial
coordinating organization, the Swiss Watch Chamber. A Collective Agreement, signed in 1928 by representatives of these
various organizations and since amended, effectively regulates
production, sales and exports of watches, watch movements
and component parts. A tax imposed on all exported movements provides a fund for advertising and propaganda in
foreign markets. Through the Collective Agreement, as well
as through its close association with firms importing watch
movements into the United States, the Swiss watch industry
has been able to exercise a large measure of control over the
volume of watch movements exported to this country, and
over minimum prices. On account of these activities the U. S.

Department of Justice has charged the Swiss trade associations, and the principal firms engaged in importing watch movements into the United States, with restraint of trade in violation of the Sherman Act and certain provisions of the Wilson Tariff Act (1894).[11]

Specifically, the government asserted, *inter alia*, that the importers had agreed not to set up facilities to manufacture watches and watch parts in the United States and that they had participated in an agreement to limit the number of certain brand-name movements which would be shipped into this country. Furthermore, the importers were charged with having conspired to fix the prices of the Swiss movements. "Combination and conspiracy," the government alleged, (1) had retarded the growth of watch manufacturing in the United States, and (2) had also maintained the prices of Swiss watches in the United States at "arbitrary and non-competitive levels." These two charges hardly seem compatible, for, if the cartel had actually been able to sustain the prices of Swiss movements above a normal or competitive level, it must have improved the market for American-made watches and thus helped rather than hindered the American industry.

Swiss costs of manufacture of comparable watch movements, according to statements of both the manufacturers and the importers, are substantially lower than the American. The scale of wages is much lower than in the United States, and labor makes up a large part (80 percent in the United States) of the cost of the finished movement. According to testimony presented to the Tariff Commission, the highest paid workers in Swiss factories in 1954 were earning from

[11] For particulars of the charges and a list of the defendants, see Civil Action No. 96-170, filed October 19, 1954 in U. S. District Court, Southern District of New York.

The Bulova Watch Company was named as a defendant but not Waltham, Hamilton or Elgin, although all four manufacturers have been engaged in importing Swiss movements.

A second antitrust suit, which the Department of Justice filed on December 2, 1955, charged that Swiss manufacturers of watchmaking machinery had conspired with the four American producers of jeweled-lever watches to restrain trade in watchmaking machinery. Specifically, the government alleged that the American firms had agreed not to use *for watch manufacture* certain machinery imported from Switzerland. The American defendants have replied that they signed under duress in order to obtain equipment necessary for carrying out defense contracts.

90 cents to $1.10 an hour; in the United States the rate for these workers ranged from $1.72 to $2.85. Less skilled workers earned 85 cents in Switzerland and $1.65 to $2.10 in the United States. Unskilled workers in Swiss factories were paid only one-third the American rate. Because watchmaking in Switzerland has a history going back several hundred years, there is available a large supply of labor brought up in the tradition of the industry.

The system of interchangeable parts, originally an American invention, has been adopted in Swiss factories. In both countries watch parts are made by mass-production methods on identical machines or machines of the same type. The output per worker in the United States is somewhat greater but not nearly enough to compensate for the higher scale of wages. As a result, the cost of producing a typical 17-jewel watch movement in Switzerland may be as much as $4 less than the corresponding American cost.

Lower labor costs, however, have constituted only a part of the economic advantage of the Swiss manufacturers. They proved more ingenious than their American rivals in designing new types of watches. The wrist watch was first introduced by Swiss manufacturers; they also pioneered in making antimagnetic, shock-resistant and self-winding movements. As important as any of these achievements was the success of the Swiss manufacturers, in cooperation with the importers, in their analysis of the American market. For many years American manufacturers of jeweled-lever watches had been content to sell a limited number of rather expensive watches. They generally marketed their product through jobbers and wholesalers to retail jewelers. Pin-lever watches, a much cheaper product, were sold in hardware stores, department stores and chain drug stores.

The importers, observing the wide gap between the price levels of the two types of American products, proceeded to fill it with millions of medium-priced watches. They by-passed the wholesalers,[12] selling their watches directly to a

---

[12] In fact, the big jobbers and wholesalers refused to handle watches with Swiss movements for fear of losing their Waltham, Elgin and Hamilton business. Hence, in devising the new method of marketing watches, the importers were making a virtue of necessity.

wide variety of retail dealers, department stores, chain stores, hardware stores and drug stores. They sought a wide market by aggressive advertising, first in newspapers and on the radio, and recently on television, and by time-payment sales. At a time when the American manufacturers were fair-trading their watches, many of the importers left the retailers free to fix their own selling prices.

The Tariff, a Weak Defense Against Swiss Competition

In their attempts, within the past 25 years, to ward off competition from abroad, the domestic manufacturers found tariff protection of little value, except for a few years in the early 1930's. This was surprising, for it seemed that in the complicated watch paragraphs of the Act of 1930 Congressional committees, guided by representatives of the industry, had constructed a practically impassable barrier to imports. The barrier had two levels of duties, all of which were specific:

(1) A duty on the movement itself, varying with size and jewel count. Thus a movement with 17 jewels, of a width of over 1 inch but not over 1.2 inches, paid $3.05.

(2) An additional duty of $1.00 levied on each "adjustment." [13] Thus the tariff makers intended that a typical 17-jewel movement with five adjustments would pay $8.05 in import duties (3.05 + [5 × $1.00]). The duties on watches with fewer jewels and fewer adjustments would, of course, be proportionately less.

But the second layer of the tariff barrier proved no barrier at all, for the tariff makers failed to take into account the ingenuity of the Swiss watchmakers. By changes in the technique of manufacturing they produced watch movements which need no adjustments. Such watches they marked "unadjusted." This marking was permitted by the U. S. Treasury, and the watches were imported without payment of the additional duties prescribed in the Tariff Act of 1930. Later, the Swiss manufacturers, by constructing watch movements which, at slight expense, can be "upjeweled" after importa-

---

[13] The principal adjustments were for changes in temperature, changes in position, and isochronism (to insure uniformity in time keeping as the watch runs down after winding).

tion, found another loophole in the tariff wall.[14] (See pp. 111-113.)

By changes in their manufacturing processes, it has been asserted, the Swiss producers have circumvented tariff legislation and have fraudulently deprived the U. S. Treasury of revenue. This charge, however, seems unjustified. We are concerned here with "tax avoidance," not "tax evasion," for in U. S. customs law the principle is well established that the importer is justified in preparing his shipments so as to incur the minimum of duty payments. Smuggling is, of course, a horse of a different color.

Smuggling upset the calculations of the architects of the 1930 tariff. They failed to take into account the principle, established by centuries of experience of customs officials in all countries, that when import duties rise above a certain point they defeat their own purpose by making smuggling a richly rewarding enterprise. This is exactly what happened after 1930. Like diamonds, watch movements, especially the smaller movements which are the more valuable, have great value in proportion to their bulk and hence can readily be concealed in baggage or on the person. According to a Tariff Commission report:

. . . smuggling rose to such proportions that recorded imports for the first half of the 1930's considerably understate the number of watches and watch movements which actually were brought into the United States in that period. Customs officials seized large numbers of smuggled watches, but even the seized watches finally reached regular trade channels as, under the law, they had to be sold at auction.[15]

After the 1936 trade agreement had reduced duties, illegal operations became less profitable. The Swiss government, as a *quid pro quo*, set up various controls on exports designed to keep the business of exporting watch movements within legitimate channels.

Another weakness in the 1930 Act, viewed as a measure for

[14] Additional jewels can be inserted in any watch movement. The Swiss manufacturers, by preparing the movement in advance, have substantially reduced the cost of the upjeweling process.
[15] U. S. Tariff Commission, *Watches*, War Changes in Industry Series, Report No. 20 (Washington: GPO, 1947), p. 40.

the protection of the domestic industry, was its reliance on specific rates of duty. During the middle 1930's, when prices of imported movements were falling, the specific duties were an increasing handicap to importers and afforded increasing protection to domestic manufacturers. In 1931-1935 the duties collected on imported watches averaged 83 percent of

Table 18

U. S. RATES OF DUTY ON WATCH MOVEMENTS

(dollars and cents per unit)

	Act of 1930	Trade agreement 1936	1955 rate
Par. 367(a)			
Having more than 17 jewels	$10.75	$10.75	$10.75
Having more than 1 and not more than 17 jewels:			
Over 1.5 inches wide	1.25[a]	.90[b]	1.25[c]
Over 1.2, not over 1.5 inches wide	1.40[a]	.90[b]	1.35[c]
Over 1, not over 1.2 inches wide	1.55[a]	.90[b]	1.35[c]
Over 0.9, not over 1 inch wide	1.75[a]	1.20[b]	1.75[c]
Over 0.8, not over 0.9 inch wide	2.00[a]	1.35[b]	2.00[c]
Over 0.6, not over 0.8 inch wide	2.25[a]	1.35[b]	2.02½[c]
0.6 inch or less wide	2.50[a]	1.80[b]	2.50[c]
Having no jewels or only 1 jewel:			
Over 1.5 inches wide	.75	.75	.75
Over 1.2, not over 1.5 inches wide	.84	.75	.84
Over 1, not over 1.2 inches wide	.93	.75	.93
Over 0.9, not over 1 inch wide	1.05	.75	1.05
Over 0.8, not over 0.9 inch wide	1.20	.75	1.12½
Over 0.6, not over 0.8 inch wide	1.35	.75	1.12½
0.6 inch or less wide	1.50	.90	1.35

[a] Plus $.15 for each jewel in excess of 7.
[b] Plus $.09 for each jewel in excess of 7.
[c] Plus $.135 for each jewel in excess of 7.

Note: In addition, a movement with 17 jewels or less was subject to additional duties, as follows:

	Act of 1930	Trade agreement 1936	1955 rate
Each adjustment (treating adjustment to temperature as two adjustments)	$ 1.00	$ .50	$ .50
A movement designed to operate more than 47 hours without rewinding, or a self-winding movement, or one in which a self-winding device can be incorporated	1.00	.50	.75

the foreign value. But this situation was soon reversed. The upturn in prices beginning in 1936 and 1937 would have weakened the protective effect of the watch duties, even if no change had been made in the rates themselves.

The 1936 trade agreement with Switzerland simplified the structure of the American tariff on watches and reduced rates in most categories. (See Table 18.) For example, on movements containing 15 or 16 jewels, specific import duties in 1930 had ranged from $2.45 to $3.85 each, according to size; after the 1936 agreement the rates were $1.62 to $2.61. The over-all average duties collected under this agreement in the years immediately preceding World War II averaged about 64 percent of the foreign value of the imported movements. The subsequent decline was the result of rising prices and changes in the kinds of watch movements exported. (See Table 19 and Chart G.) The reduction of duties in 1936 was followed in 1937 by a substantial increase in officially recorded

Table 19

U. S. IMPORTS OF WATCH MOVEMENTS: AD VALOREM
EQUIVALENTS OF RATES OF DUTY AND UNIT
VALUES, 1929-1954

Year	Ad valorem equivalent (percent)	Unit value	Year	Ad valorem equivalent (percent)	Unit value
1929	52.4	$2.25	1942	49.0	$3.63
1930	60.1	2.45	1943	42.3	4.38
1931	85.5	3.23	1944	37.0	5.39
1932	94.5	2.94	1945	37.3	5.04
1933	80.3	3.26	1946	35.4	5.37
1934	78.1	3.08	1947	35.4	5.53
1935	80.7	3.06	1948	35.4	5.21
1936	63.4	2.64	1949	37.0	4.90
1937	68.3	2.62	1950	37.0	4.80
1938	62.4	2.75	1951	36.6	4.68
1939	62.9	2.76	1952	35.4	5.05
1940	60.8	2.89	1953	33.2	5.29
1941	54.6	3.20	1954	38.4	5.19

Source: Ad valorem equivalents—U. S. Tariff Commission. Unit values—calculated from quantities and foreign values of imports, as reported by the U. S. Bureau of the Census

CHART G

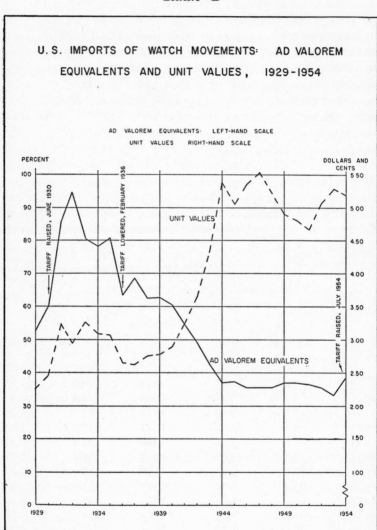

U. S. IMPORTS OF WATCH MOVEMENTS: AD VALOREM
EQUIVALENTS AND UNIT VALUES, 1929-1954

Source: Table 19

imports. The actual increase was somewhat less, owing to the decline in smuggling.

During World War II and for several years thereafter, the tariff had little effect either on imports or on domestic production. After Pearl Harbor the orders placed by the Army and Navy for fuses, watches, clocks and other timing devices occupied an increasing share of domestic manufacturing facilities. There was practically no production of watches for civilian use after the middle of 1942, although sales from existing stocks still continued. The result was a great boom in imports, stimulated by Army and Navy purchases and by rising civilian demand. From a prewar average of 2.8 million movements a year, *total* imports rose to 8.8 million in 1946. In that year nearly 60 percent of all watches sold in the United States had imported movements. If the comparison is limited to *competitive* imports,[16] foreign suppliers provided 83 percent of the jeweled-lever watches sold in the United States.

Attempts to Restrict Imports

American manufacturers looked about for ways of restricting imports. But without an act of Congress there was no possibility of raising duties or imposing quotas on Swiss watches, for the 1936 agreement contained no escape clause.[17] However, the U. S. State Department persuaded the Swiss government to impose a *voluntary quota* on exports, limited for a period of 15 months, January 1, 1946 to March 31, 1947, assumed to cover the reconversion period in the American industry. During this period Switzerland agreed to prevent direct exports of watches to the United States in excess of the annual rate of 1945 and also undertook to prevent indirect shipments. The next step was taken by the U. S. State Department in August 1950 when it gave six months' notice of denunciation of the 1936 trade agreement, indicating, however, that if the Swiss government consented to the insertion of an escape clause it would revoke the denunciation. Faced with

[16] See footnote, p. 93.
[17] For a description of this mechanism see p. 29n. The original "escape clause" had been inserted in the 1942 agreement with Mexico. An Executive Order of February 25, 1947 had required the insertion of a similar clause in all future trade agreements.

this alternative, the Swiss gave way, and the agreement was revised accordingly.

American watch manufacturers were not slow in taking advantage of their opportunity. In February 1951 the Elgin and Hamilton companies and the trustees of the bankrupt Waltham concern filed an application with the Tariff Commission looking to the restoration of the 1930 duties. After an exhaustive investigation (hearings lasted eight days and the stenographic record ran to over 1,500 pages), the Commission rendered a split decision. Three Commissioners found that the 1936 reduction in duties had resulted in injury to the domestic industry; three Commissioners found no evidence of injury, but one of them joined the first group in recommending an increase in the tariff, on the ground that the increased imports *threatened* to cause serious injury.

President Truman, in August 1952, rejected the majority recommendation. He pointed out that the domestic manufacturers were making good profits. Their production of watches had not declined. They had not cut wages or dismissed employees. He recognized that their share of the domestic market had fallen, but, as he interpreted the law, that fact did not constitute proof of injury or threatened injury. He based his decision on broad considerations of national interest, particularly the need for sustaining in foreign countries confidence in the sincerity of the much advertised American policy of promoting freer world trade. He called attention to the damage which raising the import duties on watches might inflict on the Swiss economy and on U. S. trade relations with that country. He took note of the argument that defense considerations required the maintenance of a healthy American watch industry, but doubted whether an increase in import duties constituted an "effective approach to that objective."

Not daunted by this defeat, the American manufacturers, a year later, returned to the attack. In September 1953 Elgin, Hamilton and Waltham filed with the Tariff Commission a second application for restoration of the 1930 duties. The application referred only to watches containing 7-17 jewels, but the Commission extended its investigation to cover the imports of all types of watches. The investigation showed that the conditions about which the manufacturers had originally complained (decreasing production and increasing imports) had meanwhile worsened. Again the Commission, by a vote of 4 to 2, recommended an increase of 50 percent on imports of watch movements, but in no case were the new rates to exceed those imposed by the Act of 1930. No increase was recommended on movements with more than 17 jewels on which the duty was already prohibitive. In accepting this recommendation, President Eisenhower indicated that considerations of national defense had influenced his decision.

Over 17 Jewels—A Privileged Sanctuary

Imports did not destroy the American watch industry. In spite of the decline which began in 1952,[18] average annual production for the six years 1950-1955 was 2,347,000 units, a figure 40 percent above the 1936-1940 annual average. But an important change took place in the character of the American product. In prewar years, watches with 8 to 17 jewels made up 73 percent of the domestic output; watches with more than 17 jewels accounted for only 13 percent. In 1955 the group with more than 17 jewels made up 62 percent of all watches produced in American factories. (See Table 20.)

Progress in manufacturing techniques, stimulated by the high import duties on movements with more than 17 jewels, accounts for the change in the composition of the domestic product. American firms discovered that by using a new method of setting jewels, the so-called friction setting, they could produce movements with 17 jewels and more at costs lower than those incurred in making 7- and 15-jewel models by methods formerly employed.

The peculiar structure of the watch duties made the new process a profitable venture. The Act of 1930 had imposed an extraordinarily high duty, $10.75 each, on movements with more than 17 jewels, which had practically eliminated imports in that category. In recent years only a few of the most expensive Swiss watches with more than 17 jewels have been able to surmount the tariff barrier.

For the domestic manufacturers, under strong pressure from imports of 16- and 17-jewel movements, the over-17-jewel business has proved "a privileged sanctuary." The cost

[18] The unusually low production in 1954, 1,716,000 units, is attributable to an inventory situation.

Table 20

U. S. PRODUCTION OF JEWELED-LEVER WATCH MOVEMENTS, BY JEWEL COUNT, 1934-1955

Number of jewels
(as percent of total)

	2-7	8-15	16-17	More than 17
Average:				
1934-35	37.9	22.2	35.6	4.3
1936-40	13.3	28.0	45.5	13.2
1941-45	6.3	32.8	41.6	19.3
1946-50	—	12.3	46.0	41.7
Annual:				
1951	—	1.2	58.1	40.7
1952	—	1.3	62.6	36.1
1953	—	1.6	47.0	51.4
1954	—	—	50.0	50.0
1955	—	—	37.7	62.3

Source: U. S. Tariff Commission, *Watches, Movements, and Parts* (Washington: Author, 1954), Table 7; U. S. Bureau of the Census

of the extra jewels is only a few cents each, and the additional labor cost of constructing a 21-jewel movement is a negligible percentage of total manufacturing cost.

Horological experts agree that jewels above 17 add little or nothing to the time-keeping qualities of the conventional watch. Watches which take prizes for accuracy rarely contain more that 17 or 18 jewels, often only 15. Yet through persistent and persuasive advertising, American manufacturers have been able to sell watches with 21 or more jewels at a substantially higher price than they can obtain for the 17-jewel timepiece. This is a joint-cost situation familiar to accountants and economists. The price of the 17-jewel watch, it seems, is held down by Swiss competition to a level where it covers labor and material costs but contributes little to overhead expense. The latter is covered by sales of timepieces with over 17 jewels. By restricting output of these watches, manufacturers can maintain prices above the 17-jewel level.

The following excerpt from the testimony of Mr. Arde Bulova before a Congressional committee is instructive. Mr.

Bulova is chairman of the board of the Bulova Watch Company which is both an importer and manufacturer. He stated that his company imported 1,600,000 watch movements in 1954 and manufactured in its Long Island factory 400,000 watches, all with 21- or 23-jewel movements.

Mr. McCarthy.[19] With an increase in the production cost of 10 cents or 20 cents, a 23-jewel watch on the market is worth anywhere from $10 to $25 more than a 17-jewel watch?
Mr. Bulova. That is correct.
Mr. McCarthy. Although the cost [of] production is only 20 cents more?
Mr. Bulova. It is not only that. The cost of production here, because of the high cost of labor, versus our cost in Switzerland, is so much higher that we cannot afford to produce a 17-jewel watch here and compete with the Swiss imports of 17-jewel watches. We would be out of business.
Therefore, the higher range is the only watch we can make in the United States.[20]

Later Mr. Bulova said:

I might explain the economics of that problem. You will find that most of the American watch manufacturers, based on a formula that was worked out so that they could sustain themselves in business, produced about 50 percent of their watches in higher jewels and 50 percent in 17 jewels because they can sell their entire production in that field but from an internal cost standpoint they plussed their 23-jewel watches, they plus them $2 and decrease the cost on their 17-jewel watches by that $2.
In that way they are able to balance the production and keep in business.[21]

But the manufacturers' privileged sanctuary may not prove inviolable. Seventeen-jewel movements have recently been imported, so constructed as to permit the insertion at small expense of additional jewels, *after importation*. American manufacturers, fearing that watches containing such "upjeweled" movements might cut deep into their sales of 21-jewel

[19] Representative Eugene J. McCarthy of Minnesota.
[20] U. S. House, Committee on Ways and Means, *Jewel Substitutes in Watch Movements*, Hearings, 84th Cong., 1st sess., on H. R. 7466 and H. R. 7467 (Washington: GPO, 1955), pp. 57-58.
[21] Same, p. 59. Only Bulova, among the American producers, makes a 23-jewel watch.

watches, lodged strong protests with the U. S. Bureau of Customs, stating that the "doctored" movements should pay the full $10.75 duty. To allow them to enter at the 17-jewel rates, they argued, would nullify the intent of Congress.

In the course of the ensuing discussion, it developed that upjeweling was not a new practice, but in recent years it had been forbidden by the Swiss watch trust to its members. On September 9, 1954, however, less than two months after President Eisenhower's proclamation of higher import duties, the Swiss organization lifted the ban. At once importers brought in several new kinds of movements devised so that upjeweling could easily be accomplished. Spurred by manufacturers' protests, the Bureau of Customs ruled that these movements contained "substitutes for jewels," and hence they should be assessed at the $10.75 rate. This decision, however, did not daunt the importers. They soon presented other types of movements designed to circumvent the unfavorable ruling.

At this point the Bureau of Customs, apparently lacking confidence in its ability to cope with the seemingly inexhaustible ingenuity of the Swiss manufacturers and the importers, turned to Congress for assistance. It arranged for legislation to be introduced in the House[22] which was designed to "plug the tariff loophole." The Department of Commerce lent its support and the Department of State offered no objection, but the Tariff Commission was severely critical. The Commission asserted (1) that the proposed legislation would conflict with treaty obligations to Switzerland, and (2) that it violated a long-established principle of customs law, viz., that for tariff purposes imported articles are classified according to their character and condition *when imported*. The Commission also held that the administration of the proposed legislation would prove burdensome both to the government and to the importers. Finally, it warned that it would not be effective against new practices which the importers might devise.[23] Although adopted by a majority vote of the Ways and Means Committee, the bills did not reach the floor of the House before its adjournment. In the 84th Con-

[22] Two identical bills were introduced, H. R. 7466 and H. R. 7467, to amend paragraph 367 of the Tariff Act of 1930.
[23] U. S. House, Committee on Ways and Means, *Jewel Substitutes in Watch Movements*, Hearings, cited, pp. 4-5.

gress, second session, Representative Daniel Reed proposed a novel method of suppressing upjeweling. By an amendment to the Internal Revenue Act of 1954 he would impose an $8.00 "processing" tax on all movements to which jewels had been added after importation.

Effects of 1954 Tariff Increase

After the higher rates went into effect, imports of jeweled-lever watch movements, in the categories competitive with the domestic product, fell from 6.6 million in 1954 to 6.3 million in 1955. How far the higher duties were responsible for this change is not clear. Importers had brought in large quantities of watch movements in early 1954 in anticipation of the tariff change. Then business recession left them and the retailers overstocked. The need for working off inventories exerted a depressing effect on 1955 imports.

Instead of falling, imports of the cheaper pin-lever watches rose in 1955. Consequently, the proportion of 16- and 17-jewel watch imports in the total fell from 59 percent in 1954 to 52 percent in 1955 and 49 percent in the first quarter of 1956. This shift was directly related to the tariff change, for the President's proclamation, which had raised rates on the most popular categories of 16- and 17-jewel movements by 50 percent, had made smaller increases (and, in one case, no increase) on watch imports in the "0-1 jewel" category.

Domestic production of jeweled-lever watches, in total, showed a gain, from 1,716,000 units in 1954 to 1,926,000 in 1955. This gain seems unrelated to the increase in the tariff, since it occurred in watches with more than 17 jewels, on which duties had not been raised. Domestic production of watches with 17 jewels or less, on which the import duties were raised, actually fell by about 12 percent. The explanation probably lies in the increased demand in the United States for 21- and 23-jewel watches, which altered the manufacturers' calculations of the most profitable division of their output.

In assessing the effects of a tariff increase, attention should be given to changes in prices as well as in the volume of imports and production. Unfortunately, reliable price comparisons over time are hard to come by because of frequent changes in the styles and models of watches put on the market.

Within a month after the President's proclamation, one large importer announced a flat increase of $1 per movement in prices to retailers. His "recommended" retail prices to consumers showed an increase of $3 to $5 per movement. Another importer made advances of $.50 to $1.00 on prices to retailers and suggested that prices to consumers should be raised by $3.00. In many cases, however, importer-assemblers continued to sell at the old prices until inventories were exhausted, and after that they raised them gradually. Often the increased duty was passed on to the consumer by cutting the quality of the case, bracelet or strap rather than by raising the price of the watch.

Remarks about the effects of tariff change ought always to be accompanied by a word, or several words, of caution. There is usually a lag before the new duties can work out their effects. Moreover, tariff change never operates in a vacuum but always in conjunction with other changes. One must always take account of fluctuations in the level of American business activity. The 1953-1954 recession had a depressing effect on sales of watches, both imported and domestic. Chart E shows similar effects in the depression of the 1930's, and in the recessions of 1938 and 1949. Imports profited by the wartime prosperity while domestic watch factories were engaged in defense production. In the 25-year period it appears that the major swings in imports and production are to be explained by cyclical variations in business activity, with resulting changes in consumers' incomes and in their propensity to buy watches, rather than by changes in import duties.

Diversification of Products

American watch factories are still in business and prospering because of their ability to successfully adjust their operations to the new conditions created by strong foreign competition. They have shifted the bulk of their production into high-priced watches with more than 17 jewels and have made other significant changes and improvements in their products. Assembly-line techniques, introduced in 1946, reduced man-hour requirements. "One company used to require 400 workers to assemble 1200 watches per day; it now can assemble the same number with only 45-50 workers.

However, reduction of assembly workers has, to some extent, increased the requirements for parts manufacturing workers due to the increased precision of components required for mass production assembly." [24]

At present watches make up a diminishing share of the total sales of manufacturers of jeweled watches. The trend toward diversification has a long history; Waltham made speedometers in the early days of the motor car. World War II gave diversification a strong push by opening profitable opportunities for making many types of defense items, and the manufacturers never wholly reconverted their plants to production of watches. After the war, they found the Swiss watches firmly entrenched in civilian markets. When attempts to dislodge them through tariff restriction proved unsuccessful, domestic firms began to invest in production of "nonwatch" items. Waltham began the production of gyroscopes and electrical tachometers. Bulova made radio apparatus for household use and experimented with an electric shaver of new design. A change of management in 1954 put Hamilton somewhat belatedly on the road to diversification. The new president, although an able and sincere advocate of high import duties on Swiss watches, recognized the danger of relying on the tariff to save the watch industry. He is said to have discovered that "you can't run a Lancaster [Pa.] company from a room at the Mayflower in Washington." [25] Hamilton in 1954 acquired the stock of the Hathaway Instrument Company, a producer of electronic instruments, as a step toward development of work in automation. The company has also set up a completely integrated steel mill to supply its watch division with special steels which will also be marketed outside.

The Elgin National Watch Company, the largest American manufacturer of jeweled watches, carried diversification even further. The company's president, Mr. J. C. Shennan, in his 1952 year-end statement said that Elgin was meeting foreign competition by increased diversification. "We are expanding our research, manufacturing and sales activities into products

[24] Interdepartmental Committee on the Jeweled Watch Industry, *The Essentiality to National Security of the American Jeweled Watch Industry*, Report to the Director of the Office of Defense Mobilization (Washington: Author, 1954), p. 12.
[25] Mr. Arthur B. Sinkler, as quoted in *Business Week* (July 3, 1954).

other than American-made watches, in the belief that diversification provides the only real source of economic security."
In line with this policy, Elgin bought two firms which made
watch cases and watch bracelets, women's compacts and
men's jewelry. But Elgin's principal investments outside the
watch industry were in the field of miniature electronics,
where tool-making facilities and workers' skills had been developed in defense work. After 1954, the company has acquired
three going concerns in the electronics field. As a result of
the continuation of military work and "external" diversification, about 40 percent of Elgin's business at the end of 1954
lay outside the manufacture of commercial watches.

In the total 1953 sales of the four American manufacturers,
watches with American-made movements accounted for only
45 percent, watches with imported movements 23 percent,
and other articles, principally defense products, 32 percent.[26]
Employment figures tell the same story. In April 1954, firms
making jeweled watches employed 9,754 workers, but of
these only 4,242, less than one-half, were engaged in making
watches. This shift occurred very rapidly; in 1950, only 50
workers had been engaged in nonwatch production.

Manufacturers Are Also Importers

The Bulova company was an importer before it became
a manufacturer. Recently the pressure of Swiss competition
has induced Elgin, Hamilton and Waltham to go into the importing business. Like the importer-assemblers, all four of the
American manufacturers bring in movements from Switzerland which they put in cases and market either under their
own, or different, brand names. On these watches the word
"Swiss," required by customs law, is inconspicuous. Of the
6.2 million 16- and 17-jewel movements imported in 1954, a
single firm, Bulova, says it brought in 1.6 million. Both Elgin
and Hamilton have been selling complete lines of watches
with imported movements, as well as self-winding, chrono-
graph, calendar and other specialized watches which supplement rather than compete with their own lines.

[26] U. S. Tariff Commission, *Watches, Movements, and Parts*, cited, p. 13.

Financial Condition of American Manufacturers

By importing Swiss movements and diversifying their operations, three of the four domestic manufacturers prospered in postwar years, notwithstanding the severity of foreign competition.

Elgin's net sales from all operations show a straight-line upward trend, from $17.7 million in 1946 to $60.1 million in 1954. In this period net income increased by 63 percent before taxes, or 38 percent after taxes. However, the ratio of the company's net income, before taxes, to sales declined:

1946	11.2 percent		1951	8.1 percent
1947	10.1 "		1952	5.7 "
1948	10.2 "		1953	7.0 "
1949	9.2 "		1954	5.4 "
1950	9.5 "			

Hamilton's sales, after a 200 percent gain between 1946 and 1953, from $11 million to $33 million, fell off slightly in 1954. Net income, both before and after taxes, showed substantial gains in the postwar years.

The Bulova company also prospered; sales rose from $41 million in 1946 to $69 million in 1954, and total assets from $26 million to $57 million. Bulova's figures, however, are of little value as an indication of the state of watch manufacturing in the United States since its principal business is the assembling of imported movements.

The Waltham balance sheets and profit and loss accounts in postwar years give a tragic story of repeated attempts to re-establish an old and respected enterprise which had been wrecked by years of mismanagement.[27] War orders gave the century-old company a brief period of prosperity, but after heavy losses in 1946 and 1947 it went bankrupt in 1948 and closed its doors. Reorganized with R.F.C. aid, it resumed operations in 1950 and was able to show, for three years, increasing sales and small profits.

The fourth year, 1954, was disastrous, resulting in a net

[27] See Charles W. Moore, *Timing a Century* (Cambridge: Harvard University Press, 1945); also "The Waltham Mess," *Fortune*, v. 39, no. 4 (April 1949).

loss, before taxes, of $210,000 on sales of less than $4 million. In early 1955 the company emerged from bankruptcy and was discharged of all debts and liabilities. (The income statement for that year showed a profit of $70,000.) The Bellanca Aircraft Corporation, which acquired control through purchase of shares, made a 50 percent price cut in order to reduce excessive inventories. Waltham in March 1955 employed 450 workers, in all operations. In 1938 the number had been 2,500.

The Defense Issue

In the formulation of postwar tariff policy on watches, the national defense issue has received increasing attention until it now overshadows economic considerations. The manufacturers of jeweled-lever watches, particularly, have based their demand for restriction of imports on the unique and indispensable character of the services which their industry is prepared to furnish in a war emergency.

As early as 1934 Elgin, Waltham and Hamilton protested against tariff reduction, alleging that the jeweled watch industry was essential to national defense. In subsequent appearances before Congressional committees, they have consistently argued for increased tariff protection on this ground.

The Tariff Commission based its 1952 and 1954 recommendations for higher duties on economic considerations, as required by statute. President Eisenhower, however, in explaining why he had accepted the Commission's second report, indicated that considerations of national security had influenced his decision. He said that watchmaking represented an essential skill which must be preserved in the national interest. In the press release, of July 27, 1954, which accompanied his proclamation we read: "The President's action will have an important collateral effect in contributing to the maintenance of a satisfactory industrial mobilization base for the domestic production of watch movements and other precision devices necessary for national defense." The release also referred to a report of the Interdepartmental Committee on the Jeweled Watch Industry which held that "preservation of the unique skills of this industry is essential to the national security."

Conflicting Opinions

The report to which the President referred was the most recent of a series prepared by various government agencies on the relation of watch manufacture to national defense. President Truman, in September 1952, requested the National Security Resources Board to make a study of essential manpower skills in the watchmaking industry.[28] The Board, in a report filed on January 8, 1953, found that precision jeweled movements were essential to national security in wartime and that these movements were uniquely produced in the United States by firms in the American jeweled watch industry. But the Board recommended no government action. It found that *at current levels of production* and employment the industry furnished "a base of skilled workers upon which expansion could be built. . . ." It advised, however, "that the production levels of this industry be kept under review" and that the government should take action "if production falls below the safety level." [29]

Six months later, in July 1953, President Eisenhower appointed an Interdepartmental Committee on the Jeweled Watch Industry under the chairmanship of the Office of Defense Mobilization. This Committee, in its report published June 30, 1954, about a month before the President proclaimed the increase in watch duties, reached conclusions which differed from those of the N.S.R.B. The Interdepartmental Committee found: "The levels of production and employment in jeweled watch manufacturing are now *below* the levels which would enable the industry to expand quickly and effectively to meet the requirements of full mobiliza-

[28] All the reports of administrative agencies, to which we are referring here, are directed specifically to the relation of the jeweled-lever watch industry to national security. The problems affecting this segment of the industry, according to the Interdepartmental Committee, were considered "most acute and most immediate," but the Committee explained that it did not wish to imply that other segments of the watch industry, viz., the manufacture of pin-lever watches and clocks, were "necessarily any less essential to national security." Only the Senate Preparedness Subcommittee included in its inquiry the whole horological industry.

[29] Declassified excerpts from a memorandum of the chairman of the National Security Resources Board to John R. Steelman, Assistant to the President, January 12, 1953; reprinted in *Congressional Record*, 83rd Cong., 1st sess., v. 99, pt. 2 (March 4, 1953), p. 1623.

tion." [30] (Italics supplied.) It recommended government action to assist the industry and suggested five alternative methods: advanced procurement of military timepieces, preferential procurement of other products (fuses, etc.), tariff relief, quotas and subsidies. The report implied that the Committee preferred subsidies to tariffs or other methods of assistance.

The Defense Department's Views

The Department of Defense, one of the participating agencies, seemed to have reached different conclusions. Its Defense Task Group, after an exhaustive study of mobilization requirements for jeweled movements and timing mechanisms for the ammunition program, reported:

It is clear that the jeweled watch industry affords some of the finest manufacturing facilities and technical abilities in the country for small, close tolerance work. The tool and die making facilities for small parts are perhaps unsurpassed. The fabrication of parts, together with technical knowledge of mechanical transmission of movement within precise and steady time limits and confined spaces, is the basis of their ability to manufacture jeweled movements.[31]

But the Department found that in the manufacture of devices used in the ammunition program the watch industry had no advantages over firms "completely outside the horological group. There does not appear," the report stated, "to be any part of the manufacture or assembly of mechanical time fuses that is peculiar only to the jeweled watch industry."

In the conclusions of the report we read:

While the jeweled watch facilities visited clearly represent excellent and desirable capacity, the needs of the Department of Defense for industrial capacity clearly demonstrate that no special nor preferential treatment for the industry is necessary. It is true that no other industry can show conclusively its ability to produce jeweled watches or chronometers, but these requirements

[30] *The Essentiality to National Security of the American Jeweled Watch Industry*, cited, p. 28.
[31] *Department of Defense Report on the Essentiality of the Jeweled Watch Industry*, April 26, 1954 (adjusted for declassification February 28, 1955), p. 2. (Mimeographed.)

to the Department of Defense are nominal. The Defense Department can, therefore, at this time, reasonably assume that sufficient capacity will remain and can be used for current procurement needs and be the basis for supplying the mobilization requirements. If in the future it should become apparent that sufficient capacity will not be maintained and available, the Defense Department can then procure all of its requirements of jeweled movements for the mobilization reserve.[32]

The Department's report was a "classified" document. Its publication in February 1955, after declassification, created a mild sensation, since it appeared to contradict the position taken by the Office of Defense Mobilization and the Interdepartmental Committee.[33] But Secretary of Defense Wilson, in a letter replying to nine Senators who had requested an explanation, said that the report had given an erroneous impression.[34] The Pentagon's view, he asserted, was that the entire domestic watch industry, *and not only the jeweled-lever branch*, was essential to national defense.

Senator Saltonstall's Committee

In early 1954, while the Tariff Commission was considering the watch industry's second application for higher duties, and while the Interdepartmental Committee's investigation was under way, pressure for quick action began to build up in Congress. In response, Senator Saltonstall, Chairman of the Senate Armed Services Committee, appointed a subcommittee on the Essentiality of the American Watch and Clock Industry. In a three-day hearing, Senators and Congressmen expressed their opinions, as well as high government officials, domestic manufacturers and a representative of the importing interests. Although the Chairman announced that foreign competition was not a matter within the Committee's terms of reference, Senators and Congressmen from watch-producing constituencies, and other witnesses, discussed the subject

---

[32] Same, p. 6.

[33] In Congress, Representative Lankford (Democrat, Maryland) said: "It now appears . . . that we have been subjected to a gigantic hoax. . . ." See *Congressional Record*, 84th Cong., 1st sess. (March 24, 1955), p. 3142. (Daily edition.)

[34] See *New York Times*, May 2, 1955.

freely. Several expressed the hope that the Tariff Commission would "provide relief" for the domestic watch industry.[35]

On July 23, four days before the President's proclamation, the Committee reported that "The highly skilled workers in the American watch and clock industry . . . are essential to the national defense. Therefore, it is in the interest of national defense to keep this essential industry alive and vital." [36]

Is Watchmaking an Essential Industry?

Three possible reasons for declaring the watch industry essential to national defense emerge from the preceding discussion: (1) the need for maintaining, in peacetime, minimum facilities for the production of watches and other time-keeping devices, as a basis for wartime expansion; (2) the ability of the watch manufacturers to convert their facilities in wartime to the production of weapons requiring precise engineering of miniature components; and (3) the need for preserving for use in a war emergency the skills of a small group of exceptionally qualified tool and die makers by employing them continuously in work which demands the highest degree of precision.

Arguments respecting defense essentiality have no validity except with reference to some assumption regarding the nature and duration of future wars. (See Chapter 11, p. 279.) In what follows we accept the assumption, which is implicit in the arguments of the watch industry, and which is most favorable to its position, that the next war will be a long, drawn-out struggle resembling World War II.

We shall examine the arguments in order. Reliable and accurate watches are indispensable in wartime for use by members of the armed forces and by civilians in key occupations. The watch factories obviously are better equipped than any other industry to make these timepieces.

On the second count the available evidence does not sus-

---

[35] U. S. Senate, Committee on Armed Services, Preparedness Subcommittee No. 6, *Essentiality to the National Defense of the Domestic Horological Industry*, Hearings, 83rd Cong., 2d sess. (Washington: GPO, 1954). See particularly p. 107.

[36] U. S. Senate, Committee on Armed Services, Preparedness Subcommittee No. 6, *Essentiality of the American Watch and Clock Industry*, Report, 83rd Cong. (Washington: GPO, 1954), p. 2.

tain the watch manufacturers' claim of defense essentiality. Watchmaking skills and equipment, it is true, have been successfully employed in making fuses for artillery shells and other military items of small dimensions where close tolerances are required. But in work of this sort the watch industry has no pre-eminent qualifications. Manufacturers of cameras, adding machines and other products have shown equally satisfactory performance.

Watch firms supplied great quantities of small, precisely made parts, such as springs, pinions, gears, etc., to other contractors. But all these parts, according to various official reports, could have been procured from other sources. For example, regarding mechanical time fuses the Interdepartmental Committee, in its 1954 report, said: "Surveys of the degree of dependency of other prime contractors on the jeweled watch industry as a source of supply for military end item production indicate that there is no item or product which is not being made or procured in some quantity outside of the jeweled watch industry. However, where parts have been purchased from the jeweled watch industry, the reasons given in most cases were that the watch companies represented an excellent and dependable existing source with favorable cost relationship. Many contractors have stated that they could produce the parts which they are procuring from the watch industry, if necessary, but since the facilities of the watch manufacturers have been available to date, there has been little incentive for them to attempt to do so." [37]

Available evidence does not appear to support the third contention, that based on skilled labor. Among the employees in every jeweled watch factory there is, it is true, a small group—10 or 12 in a factory employing 1,200 persons—who possess skills of great value for work on some of the newer types of weapons. These are the tool and die makers. They do not make watches; they make only certain parts, of extremely small dimensions, which fit into machines which make parts for watches. To acquire the accuracy (to 1/10,000 of an inch) required in this type of work, the tool and die makers need a training or learning period which may vary from six

[37] *The Essentiality to National Security of the American Jeweled Watch Industry,* cited, p. 16.

to ten years. Their ability to work to the closest tolerances deteriorates rapidly when not used.

The watch manufacturers assert that only their factories require the kind of work which will keep the tool and die makers employed at tasks which demand the exercise of their highest skills. A generation ago this statement would have been accepted at face value, but today experts in microengineering are inclined to discount it, because of the technical advances made in their field in recent years. At present the manufacture of miniature ball bearings, fuel-injection pumps for gas engines, and various other products employs workers with skills equal to those found in watch factories.

But even if we grant that the tool and die makers employed in the watch factories have skills essential for defense work, they are essential for watch production also, especially when the industry is expanding to supply wartime needs. It is difficult to see how this small group could serve in both capacities.

In summary, it seems that the watch industry is important to national defense primarily because it is uniquely qualified to produce watches and other time-keeping devices. In a period of emergency, the country would be better off with a watch industry than without one, since it is not certain that we could again obtain adequate supplies from Switzerland. Furthermore, the industry is vulnerable to foreign competition. For these reasons a prudent policy should provide safeguarding measures to make sure that in peacetime watch production is maintained at a level which would provide an adequate base for wartime expansion.

Two important questions must still be answered: (1) How big a watch industry do we need, and (2) how can we make sure that an industry of the necessary size is maintained and kept in operation?

The Interdepartmental Committee estimated that an average annual production of 2 million jeweled watches would meet security requirements; an industry of that size, it judged, would form an adequate base from which production could expand in wartime.[38] An average production of 2 million

[38] Stockpiling of watch parts might reduce the production requirement. In addition, several million watches might be obtained in an emergency from stocks in the hands of importers, department stores, chain stores, mail order houses and retail jewelers.

watches would employ about 4,000 workers, including perhaps 50 tool and die makers.

It is worth noting that the armed services have scaled down their requirements for time-keeping devices from World War II levels. The Army has on hand large supplies of watches left over from the last war, and it will not issue jeweled watches as liberally to the troops in the next war. The Navy also finds that it has on hand an adequate supply of ships' chronometers, durable items which are constantly being overhauled and reissued.

Alternatives to Tariff Protection

How, considering the strength of foreign competition, can the production of jeweled watches be maintained in the United States at the safe level of 2 million units per year? The industry itself cannot do much to narrow the gap between its costs and those of the Swiss manufacturers. Mechanization of production has already been carried to a high degree of perfection in at least three of the four American factories. New technological developments are always possible, but they probably would give the American industry only a temporary advantage in competition with the Swiss manufacturers. The same may be said for economies in marketing, a field in which the importer-assemblers have displayed great ability. If we were concerned simply with making the total business of the four firms profitable, diversification of products might be the answer. But diversification, in which the watch firms have already made rapid progress, does not guarantee watch production. On the contrary, it has enabled the manufacturers to expand their business by substituting other products for watches.

Restriction of imports by tariff duties has been the traditional method of giving government assistance to the watch manufacturers. This is the kind of help to which they are accustomed. They would like it continued and increased. But our review of the experience of the past 25 years throws doubt on the efficacy of import duties as a means of sustaining domestic watch production. The high duties of the Hawley-Smoot Act made smuggling profitable. They also stimulated Swiss manufacturers to circumvent, legally, the

American tariff barriers by ingenious innovations in watch manufacture. The revival of "upjeweling," an immediate response to the 1954 increase in import duties, indicates that the Swiss watchmakers have not exhausted their supply of new ideas and devices for "tax avoidance."

The 1954 increase in duties was followed by a decline in imports of watch movements most nearly competitive with the domestic product. The latter showed a slight gain, the first since 1951. How far the tariff increase was responsible is not clear. (See p. 113.)

Quotas

Fixing a quota on imports of watch movements would restrict Swiss competition more effectively than import duties. But quantitative restrictions on imports, even more than high import duties, encourage smuggling. Moreover, the United States has repeatedly announced its disapproval of quotas, when used by foreign countries to restrict their imports of American goods. At present it is a prime objective of U. S. trade policy to rid international trade of these interferences. In pursuit of this goal the United States in the General Agreement on Tariffs and Trade (GATT) has renounced the use of quantitative restrictions. (An exception permitted in the agreement covers our quotas on certain farm products.)

But even assuming that the legal difficulties could be surmounted, or circumvented, the limitation of imports of watch movements to a fixed quantity per year would have undesirable economic results. By preventing fluctuations in the numbers of watch movements received from year to year, or from month to month, the quota system would isolate the American market from the world market. Thus it would deprive domestic buyers of the benefits of possible reduction in the costs and prices of Swiss watches. By the same token, domestic manufacturers would have less incentive to introduce technical improvements.

The use of quotas as a protective measure involves administrative difficulties, for example in the allocation of licenses among importing firms. Added obstacles would be encountered if the quotas were employed to maintain minimum production of watches at an agreed level. No formula would produce exact results. Hence, the quotas would have to be flexible, with periodic adjustments which both manufacturers and importers would find disturbing factors in their operations.

Restriction of imports, by tariff duties or by quotas, is not the only means by which the government may grant assistance to the watch industry. A variety of alternative policies are available. Defense contracts, which have contributed substantially to the postwar prosperity of the watch companies, are in effect a form of subsidy. They enable the companies to obtain experience in making items which they may be asked to supply in a war emergency. But they also help to carry overhead expense and so diminish the cost of producing watches. Manufacturers, however, cannot count on defense business, which fluctuates with the changing climate of international affairs, as a reliable source of income. Other types of government assistance, such as advanced buying of military timepieces, preferential procurement of other products, and accelerated amortization of new equipment, are useful stopgap devices, but they offer no permanent solution to the problem of maintaining a minimum level of watch production.

Subsidies

The payment of cash subsidies to American watch manufacturers would be a simple, direct and effective means of maintaining a minimum level of production. The federal government is now subsidizing private firms engaged in building and in operating merchant ships, and in air transport. In each case assistance by means of import duties was impracticable; the subsidy takes the place of tariff protection. The principal justification of the payments in each case is the need of maintaining an industry essential to defense. National defense, also, is the ostensible, if not the real, reason for subsidizing the tungsten miners.

In paying a subsidy to watch manufacturers, the United States would violate none of the provisions of its bilateral or multilateral trade agreements, as long as the payments did not stimulate export trade, a result which could be easily avoided. The subsidy could either supplement or replace the present import duties.

Subsidies, although they avoid the disadvantages of tariffs

and quotas, have faults of their own. Their administration adds to the number of federal civil servants and requires elaborate and expensive cost-accounting systems. The bitter struggles that mark periodic reviews and revisions of the subsidies now in force absorb legislators' time and energies.

The Interdepartmental Committee, without explicitly recommending subsidies in its report, implied strong approval. "Subsidies," the Committee stated, "if carefully applied, would not inhibit competition by the firms in the industry or discourage efforts to improve the efficiency of production processes or marketing techniques." [39]

The substitution of subsidies for import duties would enable American consumers to buy their watches, both imported and domestic, at world market prices. Their gain, it may be objected, would be offset, and more than offset, by the Treasury's loss of customs revenue, and by the cost of the subsidy. This reasoning, however, is fallacious. The Treasury collects duties only on imported watch movements, but the tariff raises not only their prices but those of the American watches as well. (That, in fact, is its purpose. Otherwise the domestic producers, because of their high costs, would not be able to market their timepieces.) Consequently, the consumer's gain from replacing the import duty on watches with a subsidy would exceed the Treasury's loss of customs revenue.

But even assuming that, when gains were balanced against losses, subsidies proved to be more expensive than import duties, or other methods of supporting the watch industry, they should still be preferred if they do the job better, and this, I believe, can be demonstrated.

A subsidy is a cost which can readily be identified in government accounts as so many million dollars a year paid out to a group of American business firms (in this case the manufacturers of jeweled-lever watches). But import duties impose on consumers costs which can only be estimated. Furthermore, and more important, since the subsidy is paid for a specific purpose, viz., to maintain watch production at a certain level, payment can be checked against performance.

The purposes of tariff protection, on the other hand, can-

[39] *The Essentiality to National Security of the American Jeweled Watch Industry,* cited, p. 27.

not be as clearly defined. When the President raises an import duty, he does not require a *quid pro quo* from the protected industry. He cannot exact any guarantee that watch manufacturers will maintain production at a level adequate to satisfy defense requirements.

Finally, subsidy payments place the cost of maintaining a defense-essential industry squarely where they belong, on the whole body of taxpayers, while import duties and quotas put the burden on a relatively small group, in this case the purchasers of watches.

*　　*　　*

On purely economic grounds it would be difficult, I believe, to justify government assistance to the watch industry either through tariffs, subsidies or in any other way. Except for one firm which is still struggling to overcome the disastrous effects of years of bad management, the industry is prosperous. Most of its profits, it is true, are earned not from the manufacture of watches but from other operations, including the importing of watch movements. Through these various activities, employment in the watch factories has been well maintained, and there is no evidence of distress in the communities in which they are situated. In sum, the watch manufacturers have done an excellent job of adjustment to increased foreign competition.

But defense, as Adam Smith remarked, is more important than opulence. If the President and his advisers should decide that the watch industry is essential to national security, it should be maintained, irrespective of economic gain or loss. For this purpose subsidies appear to be the most appropriate means.

Chapter 6

WOOLENS AND WORSTEDS: AN INDUSTRY IN TRANSITION

For the past 30 years the American woolen and worsted industry has not kept pace with the general development of American manufactures. Government orders brought sudden bursts of prosperity in 1942-1945 and again in 1951, but production then fell to about the prewar level. Idle machinery and unemployed workers, the liquidation of unprofitable mills, falling prices and uncertain profits were cited as symptoms of a sick industry.

A careful examination of the patient's condition, however, gave some indications of health and strength. The explanation of the conflicting diagnoses is found in certain revolutionary changes, technical and economic, which began in the middle 1930's but whose full effects became apparent only in postwar years. The more important of these changes were:

1. The rapid rise, with violent fluctuations, in the price of wool;
2. The appearance of the "man-made" fibers and their use in blended fabrics;
3. The introduction of improved labor-saving machinery in spinning and weaving;
4. The building of new mills in the South which, for a number of reasons, operated at lower costs than the older Northern mills;
5. The mergers of woolen and worsted mills with firms engaged in manufacturing cottons and blended fabrics.

Had the woolen and worsted industry been blessed with an expanding domestic market, it might have taken these changes in its stride. But the demand for woolens and worsteds proved stagnant, despite the growth of population and national income. American families chose to spend their new dollars on housing and household appliances, on automobiles, radios and television sets rather than on wearing apparel, and they turned from woolens and worsteds to cottons and blended fabrics. The result was overcapacity and increased competition in an industry already strongly competitive. Progressive firms, well managed and adequately financed, were able to adapt their operations to the new conditions; others either closed their mills or were eating up their capital.

Manufacturers and workers asserted that tariff reduction was one of the prime causes of their troubles. The concessions made in the 1939 trade agreement had no effect while trade was cut off during World War II. But after 1946 imports increased rapidly. The wool manufacturers' association and the principal trade union organization strongly opposed the tariff reductions of 1939 and those negotiated at Geneva in 1948. They have demanded that while the industry is going through a difficult period of transition the State Department's negotiators make no further tariff cuts. They have asked that imports be kept down to five percent of domestic production, which is about the 1953-1955 level. To accomplish this both management and labor have petitioned the President to apply higher tariff duties.

How far can tariff reduction be held responsible for the postwar difficulties of the woolen and worsted industry? What is the outlook for the future? What sort of tariff policy is best suited to develop a progressive, efficient industry? These are the principal questions to which this chapter is addressed.

* * *

Processes of Manufacture[1]

Wool as it comes from the sheep's back is greasy and full of dirt and burrs. After it is sorted, the wool is washed or "scoured" in a solution of soap and soda and treated with chemicals (carbonized) to remove burrs and other vegetable matter. The wool may then be dyed and blended for shade

[1] The following paragraphs describe the operations in a fully integrated mill which performs all the processes of manufacture. Actually, scouring, spinning, weaving and finishing are often carried on by independent firms in separate plants.

and quality, or it may be dyed later when in the form of yarn or fabric. Next comes carding, a process in which the blended fibers are fed between large cylinders and rollers studded with short wire teeth. Revolving in opposite directions, the rollers open the fibers and remove remaining foreign substances.

Yarn spinning comes after carding, but at this point the processes diverge, depending upon whether the yarn is to be produced for woolen or for worsted fabrics. Woolens are loosely woven fabrics of rough texture, increasingly popular for sportswear and overcoats. The more closely woven worsteds, with their smoother finish, are used for men's business and formal wear and also in women's "style" garments.

Yarn manufactured on the woolen system is spun directly from the strands delivered from the card, but worsted yarn must first be "combed," a process which removes short fibers (noils) and lays the remainder in parallel strands, known as "tops." (Noils are used in woolen yarns and pressed felts.) Worsted yarn is characterized by its smooth, even texture and by its high "twist." Woolen yarn is comparatively loose and has less parallelization of fibers.

After the yarn is woven into cloth, there follows a series of finishing operations. Defects in weaving are removed by mending; then the fabric must be scoured and fulled. In fulling, the cloth is subjected to heat, moisture and pressure which cause it to shrink in length and width but gain in body. Usually the fibers on the face of woolen fabrics, after fulling and drying, are raised by brushing or napping and then sheared.[2]

The Domestic Industry

The American wool manufacturing industry comprises some 650 or 700 separate establishments in which about 100,-000 persons are employed. Net sales in 1954 were valued at approximately $2 billion. These figures refer to the operations of the entire industry, including scouring, dyeing and finishing establishments, knitting mills, yarn spinners and manufac-

[2] The preceding paragraphs have been condensed from *Wool in the United States*, published by the National Association of Wool Manufacturers (New York: Author, 1947), pp. 12-21.

turers of blankets, as well as mills producing woven woolen and worsted apparel cloths, the branch of the industry with which this chapter is concerned. The latter comprises about 350 woolen and worsted mills, strictly so called, which employ approximately 50,000 production workers.

The geography of wool manufacturing shows concentration on the North Atlantic seaboard, with secondary clusters of mills in New Jersey and in Pennsylvania near Philadelphia. Recently this pattern of distribution has been disturbed by the migration of Northern mills to the Piedmont region of South Atlantic states and by the establishment of new enterprises in that area. (See map, p. 134.)

Wool manufacturing traditionally has been a small-scale industry.[3] The 1947 census found that almost half of the 495 establishments making woolen and worsted fabrics in that year employed less than 100 workers each. There were 219 mills which employed 100-499 persons, 27 with 500-999 employees, and 24 employing more than 1,000. The typical financial units were small or of moderate size. Usually a company operated a single mill, or at most two or three. A few firms, however, owned a larger number of mills, and, when analyzed on the basis of financial control, the industry showed a moderate degree of concentration. In 1947 the four largest companies accounted for 28 percent of the industry's total shipments; the first eight accounted for 40 percent, and the first twenty, 56 percent. Concentration in the woolen and worsted industry was considerably greater than in the manufacture of cotton but less than in rayon and related broad fabrics. A corresponding amount of concentration was apparent in the ownership of equipment. In 1952, three percent of the companies (with 500 or more looms each) had 35 percent of the total looms. At the other end of the scale were 95 companies with less than 25 looms each; they had only 4 percent of the total.

The industry, nevertheless, was characterized by active

[3] Woolen mills are more numerous than worsted mills and are usually smaller enterprises. The typical woolen mill is an integrated organization which performs every step in the process of transforming raw wool into finished cloth. Worsted mills often purchase tops from combing plants and confine their operations to spinning yarn and weaving and finishing cloth.

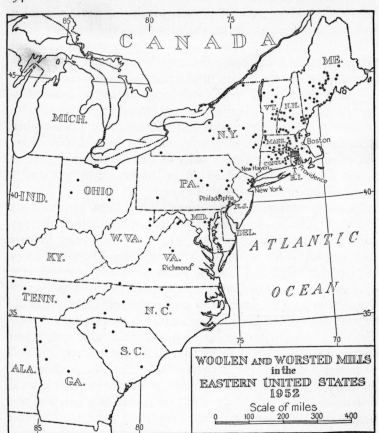

WOOLEN AND WORSTED MILLS
in the
EASTERN UNITED STATES
1952
Scale of miles

Source: *Davison's Textile Blue Book*, published by the Davison Publishing Company

competition among the various units. There was little evidence of price leadership, and only a few firms attempted nation-wide advertising of their brand names.

The American Woolen Company was an early example of large-scale production and management in wool manufacturing. Organized in 1899 as a consolidation of 26 mills, it became one of the world's largest producers of woolens and worsteds and at one time turned out 15 percent of total American production. But this experiment in horizontal combination did not prove successful. The company sustained heavy losses in the 1930's when it was forced to liquidate nearly half of its plants. Government orders in World War II brought short-lived prosperity, but the management failed to adapt itself to postwar developments, particularly in the use of synthetic fibers. "Its enormous old New England mills betrayed it for what it was—a mass producer of staples in an age of style." [4]

In early 1955, after protracted negotiations, American Woolen was merged with Textron, Inc. and Robbins Mills. This consolidation, which brought together 15 woolen and worsted mills with 5,000 employees, was one of a "rash of mergers" which broke out in the textile industry in 1953-1954. Typical new combinations were the acquisition by Burlington Mills, a leading producer of synthetics, of Peerless Woolen Mills, and Pacific Mills and the Goodall-Sanford Corporation, both leaders in worsteds. The *Journal of Commerce* estimated that within a period of 18 months more than 100 textile mills employing nearly 40,000 workers were drawn into larger organizations.[5] A later estimate, by Solomon Barkin of the Textile Workers Union, raised the figure to 171 mills owned by 70 companies.[6] Mr. Barkin's figures, as well as those of the *Journal of Commerce*, referred to the entire textile industry, including firms producing cottons and fabrics of rayon and other synthetic fibers, in addition to woolen and worsted mills. The causes of the mergers and their significance for wool manufacturing will be discussed later. (See pp. 156-157.)

Postwar Disturbances

Postwar conditions in the woolen and worsted industry, particularly in the years 1949-1954, have generally been described as "bad." Ames Stevens, veteran manufacturer, said in 1953 that the distress was the worst in his 34 years of experience. To some extent the manufacturers' difficulties were symptoms of contraction from wartime expansion. With ris-

[4] Dero A. Saunders, "The Twilight of American Woolen," *Fortune*, v. 49, no. 3 (March 1954), p. 200.
[5] August 18, 1954.
[6] Testimony before the Senate Anti-Trust Subcommittee, reported in the *Wall Street Journal*, June 30, 1955.

ing national income after 1939, demand for woolen and worsted fabrics had strengthened, and then the entrance of the United States into World War II brought a flood of government orders. Production, which had been 440 million square yards in 1940, rose in 1942 to 685 million, of which 316 million, nearly one-half of the total, were for government account. (See Table 21 and Chart H.)

In 1946, government purchases practically disappeared, but the release of civilian demand from wartime restrictions carried total output in that year to a record figure of 786 million square yards. The following years brought rapid contraction. With the outbreak of the Korean war, government purchases again became important, amounting in 1951 to 156 million square yards of apparel cloths, but in the following year they fell to 96 million, and civilian consumption continued to fall. Production in 1955 was only 464 million square yards, marking a decline of 40 percent in nine years.

The decline in production is reflected also in figures showing machinery in place and in operation:

		1946	1952	1954
			(in thousands)	
Broad looms:	In place	37.2	33.3	26.9
	In operation	33.9	24.3	20.0[a]
Spindles				
Worsted:	In place	1,917	1,692	1,000
	In operation	1,790	1,180	n.a.
Woolen:	In place	1,600	1,124	900
	In operation	1,508	970	n.a.

[a] Estimated.

The decline in the number of looms and spindles *in place* is an indication of the process of scrapping obsolete machinery and is related to the liquidation of mills, to be discussed later. The decline in machinery *in operation* is significant only when related to the number of hours operated. In this respect the postwar years witnessed a remarkable change. In 1946, only 21 percent of the looms were operated on three shifts; in 1952, the latest date for which comparable figures are available, the percentage was 43. Only 30 percent of woolen spindles were operated on three shifts in 1946, and 39 percent six years later. In worsted spinning the percentage on three shifts rose from 8 to 34. Obviously, in this period of decline some manufacturers were cutting their overhead by more intensive use of capital invested in machinery.

The number of *production* workers in woolen and worsted mills declined from 122,500 in 1947 to 78,000 in 1953, according to Census figures. Trade union estimates place the 1955 employment of these workers at 50,000. Throughout the post-was period unemployment has been severe in the principal centers of the industry, particularly in New England. Average hourly earnings, which were $1.16 in 1947, rose to $1.56 in 1952. Formal wage reductions did not begin until 1953,

Table 21

U. S. PRODUCTION OF WOVEN APPAREL CLOTHS CONTAINING
BY WEIGHT 25 PERCENT OR MORE WOOL,
1939, 1942-1955

(in millions of square yards)

Year	Total production	For government	For all others
1939	482		
1942	685	316	369
1943	661	279	382
1944	661	136	525
1945	602	174	428
1946	786	1.5	784
1947	655	15	640
1948	651	17	634
1949	527	26	501
1950	586	15	571
1951	509	156	353
1952	501	96	405
1953	470	30	440
1954	414	4	410
1955 [a]	464	10	454

[a] Preliminary.
Source: U. S. Bureau of the Census

CHART H

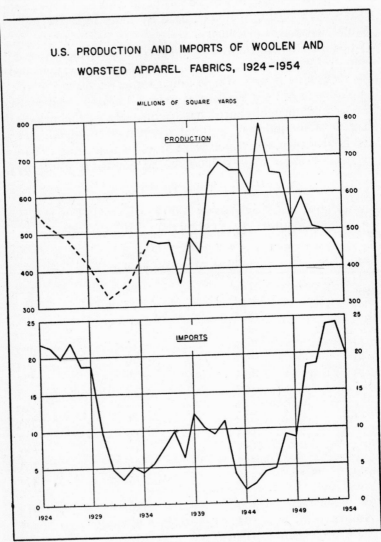

U.S. PRODUCTION AND IMPORTS OF WOOLEN AND
WORSTED APPAREL FABRICS, 1924–1954

MILLIONS OF SQUARE YARDS

PRODUCTION

IMPORTS

Source: Tables 21 and 24 and U. S. Bureau of the Census

although the number of mills paying less than the union scale was increasing.

Prices of finished cloth followed the upward trend of all commodity indexes (see Table 22) but did not rise fast enough to cover rising costs of wool and increased labor costs. Demand fell off, inventories accumulated and many firms, including some of the largest, showed declining sales and falling

Table 22

WHOLESALE PRICE INDEX OF WOOL, SYNTHETIC AND COTTON PRODUCTS AND ALL COMMODITIES, 1939, 1946-1955

(1947-49 = 100)

Year	Wool products	Synthetic textiles	Cotton products	All commodities
1939	56.6		36.6	50.1
1946	82.1		81.9	78.7
1947	90.6	96.6	103.1	96.4
1948	104.4	108.3	105.1	104.4
1949	105.0	95.2	91.8	99.2
1950	112.9	95.3	99.5	103.1
1951	144.6	97.0	111.5	114.8
1952	113.0	88.9	98.5	111.6
1953	111.8	87.1	93.5	110.1
1954	109.1	85.7	89.2	110.3
1955	104.7	86.5	91.5	110.7

Source: U. S. Bureau of Labor Statistics

profits. Scores of small mills sold out or went bankrupt. A wave of liquidations swept over the industry. The National Association of Wool Manufacturers in December 1953 listed 132 woolen and worsted mills, employing 48,000 workers, "liquidated or gone out of business" since January 1, 1949.[7] These often-quoted figures, however, include firms making

[7] Statement submitted to the Randall Commission in December 1953; reprinted in *Trade Agreements Extension*, Hearings, 84th Cong., 1st sess., on H. R. 1, U. S. House, Committee on Ways and Means (Washington: GPO, 1955), p. 1727.

blankets and automobile fabrics and other specialized firms.[8] Moreover, the information submitted by the manufacturers' association makes no mention of new mills established during the five-year period, some with machinery from the liquidated mills and others with new equipment.[9] The net loss to the industry was therefore less than the gross figures would indicate.

The liquidations were brought about by a variety of causes. Some mills which had sustained losses were bought and closed so that the purchaser could take advantage of the carry-over provisions of tax laws. Speculative operators seized opportunities to make quick profits from buying unprofitable mills, closing them and selling the real estate and equipment. The liquidations thus removed much dead wood from the industry.

Tariff Reduction

Tariff reduction is regarded by the wool manufacturers as an unnecessary and pernicious aggravation of their postwar troubles. Through their association they have repeatedly opposed the extension of the Trade Agreements Act, and in hearings before the Tariff Commission and the Committee for Reciprocity Information they have protested against further reductions in import duties.

Until 1939 the industry had enjoyed over a century of tariff protection at rates which showed a marked upward trend, particularly after 1860. Although the Underwood Tariff (1913) made substantial reductions in the duties on woolens and worsteds, they had little effect on imports. World War I, and its aftermath, prevented foreign manufacturers from increasing their shipments to the American market. The Fordney-McCumber Tariff (1922) restored high protection. The duties collected in the next eight years averaged 72 per-

[8] Makers of automobile fabrics were generally not in the woolen and worsted business. However, they used the same machinery, and when their own sales declined they turned to making woolen and worsted cloth for apparel. Often a maker of automobile fabrics came through unscathed when he turned to woolen and worsted cloths, while the original woolen and worsted mills had to close. Perhaps 90 percent of the mills liquidated were manufacturing cloths.

[9] Mr. Barkin told a Senate Committee in June 1955 that 18 new yarn and weaving mills had been established since the end of the war. A somewhat larger number were listed a year and a half earlier by Bartholin A. Neese (in the *Daily News Record*, November 25, 1953).

cent of the foreign value of the imports. The high-water mark was reached under the Hawley-Smoot Tariff of 1930 when the nine-year average, 1930-1938, was 87 percent. The trade agreement with the United Kingdom, effective January 1, 1939, set in motion a downward trend which, combined with the upward movement of import prices, brought the 1954 ad valorem equivalent of the duties down to less than one-half the 1930 level.

Raw wool has long been subject to substantial duties in the American tariff, but in the United Kingdom and other industrial countries it enters free of duty. Thus manufacturers in this country, who are large buyers of foreign wools, are handicapped in competition with mills abroad which pay less for their raw material. To offset this disadvantage the American tariff levies a compound duty on woolen and worsted cloths. One part, the specific or compensatory rate (now 37½ cents per pound of cloth), is designed to offset the higher costs of the raw wool.[10] In addition, an ad valorem rate, 25 percent of foreign value, is levied to cover higher conversion costs in this country.

In the 1939 trade agreement with the United Kingdom, the compensatory element in the cloth duties remained unchanged, but protection on the conversion costs was reduced substantially. When, in 1948, the Geneva agreement cut the import duty on raw wool from 34 to 25½ cents a pound, it made a corresponding reduction in the specific rate on woolens and worsteds, and also lowered the ad valorem rate. (No changes in these rates were made between 1948 and 1955. See

[10] For a variety of reasons the specific duty has often been more than adequate to cover the added costs of the raw material. Shrinkage ratios (the loss of weight in the conversion of scoured wool fabrics), being based on estimated average manufacturing losses, were larger for some fabrics than for others. Also, the compensatory duty was fixed on the assumption that the price of domestic raw wool would always exceed foreign wool by the amount of the duty. This, however, has not generally proved true; hence the specific duty has afforded a varying amount of concealed, extra protection. "The compensatory rates have been planned to offset the most extreme competitive disadvantages entailed, in a substantial number of cases, by the duty on raw wool. Therefore, they have been often, if not generally, overcompensatory and have contained an element of protection to the manufacturer." U. S. Tariff Commission, *Woolens and Worsteds*, War Changes in Industry Series, Report No. 29 (Washington: GPO, 1949), p. 66. For an earlier and more detailed discussion, see F. W. Taussig, *Some Aspects of the Tariff Question* (4th ed.; Cambridge: Harvard University Press, 1924), pp. 296-365.

Table 23

U. S. RATES OF DUTY ON WOOLEN AND WORSTED FABRICS

(cents per pound; percent ad valorem)

	Act of 1930	1955 rate[a]
Par. 1108		
Woven fabrics, weighing not more than 4 ounces per square yard, wholly or in chief value of wool:		
Without warp of cotton or other vegetable fiber:		
Valued at not more than $1.25 per pound	50¢ + 50%	
Valued at more than $1.25 but not more than $2 per pound	50¢ + 55%	37.5¢ + 25%
Valued at more than $2 per pound	50¢ + 60%	
Par. 1109(a)		
Woven fabrics, weighing more than 4 ounces per square yard, wholly or in chief value of wool:		
Valued at not more than $1.25 per pound	50¢ + 50%	
Valued at more than $1.25 but not more than $2 per pound	50¢ + 55%	37.5¢ + 25%
Valued at more than $2 per pound	50¢ + 60%	

a The United States reserves the right to increase the ad valorem part of the rate applicable to any of the fabrics provided in paragraphs 1108 and 1109(a) to 45 per-centum ad valorem on any of such fabrics which are entered in any calendar year in excess of an aggregate quantity by weight of 5 per centum of the average annual production of similar fabrics in the United States during the 3 immediately pre-ceding calendar years. (T. D. 51802).

Table 23.) At the same time the rate structure was simplified.[11] Rising foreign values of imported cloths continued to
reduce the burden of the duty and its protective effect.

[11] The Act of 1930 had levied highest rates of duty on the most expensive cloths. In 1939, in order to make the trade agreement attractive to the British, the situation was reversed and the lowest rates applied to the finest fabrics. These classifications (value brackets) were abolished in the 1948 agreement.

In the Geneva agreement, the opposition of the American industry to further tariff reduction achieved a partial success. The agreement contained a safeguarding clause which provided that when the imports of any woolen or worsted fabrics exceeded five percent of the average annual domestic production of similar fabrics in the three preceding years, the United States might raise the ad valorem component of the duty *on the excess* from 25 to 45 percent. In January 1954, the Textile Workers Union of America, calling attention to the increased imports and the depressed state of the domestic industry, urged the Tariff Commission to exercise the reserved right to raise the duties. Several months later the National Association of Wool Manufacturers also asked for higher duties.[12]

In the 1955 hearings on the extension of the Trade Agreements Act, only one manufacturer appeared, representing a firm making particularly high-priced goods. He complained that his firm had been hurt, and badly hurt, by tariff reduction. In his opinion the restoration of the Hawley-Smoot rates of duty would not be a sufficient remedy. Higher duties would have to be supplemented by a "flexible quota"—a phrase which he did not define.[13]

Most of the manufacturers who make fabrics for mass consumption would be satisfied with the assurance that tariff duties would be stabilized at the present level. Their attitude is reflected in the statement of the executive vice president of the wool manufacturers' association. He attacked tariff bargaining both in principle and in practice but did not say that the industry had been injured by tariff reduction nor did he plead for higher protection. The spokesman for the manufacturers may have felt embarrassed, in the presence of Senators from wool-growing states, to plead for higher duties on finished goods, because free raw wool is a new plank in the industry's tariff platform. Manufacturers, abandoning their

---

[12] In early 1956 the Textile Workers Union called the attention of the President to the imports of 1955 which exceeded six percent of comparable domestic production of woolens and worsteds. The Committee for Reciprocity Information held public hearings in April 1956.

[13] Testimony of Gilbert H. Robinson, Forstmann Woolen Company, in *Trade Agreements Extension*, Hearings on H. R. 1, U. S. Senate Finance Committee, 84th Cong., 1st sess. (Washington: GPO, 1955), p. 481.

long alliance with the wool growers, have asked Congress to remove all import duties on their raw material. Thus, somewhat tardily, they have recognized that the wool duties, by raising the price of both raw material and finished goods, have placed woolens and worsteds at a disadvantage in competition with cotton and blended fabrics. Removal of the wool duties would logically require the elimination of the compensatory element in the duties on woolen and worsted fabrics. Otherwise, free wool would give manufacturers substantially increased protection.

Competition from Abroad

Imports of foreign-made woolens and worsteds increased from a little over 4 million square yards in 1946 to 30 million in 1955, when they amounted to about six percent of domestic production.

Some manufacturers have regarded even this minimal amount of foreign competition as injurious. Mr. Robinson of

Table 24

U. S. IMPORTS OF WOOLEN AND WORSTED CLOTHS,
1924, 1929, 1930-38, 1946-1955

Year	Quantity (million sq. yds.)	Foreign value (million $)	Unit value per sq. yd.
1924	21.70	20.48	$ .94
1929	18.78	19.53	1.04
1930-38 (average)	5.86	5.29	.90
1946	4.24	6.48	1.53
1947	4.60	8.33	1.81
1948	9.21	18.60	2.02
1949	8.88	18.30	2.06
1950	18.55	33.04	1.78
1951	18.68	43.34	2.32
1952	23.98	42.87	1.79
1953	24.23	45.62	1.88
1954	19.92	38.18	1.92
1955	29.76	54.61	1.83

Source: U. S. Tariff Commission, U. S. Bureau of the Census

the Forstmann Woolen Company told the Senate Finance Committee in March 1955: "We do not maintain that the competition of imported fabrics made by cheap foreign labor is the only worry that we face but we do say, with all the emphasis at our command, that such foreign competition is a most important factor in contributing to the present sorry state of the wool textile industry." [14] The M. T. Stevens and Sons Company of North Andover, Massachusetts warned its employees that imports were threatening their jobs and urged them to write their Congressmen: "Tell them imports are hurting you. Tell them you want higher, not lower, tariffs." [15]

Not all manufacturers, however, were equally alarmed. In November 1954, the vice president of the A. D. Juilliard Division of the United Merchants and Manufacturers said in a newspaper interview that "imports do not present a grave competitive problem." The import duty, he said, raised the prices of most foreign goods to a point where importers may "just squeak through." [16]

Imported cloths, which come principally from Great Britain (see Table 25), are in general of better quality than domestic fabrics in the same price range. Among American *worsted* mills, according to the importers, there are less than a dozen which turn out cloth of a quality comparable to that made in British and other foreign mills. The number of *woolen* mills which feel the impact of foreign competition is somewhat larger because of the recent shift of imports in their direction. (British export figures show that nearly three-fourths of exports to the United States of wool fabrics consist of woolens.)

British woolens for both men's and women's wear show great diversity, in textures, weave effects and styles. They include tweeds, homespuns, cheviots, venetians, coverts, cashmeres, meltons and flannels. "In recent years the American demand for woolens has soared as the buying public has turned more and more to casual attire, to sport jackets, tweed suits

[14] *Trade Agreements Extension,* Senate Finance Committee, Hearings on H. R. 1, cited, p. 471.
[15] Letter inserted by Representative Thomas J. Lane in *Congressional Record,* 83rd Cong., 2d sess. (March 30, 1954), p. A2390. (Daily edition.)
[16] Interview with Harold Ackerman, as reported in the *New York Times,* November 3, 1954.

Table 25

U. S. IMPORTS OF WOOLEN AND WORSTED CLOTHS, BY COUNTRY OF ORIGIN, SELECTED YEARS

	1939	1948	1950	1952	1954[a]	1955[a]
	Quantity (1000 square yards)					
Total	12,018.4	9,212.3	18,549.7	23,980.0	19,923.8	29,757.7
United Kingdom	9,996.5	7,203.8	13,925.2	18,972.6	13,112.5	18,061.5
Italy	402.2	756.7	1,487.3	2,155.5	2,009.2	3,319.4
France	892.1	564.9	694.5	824.7	1,298.7	1,690.4
Japan	390.2	1.3	222.1	116.5	826.3	2,875.8
Germany	20.8	13.3	237.4	149.7	212.3	195.2
	Foreign value (1000 dollars)					
Total	8,702.4	18,597.3	33,041.8	42,869.1	38,180.7	54,606.6
United Kingdom	7,408.6	14,832.9	24,309.5	32,896.0	25,096.7	33,246.2
Italy	301.7	1,426.8	3,203.5	4,715.5	4,271.3	6,433.6
France	569.6	795.6	1,132.5	1,998.0	3,170.4	4,146.3
Japan	162.2	2.6	483.4	228.4	1,329.7	4,784.6
Germany	15.7	18.4	543.7	348.4	465.7	363.9

[a] Total imports for 1954 and 1955 include estimated quantities for shipments of less than $250 each, which Census data do not allocate by countries. Hence the figures for these years understate the imports from individual countries.
Source: U. S. Bureau of the Census

and coats, and to softer finishes. . . ." [17] Besides the meticulous workmanship, involving large amounts of hand labor, particularly in finishing, which distinguishes the British goods, the prestige which they enjoy in the American market enables them to command high prices. Clothing manufacturers stress "British" or "imported" in their advertising.

Importers sell their English worsteds to only a few, perhaps 20 or 25, manufacturers of the higher-priced, ready-to-wear suits.[18] Occasionally, however, one of the "chains" will advertise sales of men's suits or overcoats made of imported cloth. Representatives of the American industry have disputed these estimates, asserting that the impact of the imports is felt much more widely. It is perhaps significant, however, that the firms which are the most vocal in protesting against tariff reduction are those producing fabrics of the highest quality.

[17] David L. Hurwood, British Woolens in the American Market (New York: Author, 1953), p. 15.
[18] Sales to merchant tailors make up a small fraction of the total.

Imports from countries other than the United Kingdom have made rapid gains in postwar years which have brought them very considerably above the 1939 level. The quality of the goods imported from Italy, France and Germany, as indicated by average unit values, is as good as, if not superior to, the British. Imports from West Germany and Japan have shown a rapid rate of postwar increase, but neither country seems in a position to seriously challenge American producers in their domestic market.

Japan's woolen and worsted industry, which ranked among the world's largest in prewar years, with an annual output of about 300 million square yards, suffered severely in the war and postwar years but since 1950 has shown rapid recovery. Production in 1955 was 182 million square yards. Exports, which now constitute 10 percent of production, have fallen with domestic production below prewar levels; in 1955 they were approximately 19 million square yards.

The German woolen and worsted mills suffered from war damage and dismantling. Moreover, the separation of East Germany unbalanced the structure of the industry; one-third of the wool scouring and combing firms and two-thirds of the worsted spinning and weaving mills were in the Russian zone of occupation. Domestic production in 1955 was 174 million square yards, not sufficient to meet domestic requirements. Imports are growing faster than exports; in 1955 they were 55 million square yards and exports only 11 million.[19]

Competition from abroad was not the sole cause of the postwar troubles in American wool manufacturing. In order to set imports in their proper perspective it will be useful to examine some of the other disturbing factors.

Fluctuating Prices of Raw Wool

More than most manufacturing industries, the business of making woolen and worsted cloth is "oriented" toward its raw material. The Tariff Commission has estimated that raw

[19] See *World Wool Digest*, published by the International Wool Secretariat and the Wool Bureau, Inc., for August 31, 1955, and also the article, "Capacity in the West European Wool Textile Industry," in the same publication, May 26, 1954, pp. 129-132.

materials (chiefly raw wool) constitute 40 to 60 percent of total manufacturing cost.[20] On this account the industry is particularly sensitive to fluctuations in wool prices, which have been notoriously unstable. Because wool fiber cannot be easily standardized, the futures market has been too "thin" to permit hedging operations. Worsted mills, which buy their tops from combing establishments, can hedge their purchases of this standardized product in a futures market, but manufacturers who buy raw wool have been forced to gamble on the probable trend of prices. Thus their profits have depended on their shrewdness as traders in the wool market, as well as on their capacity for good business management and their initiative in introducing economies in production.

In response to war demands, prices of raw wool rose rapidly and, after a brief check in 1946, continued their upward movement in postwar years. The outbreak of the Korean war caused wool prices to double within a year; some types of wool rose to two and one-half times the pre-Korean price. But within the next 12 months prices dropped by 50 percent. After March 1952 the wool market enjoyed a period of unusual price stability. A new decline which began in September 1954 reflected falling mill consumption, both in the United States and abroad, and prospects for increased supply. More important in the long run was the announcement of a radical change in United States policy on raw wool.

Congress in August 1954 repealed the price-support legislation which for more than a decade had reinforced the tariff as a means of keeping domestic wool prices above the world market level. Instead of price supports, the new legislation guaranteed domestic wool growers an average return of 62 cents per pound (greasy basis) and provided for cash subsidies to make up the difference between the average of the prices they received during the marketing year and the 62-cent rate. Purchases and loans by the Credit Commodity Corporation were discontinued, and 150 million pounds of greasy wool which the Corporation had acquired in price-support operations were to be sold in the open market over a period of two years, beginning November 1, 1955. The effect was to restore

[20] *Woolens and Worsteds*, War Changes in Industry Series, cited, p. 55.

a free market for wool, with prices fluctuating in response to current variations in supply and demand.

Substitution of Synthetic Fibers

In the 1930's a new cellulose fiber, rayon, was first used to supplement wool in the production of women's wear and in men's slacks. But it lacked some of wool's desirable qualities, durability and resiliency. These qualities were supplied in large measure by the new noncellulosic fibers which, in addition, had valuable qualities of their own.

Nylon was introduced shortly before World War II. Other synthetics, such as Acrilan, Dacron, Dynel and Orlon, appeared on the market after the war. In fabrics for wearing apparel they have often been blended with varying proportions of wool. At first, advertised extensively as superior to 100 percent woolens and worsteds, the synthetic and blended fabrics sold at higher prices, but after a few years price reductions brought the competition nearer to an even basis.

In prewar years (1935-1939) U. S. total consumption of certain textile fibers averaged 28.1 pounds per capita. Wool (3.0 pounds) and synthetics (2.6 pounds) each had about 10 percent. In 1955, total per capita consumption had risen to 36.5 pounds. Wool, with 2.9 pounds, had only 8 percent, but synthetics had risen to 28 percent (10.3 pounds).

The eventual effect of the introduction of the blended fabrics on the woolen and worsted business is still uncertain. The first experimental purchases of blended fabrics for the armed forces, always conservative buyers, turned out badly, but recently government specifications for many basic wool cloths have been revised so as to permit the blending of 10-20 percent synthetic fibers with wool. Early enthusiasm on the part of clothing manufacturers has cooled somewhat. For the present the new synthetics are a threat to wool in the production of knit goods and carpets and in novelty fabrics (woolens) for women's wear and in men's lightweight suits for summer wear, where they are displacing a large percentage of tropical worsteds. Incidentally, the woolen and worsted business benefited from the elaborate advertising of the synthetics which has stimulated consumers' interest in apparel, generally.

Increasingly, the new fibers have proved supplementary to wool rather than substitutes for it. "After five years the battle of the fibers has subsided. Some of the former adversaries now are married to each other. . . . What has happened is that the new fibers . . . have either created for themselves new markets where they have very little competition, or they have been engineered into blends with the older fibers, and thus created better fabrics which have benefited the interests of both the traditional fibers and themselves." In men's and women's clothing synthetic fibers have succeeded best when blended with wool. "By themselves they· have made good fabrics, but wool has been necessary to bring them into the best public acceptance." [21]

Failure of Markets to Expand

The impact of technological change on the woolen and worsted industry was all the more severe because the market failed to keep pace with expanding productivity. This situation had been apparent long before World War II. As early as the middle 1920's, the introduction of central heating into homes, retail stores, business offices and public buildings and the use of closed automobiles, with heaters, caused men to demand lighter-weight suits and overcoats. Women bought fewer woolen garments and more cottons and synthetics.

Wartime regulations forbade manufacturers to furnish vests with men's suits. Most men, finding that they were more comfortable without the extra garment, are now satisfied with coat and trousers. The emigration of young families from cities to suburbs, where there is much less dressing up, stimulated buying of woolens but checked purchases of worsteds. In both city and country men and boys bought fewer suits and overcoats and more slacks, sport jackets and light raincoats, garments which require smaller amounts of wool. Synthetics also displaced wool in women's suits, jackets and skirts.

Sales of woolens and worsteds, and other apparel fabrics, suffered because other kinds of expenditures claimed an increasing proportion of the consumer's income.[22] Automobiles,

[21] *Journal of Commerce*, September 29, 1955.
[22] See Clive Howard's interview of Solomon Barkin in *This Week*, November 9, 1952.

television, payments on mortgages, house repairs and improvements demanded an increasing share of the family budget. As a result of these and other factors, the proportion of consumers' disposable income spent on clothing (not including shoes) declined from 9.5 percent in 1946 to 6.2 percent in 1955.

Compared with other fabrics, woolens and worsteds have been expensive. The 1955 wholesale price index for wool products was 104.7; for cottons, 91.5; and for synthetic fabrics, 86.5 (based on 1947-49 = 100). Between 1947 and 1955 wholesale prices of woolens and worsteds rose 16 percent; meanwhile prices of cotton goods fell 11 percent and synthetics 10 percent. (See Table 22, p. 139.)

The Second Industrial Revolution

In the second half of the 18th century a series of technical improvements revolutionized the British textile industry. In American wool manufacturing, particularly in the worsted mills, the first half of the 20th century brought changes equally dramatic, if not so far-reaching in their effects. In the space of 50 years both woolen and worsted mills have introduced important labor-saving and cost-reducing improvements. In the spinning of worsted yarn the substitution of ring frames for mules made rapid progress after 1930; in 1947 nearly three-fourths of all worsted spindles in place were of the newer type. Another significant labor-saving improvement was the introduction of the automatic broad loom. In December 1954, 84 percent of the looms in place in woolen and worsted mills were automatic; in 1935 only 50 percent had been in that category.

In postwar years a new system of spinning worsted yarns, the so-called American system, made rapid progress. With the active cooperation of makers of textile machinery, the new long-draft system of spinning, first built for rayon and acetate fibers, was adapted for worsted yarns. Under the conventional Bradford system, yarn spinning required seven separate processes. The American system cut them to three, with a large saving in the number of operatives and a substantial reduction in floor space. The new machines, also, have lower operating and maintenance costs.

Several years ago a textile engineer estimated that these economies had brought about a saving of 10 cents per pound of yarn.[23] The yarns produced were equal in quality to those produced on the older system. At the end of 1952, 300,000 spindles, about 15 percent of those in the worsted industry, were on the American system. Other innovations followed, larger spinning frames were installed, and more efficient looms.

Reinvestment of wartime profits in most cases financed the

Table 26

OUTPUT PER EMPLOYEE IN U. S. WOOLEN AND
WORSTED INDUSTRY, 1935, 1937, 1947-1954

Year	Production (millions of square yards)	Total employees[a] (thousands)	Yards per employee
1935	478	172	2,779
1937	471	166	2,837
1947	655	180	3,639
1949	527	145	3,634
1950	586	157	3,732
1951	509	138	3,688
1952	501	125	4,008
1953	470	132	3,561
1954	414	100[b]	4,140[b]

[a] Includes all employees in establishments producing woolen and worsted fabrics, yarn mills (except carpet yarns), scouring, combing and finishing plants. Prewar figures are not strictly comparable with postwar.
[b] Estimated.
Source: U. S. Bureau of the Census and estimates of the National Association of Wool Manufacturers

cost of the new equipment. But many of the smaller firms, and others lacking capital or progressive management, or both, failed to take advantage of the new technology. In the long run the woolen and worsted industry is bound to benefit from reduction in costs and improvement of product, but the process of transition has been painful. It has tended to widen the margin between the low-cost and the high-cost

[23] Robert J. McConnell, "The American System," *Papers of the Association of Textile Technologists*, v. 7. (September 1952), pp. 161-162.

firms and has been responsible for the liquidation of some in the latter category. Moreover, by raising the productivity of the individual operative, technological progress incurred a large part of the responsibility for the decline in employment. The new equipment ran faster and required less manpower per unit of output. Processes were "telescoped" and many operations omitted altogether. Automatic controls eliminated the necessity for inspectors and supervisors. The combined result has been a progressive increase in postwar years in the average output per employee. Accurate statistical comparisons over a period of years are impossible because of intervening changes in the kinds of fabrics produced. The data in Table 26 give, nevertheless, a rough indication of what was taking place.

The Shift to the South

In 1954, according to trade sources, there were 26 woolen and worsted plants in the states of Georgia, North and South Carolina and Virginia in the region known as the Southern Piedmont. Many of these had been opened by New England firms between 1939 and 1951. The migration was a part of a larger southward movement of the whole textile industry from its traditional seat in New England and the Middle Atlantic states. In the early 1920's, lower labor costs in the South (based on lower wage rates and higher work loads), a more amenable labor supply, and other advantages, such as lower taxes, cheaper fuel, etc., had attracted cotton mills. The shift in the woolen and worsted industry which began some 10 or 15 years later was influenced, also, by the rapid technological changes described above. The improved machinery, it was found, could be operated more effectively in the new one-story structures in the South than in the older three- and four-story Northern mills. Only the best machinery was transferred from liquidated Northern mills; more often the new mills were fitted out with improved modern equipment.

The decline in New England's position in wool manufacturing in general is seen in the distribution of mills liquidated. In the five years, 1949-1953, out of 132 mills closed, 74 were in New England, 38 in the Middle Atlantic states, 7 in the South East, 9 in the Middle West, and 4 on the Pacific Coast.

The Menace of British Competition

In tariff hearings American manufacturers have persistently stressed the menace of British competition. Measured by volume of output, the British woolen and worsted industry is now practically on the same level as that of the United States. Mills in the United Kingdom turned out 410 million square yards in 1955, about 10 percent less than U. S. production for that year. The output of both the British and American mills was slightly less than in prewar years.

Declining employment has characterized both the British and American industries since the middle 1920's. In 1939, 230,000 persons were employed in United Kingdom mills. Wartime conditions, which in the United States raised production and employment above any prewar figure, had the contrary effect in Britain. Employment fell considerably below the prewar level.

The American industry has often cited the low wages paid to workers abroad as evidence of its need for tariff protection. In 1954 average hourly earnings in American woolen and worsted factories were $1.53; earnings in British mills were $.45 per hour in October 1954. Figures presented at the 1955 Senate Finance Committee hearings indicate that wages paid in France, Italy and, particularly, Japan fall considerably below the British figure.

At first glance one might wonder how the domestic mills paying wages four to eight times as high would be able to sell any goods at all in competition with their foreign competitors. The explanation is found partly in the fact that direct labor cost of the ordinary run of woolens and worsteds in this country makes up not more than one-third of total manufacturing costs. But even if labor constituted 100 percent of costs, the wage differences in themselves would not be significant for they fail to take account of differences in output. These, taken together with wages, determine the cost of labor *per yard of cloth*, the essential factor in all inter-firm competition.

Reports from various sources agree that in American mills the productivity per man-hour is higher than in the British, largely because the latter have been slower in introducing improved machinery and other cost-reducing innovations. In prewar years, an English economist estimated, American output per man-hour in woolen and worsted mills was 74 to 88 percent higher than in the British,[24] and in 1947 an official British report found that the output per worker in American factories was nearly twice as great as in the United Kingdom.[25]

Since these estimates were made, the margin of advantage of the American mills appears to have widened. While in this country output per employee has continued to gain, in the United Kingdom similar progress has not been apparent. None of the British worsted mills, it seems, have introduced the revolutionary improvements in drawing and spinning which have cut labor costs in American factories. One American observer has recently stated that the best British worsted mills are now as up to date as the best American mills of 20 years ago.

British exports of woolens and worsteds declined steadily from 123 million square yards in 1937 to 103 million in 1955. Exports fell with production, so that the percentage of output sold abroad amounted to 26 percent in 1937 and in 1950 and 25 percent in 1955. The British mills lost markets in South America, India and other countries which were building up their own textile industries in the process of economic development. These losses were only partially offset by gains in sales to the United States. The proportion of exports sold in this market increased from about 6 percent in the pre-war years, 1936-1938, to an average of 15 percent in the six years, 1950-1955.

The Process of Adjustment

The postwar depression in the American woolen and worsted industry should properly be regarded as only the most recent phase of a long process of adjustment to new conditions of supply and demand. As long ago as the 1920's, changed conditions of living and working in the United States

---

[24] L. Rostas, *Comparative Productivity in British and American Industry*, National Institute of Economic and Social Research, Occasional Papers, v. 13 (Cambridge: Cambridge University Press, 1948), p. 141.
[25] Board of Trade, *Wool*, Working Party Reports (London: HMSO, 1947).

were shrinking the market for woolen and worsted apparel fabrics. At the same time manufacturers' costs were mounting. Their principal raw material, raw wool, was becoming steadily more expensive, owing to natural causes (the decline in wool growing) as well as to government policy (the tariff and price supports). At the same time the newly unionized textile workers were exerting an upward push on wages and labor costs.

World War II submerged the manufacturers' worries in a sea of government purchases, and for a few years woolen and worsted mills, even the most inefficient, were prosperous. Government buying suddenly stopped at the end of the war and shortly thereafter civilian demand resumed its downward course. But wages and the price of raw wool continued to rise. Caught in the squeeze between mounting costs and falling sales, scores of mills were forced out of business, and thousands of workers lost their jobs.

But, paradoxically, the 30 years of the industry's apparent sickness and decline marked a period of real progress. The more progressive and better-financed firms were able to counteract rising wages by introducing technological improvements which made labor more efficient, and by establishing new enterprises in low-cost areas of the South. By use of synthetic fibers in blended fabrics they were able to cope with rising costs of wool and, at the same time, stimulate flagging consumers' demand for wearing apparel. The most recent and, to the outside observer, the most spectacular phase of this process of adjustment is the merger movement, to which we have already referred.

The significance of new combinations such as Burlington Industries and Textron American is not to be found merely in the creation of business units operating on a larger scale than the merged firms and disposing of more ample financial resources. Many of the formerly independent units had already attained maximum economies of scale in production and marketing. Moreover, the sad experience of the American Woolen Company warns that bigness is not synonymous with economy and efficiency. A deeper meaning of the mergers can be found in the creation of an integrated American textile industry. For the first time woolen and worsted mills, cotton mills and mills producing synthetic fabrics were brought under common ownership. "Fewer and fewer companies are now engaged in exclusively producing cotton textiles or wool textiles, and most major companies now make products from all fibers, both natural and synthetic, with increasing emphasis on blended fabrics designed for specific end uses." [26]

Trade union leaders have been bitterly critical of the new mergers, claiming that they dominate price and production practices and that they have substantially reduced competition. The new "colossal corporations," they assert, have accelerated mill closings and have frequently exercised their concentrated power "to repress workers . . . to discourage unionism, and to relocate plants without concern for the destructive effects." [27] In rebuttal, J. Spencer Love, chairman of Burlington Industries, denied that the new combinations have monopoly power, pointing out that the number of firms in the entire textile industry has actually increased, from 5,400 in 1945 to about 6,800 in 1954, and that no company controlled more than three percent of total textile volume.

Whether or not the new corporations will be in a better position to meet foreign competition than independent companies is still uncertain. The more progressive American mills already had a clear advantage over foreign competitors in textile engineering, in the invention and application of new mechanical processes and in the design of new fabrics where wool is blended with synthetic fibers. With larger resources for research and experimentation the new combinations may be able to widen these advantages. On the other hand, they may lose in some measure the vigorous initiative which is essential to the success of enterprises conducted on a smaller scale.

In 1955 the American woolen and worsted business seemed to be emerging at last from its long period of depression. Indications of approaching recovery were evident in late 1954. Sales of wearing apparel increased, and manufacturers' inventories began to fall. Mills reported increased wool consumption, and their unfilled orders for cloth for civilian apparel

[26] *Textiles and Apparel,* Standard & Poor's Industry Surveys, v. 123, no. 26, sec. 2 (June 30, 1955), p. 2.
[27] Statement of Solomon Barkin to the Senate Committee on the Judiciary, Sub-Committee on Anti-Trust and Monopoly (Washington, June 29, 1955), p. 3. (Mimeographed.)

showed substantial gains over the previous year's figures. The U. S. Army, having decided to change from olive drab to green uniforms, asked the mills to bid on six million yards of cloth. Some mills raised their prices. Surveying the new situation in May 1955, Harold J. Walter, president of the NAWM, said "For the first time in three years, some cheerfulness appears warranted in the wool textile industry." [28] As the year progressed his optimism appeared justified.

Many factors contributed to the upturn in wool manufacturing. The elimination of marginal firms had concentrated a larger proportion of production in the hands of enterprises with lower costs and larger resources. Competition with synthetic fibers took a new turn. Instead of displacing wool, they proved a useful supplement. Decreased competition from abroad (imports had fallen off by 4,300,000 square yards in 1954) was interpreted as a favorable omen. Another factor in stimulating recovery in wool manufacturing was the decline in raw wool prices which followed the repeal of price-support legislation in August 1954. At the new prices, raw wool became a better bargain than the newer synthetic fibers, and wool manufacturers without raising prices were able to earn better profits. Finally, the general upturn in business brought increased demand for woolens and worsteds.

How Important Is Tariff Protection?

The history of the woolen and worsted industry in the past 30 years can best be understood, as we have remarked above, as a process of adjustment to rising costs and shrinking demand. After 1946 the reappearance of foreign cloths in the American market, and their rapid increase at a time when domestic production was declining, may have made adjustment more difficult but did not divert its course. For, in fact, the imports never exceeded six percent of domestic production and were directly competitive with the output of only a small number of American mills. The gain in imports, if measured from the abnormally low level of the war years, seems impressive. But in a longer view there was little gain. In the five years, 1951-1955, average annual imports were 23

[28] Reported in the *Wall Street Journal*, May 6, 1955.

million square yards; 25 years earlier in 1925-1929 the average had been 20 million.

Practically all the foreign manufacturers had been able to accomplish was to regain in the American market the position they had held a quarter of a century earlier. In fact, if account is taken of the intervening growth of population in the United States, imports lost ground. In 1924 they amounted to 19 yards per 100 persons and in 1955 to only 17 yards. When related to the downward trend in American production, however, imports scored a slight gain. In 1924 they supplied only 3.8 percent of total domestic consumption; 31 years later this proportion had risen to 6 percent.

The tariff reductions of 1939 and 1948 stimulated postwar imports by reducing the prices at which English woolens and worsteds became available to clothing manufacturers. Sterling devaluation in September 1949 had a similar effect. But in both cases the advantage conferred on importers can easily be exaggerated. Some British manufacturers, relying on an established, limited market for their goods in the United States, absorbed the tariff concessions by raising their export prices. Rising sterling prices, also, soon offset the advantage of the higher rate at which pounds exchanged for dollars.

The high level and upward trend of American incomes and the pervasive optimism which encouraged free spending were more important than either tariff reduction or sterling devaluation in explaining the revival of imports in postwar years. Imports of foreign-made wool fabrics, like imports in general, regularly respond to fluctuations in American business conditions. In the 1930's the Great Depression reinforced the effect of the Hawley-Smoot tariff in cutting down sales of British cloths. A similar effect, on a much smaller scale, was observed in the business recession of 1953-1954; imports fell off but came back in 1955 with business recovery. Commenting on this change, an officer of the NAWM has said, "The rise in imports, accompanying improved conditions here, bears out NAWM's long-standing contention that general economic factors rather than present U. S. tariffs are controlling so far as import volume is concerned." [29]

[29] Statement of Gordon F. Graham, quoted in the *Journal of Commerce*, October 3, 1955.

In the list of commodities on which the United States considered tariff reductions at the 1956 session of GATT, woolen and worsted woven fabrics were not included. It seems that the State Department accepted the contention of manufacturers and workers that the industry should not be exposed to a greater measure of foreign competition while it is still in a period of transition.

Transition has already been in progress for 30 years. How much longer can it be expected to last? In the dynamic American economy it is difficult to find any industry in a normal, or stable, situation. And even if we assumed that after five or ten years wool manufacturing would be "stabilized," it might plausibly be argued that tariff reduction then would prove an unwise disturbance of this desirable condition.

More competition from abroad might hasten modernization and encourage experimentation with new fibers and new processes. Neither the British, the Japanese nor other foreign mills are in a position to swamp the United States market with their products. They have lagged behind in the introduction of new machinery and have failed to keep up with the American mills in the use of artificial fibers. In the United Kingdom, as in the United States, postwar volume of production has shown a continual decline, dating from prewar years. Exports have fallen both in quantity and in value. The Japanese industry is far from attaining its prewar volume of production or of exports.

Further tariff reduction, by encouraging imports, might cause difficulties for the less efficient firms in the woolen and worsted industry. Some might have to sell out and close their mills. Their workers would have to find other employment. Eventually, a shifting of economic resources would take place which in the long run would make the national economy more productive. The transition would cause local hardships. These hardships can be alleviated somewhat by agencies, public and private. Every New England state, and some others, has a state development commission which, by loans, technical advice and other means, assists manufacturers to devise new products, introduce improved processes and find new markets. Their activities are supplemented by privately financed development corporations organized either on a local or state-wide basis. Federal agencies are devising new means of assisting firms and communities in distressed areas. In Chapter 10 we shall consider, at some length, the accomplishments and limitations of various types of assisted adjustment.

Chapter 7

IRON AND STEEL: AN INFANT
INDUSTRY GROWS UP

IRON AND STEEL provides an illustration of an American industry, sheltered from foreign competition in its early years
by protective tariffs, which later achieved independence from
this type of government assistance. Since 1890 the trend of
import duties on iron and steel products has been steadily
downward; now they average about five percent of foreign
value. With the removal of tariff protection the industry has
not declined; instead it has grown steadily bigger and stronger
with the growth of the country and the development of the
world's greatest internal market.

Steel is no longer an "infant industry," as its leaders are
well aware. Few of them regard the small amounts of iron
and steel products imported each year as injurious, or as
threatening injury. At tariff hearings spokesmen for the
American steel and iron industry have not opposed the continuation of the policy of reducing import duties in trade
agreements. But they have criticized the State Department's
negotiators for failing to obtain from foreign governments
satisfactory concessions in their tariff treatment of American
steel and iron products.

It would be inaccurate to say that the iron and steel producers have no interest in protective import duties. They
would be glad to retain them for use when, and if, serious
competition from abroad should develop. Also, they want
stronger antidumping measures and have asked for more
effective escape clause procedures. But for the present they
are much more interested in other aspects of our foreign trade
policy as it affects their industry:

(1) As consumers of raw materials, they have a direct and
unmistakable interest in opposing tariffs on imports of lead,
zinc, manganese, tungsten and other minerals essential to the

manufacture of iron and steel. Moreover, they urge restriction of exports of iron and steel scrap whenever shipments abroad threaten to create scarcity in the home market.

(2) The steel industry's purchases of paper, lumber, paint, petroleum products and many other semimanufactures and finished goods run into hundreds of millions of dollars every year. As far as import duties restrict imports of these products, or raise their prices, the iron and steel manufacturers recognize that their interests are adversely affected.

(3) As exporters, the steel men would like to see foreign governments moderate, or remove, their restrictions on imports of American products. Lowering, rather than raising, American tariffs, they recognize, would be a promising way to achieve this result. Their interest in foreign markets is not measured only by direct exports of the products of iron and steel mills. It takes into account, also, the much larger volume of American steel contained in exports of automobiles, machinery and many other products of American industries.

(4) Recently, the big iron and steel companies have shown interest in the broad effect of tariffs on national prosperity and national welfare. Some of the more farsighted steel men believe that lowering import duties will lead to a more effective use of both American and world resources of men and materials. What is good for the country must be good for one of its biggest industries. Their industry, they believe, will inevitably benefit from the resulting rise in national income.

*   *   *

From small beginnings in colonial days, the American iron and steel industry has grown until it has attained a position of unquestioned world leadership. Its annual output, at the rate of over 120 million tons yearly, is about 40 percent of world production and more than twice that of the Soviet Union, its nearest competitor. In its infancy the American industry was protected from foreign competition by import duties, but how far these duties contributed to its phenomenal growth is far from clear.

Expanding Production and Declining Protection

In the first half of the 19th century, tariff duties on iron and steel products varied widely. But for 20 years after the

Civil War a consistent policy of high protection was maintained, and at the same time the industry experienced rapid growth. Between 1883 and 1922 the trend of tariff rates on the major products of the iron and steel industry was noticeably downward. Under the influence of revived protectionism after World War I, there was a slight reaction in the Acts of 1922 and 1930, but the increases were only moderate. After 1934, trade agreements made substantial reductions. In addition, rising prices weakened the force of the duties, which are largely specific. The combined result was reduction in the average level of the iron and steel duties to about one-half the 1930 level.

A tabulation of rates effective in 1953 on 32 major imported iron and steel products is shown below.

	Number of products
On the free list....................	2
Dutiable at less than 5 percent......	11
Dutiable at 5-14 percent...........	17
Dutiable at 15 percent and over.....	2

Taking all imports together, the over-all average duty was about 5 percent of foreign value.

Table 27 shows the 1930 rates of duty and those effective in 1954 on a few major items.

Table 27

U. S. RATES OF DUTY ON CERTAIN IRON AND
STEEL PRODUCTS, 1930 AND 1954

(in dollars per long ton)

	Act of 1930	1954 rate
Structural shapes, not fabricated	4.48	2.24
Bars	6.72-78.40	2.80-39.20
Pipes and tubes	16.80-39.20	8.40-19.60
Pipes and tubes, n.s.p.f.	25%	12½%
Nails	8.96-100.80	4.48-100.80
Barbed wire	Free	Free
Pig iron	1.125	.60

In the period between the Civil War and the end of the century, the development of the industry may have been hastened by restriction of imports. The duties on tin plate afford a good example of successful protection of an infant industry. During a short period of high duties (of nearly $50 per long ton) from 1890 to 1894, production increased rapidly while imports declined, until by 1914 the country was entirely independent of foreign supplies of this commodity. By 1890 or 1900, with expanding domestic production, American costs on the major items such as steel rails and pig iron had fallen to a point where imports could not compete and tariff protection had become useless. The only exceptions to this statement are special steels, low-volume items in which the greater productivity of American labor does not fully compensate for lower wages paid abroad.

Berglund and Wright found that as early as 1896 the iron and steel industry, "so far as concerns the manufacture of tonnage products," was independent of the tariff; exception could perhaps be made with respect to establishments located near the seaboard.[1] By 1909, according to Taussig, the iron and steel duties "no longer played an important part in the tariff controversy, and were no longer of any considerable economic consequence."[2]

The relation of tariff protection to the growth and prosperity of the steel industry has been much debated. Protectionists have naturally claimed credit for their system; the industry was protected, and it grew and flourished. But observers with sympathies on the side of freer trade have pointed out that in the last half of the 19th century, irrespective of tariff policies, many natural advantages would have promoted the growth of the industry: abundant supplies of raw materials; the cheapening of inland transport which made it economical to bring them together over great distances; the creation of a vast internal market free from tariff restrictions; an abundant supply of cheap labor made possible by unre-

[1] Abraham Berglund and Philip G. Wright, *The Tariff on Iron and Steel* (Washington: Brookings Institution, 1929), p. 130.
[2] F. W. Taussig, *The Tariff History of the United States* (8th ed.; New York: Putnam's, 1931), p. 386.

stricted immigration; and, finally, technical progress and business enterprise and the climate of democracy in which both could freely develop. Professor Taussig wrote:

No one can say with certainty what would have been; and the bias of the individual observer will have an effect on his estimate of probabilities. The free trader, impatient with the fallacies and superficialities of current protectionist talk, will be slow to admit that there are any kernels of truth under all this chaff. What gain has come, will seem to him a part of the ordinary course of progress. On the other hand, the firm protectionist will find in the history of the iron trade conclusive proof of brilliant success. And very possibly those economists who, being in principle neither protectionists nor free traders, seek to be guided only by the outcome in the ascertained facts of concrete industry, would render a verdict here not unfavorable to the policy of fostering "national industry." [3]

Imports

Imports of steel mill products, which had averaged about 220,000 tons in 1937-39, reached a postwar peak of 2,178,481 tons in 1951. This was a year of shortages augmented by rearmament demands. By 1953 imports had declined to 1,674,-468, and the business recession of 1953-1954 brought them down to 787,596 tons in 1954. On a quantity basis the imports now supply something less than 2 percent of the domestic market.

In postwar years the quantity of foreign iron and steel entering American ports has regularly been less than half the amount of American products leaving those ports destined for foreign markets. Measured in dollars, imports in the five years, 1950-1954, were 33 percent of the exports. (See Table 28.)

Table 29 summarizes the competitive situation for six products in which foreign competition has been, or may be, active.

In spite of recent increases, the imports, in each category as well as in total, remain small in relation to domestic production and are sporadic, fluctuating in response to short-run

[3] F. W. Taussig, *Some Aspects of the Tariff Question* (4th ed.; Cambridge; Harvard University Press, 1924), p. 151.

Table 28

U. S. IMPORTS AND EXPORTS OF IRON AND STEEL PRODUCTS, 1936-40, 1947-1954[a]

(in thousands of dollars)

Year	Imports	Exports
1936-40 (annual average)	13,841	211,618
1947	6,576	813,652
1948	20,003	636,724
1949	32,642	721,231
1950	87,048	466,118
1951	278,414	601,722
1952	189,037	609,491
1953	222,749	483,743
1954	101,027	464,274

[a] Excluding granular iron, pig iron and iron and steel scrap.
Source: U. S. Bureau of the Census

conditions in domestic markets. Because of the high costs of inland rail transport, foreign iron and steel products can be marketed principally in the vicinity of seaports. For example, in Florida imported bars are used for reinforcing concrete in building and highway construction. Barbed wire for use in the South and Middle West enters at Gulf ports. Because of low transportation costs by water routes, the foreign wire in some years has supplied a substantial share of the purchases of American farmers, whose influence in Congress has been strong enough to keep barbed wire on the free list. In 1954 the imports, 53,000 tons, were almost 40 percent of domestic production.

The best-informed men in the iron and steel industry find no evidence that the lowering of import duties under trade agreements has had as yet any appreciable effect on the quantity of foreign steel sold in American markets or on market prices. Foreign producers who want to sell to the United States customarily price their goods at 15 to 20 percent below the American level. American producers usually make no attempt to meet these prices, but instead depend on closer

Table 29

U. S. SHIPMENTS, EXPORTS AND IMPORTS OF CERTAIN IRON AND STEEL PRODUCTS, 1954

(in thousands of short tons)

	Net shipments[a]	Imports	Exports
Concrete reinforcement bars	1,751	164	30
Other bars	7,465	50	58
Structural shapes, not fabricated	4,501	206	267
Pipes and tubes	8,158	80	465
Barbed wire	132	53	4
Nails	567	91	3
Total, steel mill products[b]	63,153	788	2,659

[a] Excluding shipments to members of the industry for conversion into further finished products or for resale.
[b] The total import and export quantities given in this table are not strictly comparable with import and export values found in Table 28. The classification, "steel mill products," employed by the American Iron and Steel Institute does not include some of the items found in the U. S. Bureau of the Census classification, "steel mill products." For example, the value of 1954 imports, given in Table 28, includes approximately $5-6 million of iron and steel products which are not included in the quantity figure of 788,000 tons given above.
Source: American Iron and Steel Institute

touch with the domestic market and quicker service[4] to maintain their dominant position. Besides the advantage of location in relation to the huge domestic market, American steel mills have easy access to large supplies of raw materials. These and other advantages more than offset lower wages paid in foreign mills.

Raw Materials: Imports and Trade Policy

The growth of the American iron and steel industry has been made possible by the availability of abundant supplies of the basic raw materials, iron ore, coking coal and limestone. Small quantities of high-grade iron ore have long been im-

[4] A contractor who wanted 15,000 tons of sheet piling for a large hydroelectric project awarded the contract to a foreign firm at a price 20 percent under the lowest American bid. The job had to be completed in about 4 months. But when after 3 months the foreign concern had made no deliveries the contract was cancelled and the business was switched to a domestic steel mill which supplied two-thirds of the order in a few days.

ported duty free, for example, from Chile and Sweden. Recently American steel makers have brought ores from Venezuela and Labrador. In 1954 blast furnaces consumed 17.7 million short tons of imported iron ore, 18 percent of the total consumption of 96 million short tons. With expanding steel production and the progressive depletion of the richest and most accessible domestic supplies, a sharp rise in imports of foreign ore is expected.

Various metals required in the process of steel making are imported, either because no significant deposits have been discovered in the United States, as for example nickel, or because of the poor quality of the domestic ores and the high cost of exploiting them, manganese, for example. Most of these metals, when imported as ores, come in free of duty; exceptions are molybdenum, manganese and tungsten.

The duty on molybdenum is of little consequence. The United States is the world's largest producer of this metal, and imports are negligible. The manganese situation is quite different. Over 90 percent of the more than 500,000 tons (metallic content) consumed each year in American blast furnaces is imported, chiefly from India, Cuba and Africa. Domestic producers have claimed tariff protection on the grounds that manganese is essential to national security, but negotiators of trade agreements have not heeded this plea. Instead they twice cut the 1930 rate on manganese ore so that it now stands at $5.60 per long ton, or about 7 percent of foreign value.

The steel industry is the largest consumer of tungsten. From 1946 to 1950 the American industries obtained about half their supplies from domestic mines and the remainder from abroad. To stimulate domestic production, Congress, in 1950, instituted a subsidy program. In the Defense Production Act of that year the government undertook to purchase from domestic mines a maximum of 11,750 tons of tungsten annually at $6,300 per ton. Under this program the domestic output has increased until, when added to imports, it is more than sufficient to supply the needs of the steel industry and other domestic consumers. The excess has gone into government stockpiles.

Restrictions on Exports of Scrap

One of the principal sources of metal for steel making is scrap—worn-out, discarded or broken items containing iron or steel—and clippings produced in manufacturing processes. Because of its great value in economizing the use of iron ore, coal and limestone, an abundant supply of scrap is a matter of much importance to the steel makers.

Twenty years ago the United States was the world's leading exporter of iron and steel scrap, but during World War II American export controls over all foreign trade almost entirely eliminated this trade. In 1948-1951 the expanded American iron and steel industry consumed more scrap than was generated domestically, so that in these years the country was a net importer.[5] (See Table 30.) The tide turned again

Table 30

U. S. CONSUMPTION, EXPORTS AND IMPORTS OF IRON AND STEEL SCRAP, 1947-1954

(in thousands of short tons)

Year	Consumption	Exports	Imports	Net exports[a]
1947	60,864	194	36	158
1948	64,968	244	435	(191)
1949	54,336	299	1,104	(805)
1950	68,904	217	738	(521)
1951	76,740	231	359	(128)
1952	69,024	342	106	236
1953	77,304	304	132	172
1954	61,356	1,507	206	1,301

[a] Figures in parentheses indicate net imports.
Source: U. S. Department of Commerce

in 1952, and since that time the United States has again become the world's principal source of ferrous scrap.

Exports in 1954 were 1.5 million tons and in 1955 about 5.0 million. Most of the scrap has gone to the United King--

[5] Imports have continued but at a greatly reduced rate. Scrap is a bulky commodity. Hence, it has no national market but rather a number of local markets, independent of each other within the limits of transportation costs. Hence, scrap may be imported into Pacific coast ports while it is being exported from the Eastern industrial area.

dom, France, West Germany and other countries in Western Europe. Their need for rapid expansion of steel production brought about radical changes in methods of production. Capital was lacking for the expansion of iron mining and the building of new blast furnaces. But by the substitution of scrap for iron ore, increased output could be obtained from existing facilities. Hence, the unusual imports from the United States, the largest source of supplies.

The American "harvest" of iron and steel scrap in the years 1950-1954 averaged 70,000,000 tons. Of this about one-half originated in the steel mills themselves; the remainder they bought from dealers. Exports in 1955 amounted to about one-seventh of the market supply.

Representatives of American steel and iron companies have complained that the exports constitute a threat to their industry, and they have asked the Department of Commerce to impose restrictions. They assert that the European steel industries receive government subsidies; hence their purchases of scrap constitute a species of unfair competition. Countervailing export duties would be a logical method of dealing with subsidies of this kind, assuming that the facts are as stated. But the constitution of the United States forbids export duties. A somewhat similar result might be accomplished by quantitative limitation on exports.

The Department of Commerce, under the Export Control Act of 1949,[6] is authorized to limit exports for the following purposes:

(a) to protect the domestic economy from the excessive drain of scarce materials and to reduce the inflationary impact of abnormal foreign demand;

(b) to further the foreign policy of the United States and to aid in fulfilling its international responsibilities; and

(c) to exercise the necessary vigilance over exports from the standpoint of their significance to the national security.

[6] Public Law no. 11, 81st Cong., 1st sess. (Feb. 26, 1949) p. 1. This act continued in force the export controls on scrap iron which were first introduced in 1940. In later legislation the provisions of the Act have been extended to 1956. See Public Law no. 62, 83rd Cong., 1st sess. (June 16, 1953).

The Department has exercised its powers only sparingly, granting export licenses freely except for shipments to Soviet Russia and its satellites and to Red China. After much discussion with iron and steel men, the Department in September 1955 seemed ready to apply quantitative controls. But a conflict of opinion developed within the administration and no restrictive action was taken.

The Interest in Export Markets

The American steel industry exports only a small proportion of its products, about 4 percent in 1950-1954. About half of the exports go to Canada. Producers take a dim view of the possibilities of increasing these *direct* exports, because their costs are not much different from those of foreign competitors and also because of tariffs and other restrictions imposed by foreign governments. They see much brighter prospects for expanding *indirect* exports in the form of automobiles and other automotive products, machinery, office equipment and other commodities in which steel is an important element. The best way to expand these important sales, according to leading steel producers, is to put more dollars at the disposal of prospective foreign buyers by lowering American tariffs on their products.

The Revival of the European Steel Industry

The postwar revival, with American aid, of European steel industries and their organization in the European Coal and Steel Community indicate, according to the American Iron and Steel Institute, strong competition in world markets.

In the eight years of post-war reconstruction the major steel producers in Western Europe and Great Britain rehabilitated, modernized and enlarged their capacity, many of them with both financial aid and the best technical advice from the United States. All of them have production capacities above pre-war levels, and their new capacity exceeds their current domestic demands. This means that not only are European markets closed to exports of steel products from the United States, but that *these modernized competitors are now in a position, more than ever before, to compete on a quality and price basis with United States producers in the world market.* In addition the Schuman Plan is deliberately designed to set up a vast supranational industry com-

posed of all the major producing countries in Western Europe
to regulate marketing within this enlarged area and to function
more efficiently in export markets. It remains to be seen, probably
in the very near future, just what kind of competitor this po-
tentially powerful group will become in the free export markets
left in the world.[7]

British production reached an all-time high in 1954 of approximately 20.7 million short tons. In that year West Germany, as the result of rapid recovery since 1949, surpassed
prewar levels in steel production. France, Belgium, Luxem-
bourg, Italy and Japan all exceeded their 1937-38 outputs as
early as 1951. (See Table 31.)

Table 31

DOMESTIC AND FOREIGN PRODUCTION OF CRUDE STEEL,
1937, 1938, 1947-1954

(in millions of short tons)

Year	United States	United Kingdom	West Germany	France[a]	Belgium-Luxem-bourg	Italy	Japan
1937	56.6	14.5	17.2	11.3	7.0	2.3	6.4
1938	31.7	11.6	19.7	9.7	4.1	2.6	7.1
1947	84.9	14.2	3.4	7.1	5.1	1.9	1.0
1948	88.6	16.7	6.1	9.3	7.0	2.3	1.9
1949	80.0	17.4	10.1	12.0	6.8	2.3	3.4
1950	96.8	18.2	13.4	11.6	6.9	2.6	5.3
1951	105.2	17.5	14.9	13.7	9.0	3.4	7.2
1952	93.1	18.4	17.4	15.1	8.9	3.9	7.7
1953	111.6	19.7	17.0	14.0	7.9	3.9	8.5
1954	88.3	20.7	19.2	14.8	8.6	4.6	8.5

[a] Including the Saar.
Source: United Nations, Economic Commission for Europe, *European Steel Exports and Steel Demand in Non-European Countries*, E/ECE/163, E/ECE/STEEL/-
75 (Geneva: Author, 1953); United Nations, *Monthly Bulletin of Statistics* and
Quarterly Bulletin of Steel Statistics for Europe

The Competitive Situation

The advantages and disadvantages of European steel producers in competing with the American industry are sum-

[7] *Statement of the American Iron and Steel Institute before the Commission
on Foreign Economic Policy* (December 1953), p. 4. (Italics in original.)

marized in a report of the Steel Committee of the Economic Commission for Europe. "Cumulative labour costs per ton of rolled steel," the report points out, "usually represent 20 to 25 per cent of total cost. In the United States, hourly wages, including social charges, are two to four times higher than in Europe . . . but as productivity is at least twice as high, total labour costs are not much higher in the United States than in Europe. . . ." [8]

As regards raw materials and transport charges, the majority of European steelworks are favorably situated. "Coalfields are not far from the major iron ore reserves and steelworks which have to import iron ore from overseas are usually situated on or close to deep-sea ports." The Europeans have failed in the past to exploit these advantages because of inefficient mining practices, abnormally high costs of rail transport, price discrimination and intra-European barriers. These are faults which the European Coal and Steel Community intends to remedy. "In the United States," the report continues, "the near exhaustion of high-grade iron ore resources in the Mesabi range and the consequent necessity to increase ore imports or possibly to use taconites on a large scale will progressively raise the cost of ores. On the other hand, the coal situation will remain favourable." [9]

In shipping to American coastal areas, European producers have benefited by low ocean freights. This advantage will disappear when new American mills are completed in districts with direct access to the sea, both on east and west coasts.

The competitive position of Europe, as respects particular groups of products, the ECE report summarizes as follows:

"Bars, wire, rails, sections and heavy plates

European steel exporters have never met with very strong competition from American exporters, as the rolling of these products has not, so far, lent itself to spectacular new methods of mechanization and the lower hourly wages in Europe

---

[8] United Nations, Economic Commission for Europe, *European Steel Exports and Steel Demand in Non-European Countries*, E/ECE/163, E/ECE/-STEEL/75 (Geneva: Author, 1953), p. 56. Much of the material in the following paragraphs has been taken from this report.

[9] Same, pp. 56, 57.

probably result in lower rolling costs than in the United States.

"Sheets, tinplate and other coated sheets

Before the war, and until recently, American steel producers had a definite advantage over the European producers, derived from their numerous continuous wide-strip mills. Now that these mills are coming into production in Europe this advantage should no longer exist to the same extent.

"Tubes

In welded tubes, the United States appears to have had an advantage over European producers before the war, whereas in the case of seamless tubes the reverse was true. Since the war improvements in technique for the production of seamless tubes have been made in the United States; production techniques for welded tubes have made great strides both in Europe and in the United States, and it is not yet clear which group of producers will be in the more favourable position in future.

"Stainless steel

The American producer, by increased standardization, appears able to produce certain types of stainless steel at costs lower than those of the majority of other producers. For special steels, of the heat-resisting and tool steel types, European producers generally have an advantage, mainly because the small tonnages involved lend themselves better to the application of specialized techniques. Although the tonnage is small in comparison with total output, the value is high. High-speed steel for cutting tools, for instance, sells at nearly $3000 per ton." [10]

The report concludes that "if European producers pursue their present efforts to modernize and rationalize their steel industry, and to use available raw materials in the most economical way, steel production costs in Europe should be competitive with those of United States producers." [11]

[10] Same, pp. 58-59.
[11] Same, p. 59.

What the Tariff Means to the Iron and Steel Industry

Our brief examination of the competitive situation leads to the conclusion that, with only minor exceptions, present import duties on the products of iron and steel mills have little economic significance. They are vestigial remnants of a protective policy which the industry has outlived. Today, they might be raised or lowered or abandoned altogether without any appreciable effect on the fortunes of the domestic producers. The industry's real interest, which it is rapidly coming to understand, lies in a liberal trade policy as a means of obtaining cheaper raw materials and expanding direct and indirect sales to foreign markets.

Further reduction in iron and steel duties from their present low levels would hardly be worth the resulting psychological disturbances. But much can be said for the simplification of the tariff paragraphs relating to iron and steel. Over the years tariff tinkering by Congressional committees and trade agreement negotiators has produced a structure of import duties so complex as to be comprehensible only to experts in the field. The substitution of a flat five percent ad valorem duty, about equivalent to the average of the rates now in force, would save money for the federal government by reducing the cost of customs administration. More important would be the educational value of this reform. It would be a demonstration, which any layman could understand, that one of our great American industries does not fear competition from foreign countries, no matter how low their wages may be. It is no longer an infant. It can stand on its own feet without tariff protection. It has grown up.

Chapter 8

SYNTHETIC ORGANIC CHEMICALS

THE TARIFF PROBLEM in the chemical industry centers on the manufacture of synthetic organic products, principally dyes and intermediates. Forty years ago American production of synthetic organic chemicals was practically nonexistent. Now it is a giant industry, greater than that of any other country, with about 600 firms and 200,000 employees. Its varied products supply more than 95 percent of the domestic market and, in addition, furnish several hundred million dollars worth of exports. Tariff protection, and the first world war, enabled the American industry to get its start; continued restriction of imports, by high duties in the interval between two world wars, sheltered it from German and other foreign competition. Trade agreements since 1936 have cut many import duties in half, but even now some of the reduced duties, because of the method of assessment, are, in effect, among the highest in the American tariff.

Technological advance and new discoveries in chemical science have led to the development of new products and new processes. Great forward strides in chemical engineering have made possible low-cost production and wide distribution in the rapidly expanding American market. For almost a decade after 1940, the interruption of imports from Europe freed U. S. producers from foreign competition and also opened new export markets.

An economist brought up on the doctrines of Alexander Hamilton and Friedrich List might jump to the conclusion that in the chemical industry he had found a perfect example of the successful application of tariff protection to an "infant industry." He would expect that the industry, having overcome initial difficulties and grown to maturity, would now feel able to dispense with government assistance. But the chemical manufacturers, although taking great pride in their

40 years of progress, assert that they are still dependent on tariff protection and will be unable to survive unless foreign competition is restricted by import duties. They admit that they have not been injured by recent tariff changes but insist that further reduction in duties would seriously weaken not only their industry but the whole national economy.

A former president of the Synthetic Organic Chemical Manufacturers Association, Dr. Cary R. Wagner, has predicted that reduction of import duties "would wipe out all plans for the industry's expansion and result in shutting down many chemical plants, reducing wages and curtailing the industry's $200 million a year expenditure for research." [1] A representative of E. I. du Pont de Nemours has said that, if tariff rates were reduced, research would be cut and repairs and replacements would be neglected. "The domestic industry will gradually drop one product after another until finally the country will be entirely dependent on foreign sources for the products, so vital to our welfare. In other words, the industry will be returned to its status of 35 years ago." [2]

Manufacturers argue that their industry is essential to national defense. They point out that the first protective duties were imposed on imported chemicals in 1916, as a measure of national security, in order to make sure that in time of war the country would have an industry capable of producing explosives. Defense considerations, they allege, still require restrictions on imports. Otherwise, the American industry will not be able to stand against competition from abroad, particularly from West Germany.

*   *   *

The purpose of this chapter is to reappraise American tariff policy with respect to synthetic organic chemicals. We shall want to consider how the expansion of the American industry in the past 40 years and its technical progress, when compared with developments in foreign countries, have affected

[1] In an address at Wooster College, reprinted in the *Journal of Commerce*, February 17, 1954.
[2] Statement of P. K. Lawrence of du Pont before the Committee for Reciprocity Information, *Hearing Concerning Trade Agreements with Australia . . .* , Panel A, *Chemicals* (Washington, May 31, 1950), v. 1, p. 124. (Stenographic transcript.)

the competitive situation. How far is the continued production of synthetic chemicals in the United States now dependent on tariff protection? What is the relation of the industry to national security? Which, if any, of its many products are essential to defense? Is tariff protection, or another kind of government aid, necessary to guarantee their continued production?

The American Chemical Industry

The American chemical industry, whether measured by value of output, capital invested or number of employees, ranks among the first half dozen American industries. Taking a few common raw materials such as coal, oil, natural gas and salt, the chemical industry converts them into thousands of complex products whose strange names are entirely unfamiliar to the man in the street.

The chemical industry is its own best customer. Many semimanufactures are used in the industry itself for the manufacture of other chemical or nonchemical products.

The organization of the industry is as complex and varied as are its products. There are no typical firms. There are large and small firms, firms with a wide range of products and specialists, independent firms and those which are closely connected through stock ownership or otherwise with other domestic, and foreign, producers. The limits of the industry are hard to define. Established firms are constantly adding new products and outsiders are constantly invading the field, oil refiners, manufacturers of synthetic rubber, iron and steel, even meat packers.

The production of chemicals is distinguished among American industries by its high rate of capital investment, high wages and low labor costs relative to its total costs and to the value of its products. Its large expenditures for research are considered vital for continued progress. In spite of the great size which it has already attained, the American chemical industry is still in a period of rapid expansion and dynamic technological change. New raw materials, new processes and new products are continually being discovered and developed. The result is keen competition for new markets, both at home and abroad.

The products of the American chemical manufacturing industry are:

(1) Basic heavy chemicals, including inorganic acids, alkalies, salts and some bulky organic products.

(2) Chemical products to be used in further manufacturing, e.g., dyes, synthetic fibers, synthetic rubber, plastic materials, solvents.

(3) "Allied products," made partly by firms producing basic chemicals and semimanufactured goods, and partly by outsiders. These are finished goods ready for immediate consumption. They include medicinal and pharmaceutical preparations, paint and varnish, soap, cosmetics, insecticides, weed killers and soil-improving products.

The "chemical industry," strictly defined, is concerned with the manufacture of producers' goods, the commodities listed in groups 1 and 2 above. The consumers' goods listed in group 3 are made by the so-called "chemical process industries," and also by some of the largest integrated firms.

A line of division running across the chemical industry separates its products, according to origin, into *inorganic* and *organic*. The latter are compounds which, like plant and animal matter, contain the carbon atom. They are obtained from coal, petroleum and natural gas, or by the fermentation of agricultural and forest products (e.g., molasses, wood). Inorganic chemicals, largely obtained from minerals and atmospheric gases, do not necessarily contain carbon. The more important include soda ash, caustic soda, chlorine, sulfuric acid, hydrochloric acid, nitric acid and ammonia.

Many inorganic chemicals, because of their great bulk in relation to value, are also known as *heavy chemicals*. But heavy chemicals are not exclusively inorganic; they include certain organic tonnage items such as benzene and methanol. Fine chemicals are the high-purity compounds, tailor-made for specialized uses, which have a high unit value in proportion to weight.

The distinction between heavy and fine chemicals is important for the purposes of this study. Turned out by mass-production methods with low labor costs, the heavy chemicals are not in general vulnerable to foreign competition. Moreover, because of their low value per unit of weight, transportation costs make importing uneconomical. For these reasons the heavy chemicals are usually found on the free list, or are subject to low rates of duty.

Competition from abroad is confined principally to fine chemicals, including intermediates and finished products, ordinarily derived from coal.[3] Intermediates are organic chemicals which have been advanced by manufacturing processes beyond the crude state and are used in producing finished products; they are derived from coal and, to an increasing extent, from petroleum and natural gas. Some intermediates are converted to finished products such as dyes, plastics and explosives; others may be sold without further processing. Finished products are grouped by the Tariff Commission into 12 categories. (See Table 32.)

Table 32

U. S. PRODUCTION AND SALES OF SYNTHETIC
ORGANIC CHEMICALS, BY CLASSES, 1954

	Production	*Sales*	
	(million pounds)	(million pounds)	(million dollars)
Intermediates	4,614	1,793	320
Dyes	143	137	160
Lakes and toners	40	35	54
Medicinals	66	53	426
Flavor and perfume materials	35	31	47
Plastics and resin materials	2,828	2,497	856
Rubber-processing chemicals	130	101	62
Elastomers (synthetic rubbers)	1,435	1,497	436
Plasticizers	301	247	82
Surface-active agents	1,026	913	196
Pesticides and other organic agricultural chemicals	419	336	125
Miscellaneous chemicals	17,408	8,092	1,213
Total, synthetic organic chemicals	28,445	15,732	3,977

Source: U. S. Tariff Commission, *Synthetic Organic Chemicals: United States Production and Sales, 1954* (Washington: GPO, 1955)

[3] The crude products, such as benzene, toluene, xylene, naphthalene and creosote oil, enter free of duty.

Growth and Expansion, 1914-1954

In 1954, some 600 American firms reported production of almost 30 billion pounds of synthetic organic chemicals. They consumed about one-half in their own plants; sales were 15.7 billion pounds of a value of $4 billion. Yet this is a new industry, having come into existence since World War I. In 1914, the American industry consisted of a few firms making dyes from intermediates imported from Germany. They supplied about 10 percent of the domestic market; German dye makers supplied the rest, as well as medicinals and other fine chemicals.

When World War I shut off the supply of foreign chemicals, prices rose and domestic production expanded to fill the gap. Recognizing the intimate association of dye production with the manufacture of TNT and other explosives, Congress, beginning in 1916, applied a vigorous policy of tariff protection—including the Dye and Chemical Control Act of 1921 and the Antidumping Act of the same year—to sustain the new industry against the return of German competition. Under the protection afforded by this legislation, the synthetic chemical industry expanded rapidly, following in general the curve of national income.

The interwar period was characterized by the consolidation of many small firms into large financial units. During the 1920's some 500 mergers were completed, bringing about advantages of lower costs through larger-scale production and economies in management. Parallel to, and connected with, larger-scale operations was the diversification of production. New raw materials were introduced—petroleum, natural gas, cellulose—and great advances were made in research and in chemical engineering. During this period also American plants mechanized their processes and developed automatic controls to a degree unknown in Germany or other competing countries.

As a result of 25 years of progress the United States, at the beginning of World War II, was independent of foreign countries for its organic chemicals. In the dye industry, particularly, domestic production had almost completely displaced imports—in 1939 imports supplied only 11 percent of the value of consumption—and produced a substantial surplus for export.

In World War II the huge military demand for products of the chemical industry gave an impetus to rapid expansion of production and investment in production facilities, and after 1945 the market was sustained by the continued rapid growth of national income. The increase in the production of synthetic chemicals far outstripped the growth of manufacturing in general. The 1939 index of production of synthetic organic chemicals was 24 (1947-49 = 100); in 1954 it stood at 164, nearly a seven-fold increase. Meanwhile total industrial production had risen from 58 to only 125.

The building of new plants during the war years and the generously financed programs of research provided, when peace returned, a multitude of new products for the civilian market. After 1950, expansion was promoted by federal tax policies which permitted liberal depreciation allowances on new plants. In 1954 a large proportion of the sales of synthetic organic chemicals consisted of products which had had no commercial existence 15 years earlier, e.g., antibiotic medicinal preparations, synthetic rubber, synthetic detergents and many plastics. But growth did not proceed evenly in all divisions of the industry; new products such as surface-active agents (detergents, etc.) and plastics grew much faster than dyes.

The Outlook for Future Growth

The rapid wartime enlargement of plant capacity in the chemical industry, which was continued in the postwar years, at times raised the specter of overcapacity, particularly in heavy chemicals and also in some intermediates, e.g., phthalic anhydride. Doubts were expressed of the ability of domestic and foreign markets to absorb the enlarged output at profitable prices. This skepticism perhaps resulted from the leveling off of sales in 1952 after the rapid expansion of the war and postwar years. However, 1953 proved to be the best year in the industry's history. (See Table 33 and Chart I.) Then, after a decline in 1954, sales rose to an all-time high in 1955. New capital investment is continuing at a rapid rate. George W. Merck, chairman of Merck & Company, estimated in 1954 that the chemical industry will double its size in the next dec-

Chart I

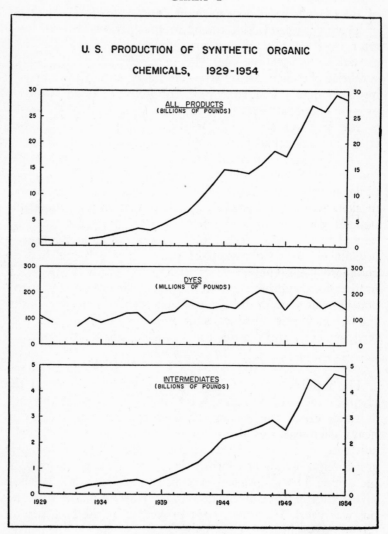

Source: Table 33 and U. S. Tariff Commission

Table 33

U. S. PRODUCTION AND SALES OF ALL SYNTHETIC ORGANIC
CHEMICALS, DYES AND INTERMEDIATES,
1929, 1937, 1947, 1950-1954

Year	Production (million pounds)	Sales	
		(million pounds)	(million dollars)
		All synthetic organic chemicals	
1929	1,155	703	171
1937	3,479	1,726	284
1947	15,910	9,997	2,201
1950	22,326	12,100	2,794
1951	27,499	14,565	3,872
1952	26,119	14,384	3,783
1953	29,129	15,637	4,030
1954	28,445	15,732	3,977
		Dyes	
1929	111	106	46
1937	122	118	65
1947	212	205	148
1950	196	188	191
1951	187	160	177
1952	145	149	171
1953	166	152	168
1954	143	137	160
		Intermediates	
1929	354	148	29
1937	576	242	36
1947	2,623	1,446	189
1950	3,397	1,484	239
1951	4,528	1,802	338
1952	4,171	1,544	290
1953	4,699	1,874	341
1954	4,614	1,793	320

Source: U. S. Tariff Commission, *Synthetic Organic Chemicals: United States Production and Sales* (Washington: GPO, 1930, 1938, 1948, 1951-1955)

ade. Looking ahead a quarter of a century, the Paley report was even more optimistic.[4]

A Large-Scale Business

The production of synthetic organic chemicals is, for the most part, a large-scale business. The bulk of the output of the principal products is furnished by a few large enterprises which turn out a wide range of products—heavy as well as fine chemicals. In 1953, 90 percent of the total output of synthetic organic chemicals was produced by less than 100 firms. Twenty-five percent was supplied by the six leading firms. Their net sales for 1947, 1951 and 1954, including organic chemicals and many other products, are shown below.

	1947	1951	1954
	(in millions of dollars)		
E. I. du Pont de Nemours & Co.	795.5	1,545.7	1,709.3
Union Carbide & Carbon Corp.	521.8	927.5	923.7
Allied Chemical & Dye Corp.	365.9	502.0	530.8
Dow Chemical Co.	170.7	407.2	470.7
American Cyanamid Co.	214.6	388.7	397.6
Monsanto Chemical Co.	143.4	272.8	341.8

Source: *Chemicals*, Standard & Poor's Industry Surveys, v. 123, no. 37, sec. 2 (September 15, 1955)

A few large companies have undertaken the production of basic raw materials, but vertical integration is not usual. "Forward integration" is a new trend. Companies formerly interested only in heavy chemicals are now turning out semimanufactured and finished products.

The industry comprises many units of small and medium size. The smaller firms are usually specialized concerns making intermediates, dyes, medicinals, insecticides, aromatic chemicals, etc. Success in these lines is dependent on close attention to techniques of production and intensive cultivation of limited markets rather than on large-scale operations.

Diversity of Products

Synthetic organic products are numbered by the thousands. More than a thousand intermediates and many thousands of

[4] *Resources for Freedom*, Report of the President's Materials Policy Commission (Washington: GPO, 1952), v. 4, *The Promise of Technology*, pp. 189, 209.

end-chemicals are now being made commercially. "Few companies enjoy more diversified markets than the chemical producers. There is almost no branch of industrial production into which chemicals do not enter directly or indirectly." [5] The operations of the larger companies show great diversity. Allied Chemical in 1955 made over 3,000 different products; its National Aniline Division made 700 dyes and 300 intermediates. Unit prices show a wide range; some chemicals sell in tank car lots for as low as $20 a ton; cortisone at one time sold for $1,500 per pound.

Some of the larger, diversified companies are upgrading their basic products and their intermediates, with the result that the stream of production has spread out ever more widely into the region of semifinished and consumers' goods.

An important structural change in the chemical industry, affecting, particularly, established producers of general or diversified chemicals, is the invasion of the field by large firms in "nonchemical" industries. Meat packers, food processors, brewers, distillers, steel mills, electrical and machinery manufacturers, rubber companies and oil refineries have set up new chemical divisions. Chemicals now account for nearly one-third of the total sales of the rubber industry. The rubber companies were attracted into the new field by the advantages they expected to derive from producing for themselves materials such as plastics and auxiliary chemicals, particularly vulcanizers and stabilizers.

Petrochemistry—A New Development

The large-scale invasion of the organic chemical industry by all the major oil companies has been called one of the most important industrial achievements of the past several decades. The possibilities of utilizing natural gas and the hydrocarbons obtained from oil cracking had been explored in this country as early as 1919, and considerable experimental work was done before World War II. Then, the establishment of a synthetic rubber industry created a demand for certain organic chemicals, e.g., benzene and butane, which could not be met from coal tar sources. This gave a strong impetus to

[5] *Chemicals,* Standard & Poor's Industry Surveys, v. 121, no. 18, sec. 2 (April 30, 1953), p. 3.

petrochemical production. In postwar years the demand for products such as plastics, synthetic fibers, paints, detergents and fertilizers not only exceeded the capacity of producers of coal tar chemicals but intensified the search for more plentiful raw materials. Thus new opportunities were opened for the oil companies and producers of natural gas.

Petrochemical production is now the fastest growing segment of the entire chemical industry. In 1954 it had more than 270 plants in operation, of which 58 were operated by oil producers, 79 by chemical companies and 6 were joint ventures. Sixty new plants were then in the planning or building stage.

Tariff History

World War I pointed to the need, for reasons of national security, for increased protection for coal tar products which at that time were the only source of synthetic organic chemicals. Congress responded by imposing in the Revenue Act of 1916 duties of 15 percent ad valorem, plus 2½ cents per pound, on intermediates. On dyes and other finished products, with only a few exceptions, the rates were 30 percent plus 5 cents per pound. This measure was designed to be only temporary. The full rates were to apply for five years, until 1921; then they were to be reduced by 20 percent annually so that by the end of the tenth year all coal tar chemicals would be on the free list.

Meanwhile, however, the United States became involved in the war, and a domestic chemical industry was suddenly built up. It demanded more effective safeguards against the anticipated postwar competition from the powerful German and Swiss producers of coal tar products. Congress again responded with a temporary measure, the Dye and Chemical Control Act of 1921. This imposed an embargo on dyestuffs, intermediates, and synthetic organic drugs and chemicals. The embargo, which was in effect for four months, applied only to those products for which a comparable domestic product was available on reasonable terms.

Protection on a permanent basis and at a high level was provided by the Tariff Act of 1922, with rates of 55 percent plus 7 cents per pound on intermediates and 60 percent plus 7 cents per pound on dyes and other coal tar products. In the Congressional debate, the defense argument played a large, perhaps a decisive, part. Professor Taussig, then Chairman of the U. S. Tariff Commission, wrote: "The cool economic considerations . . . were quite disregarded because of the stress laid on the chemical industries, and especially on the manufacture of coal tar products, for the direct service of war. The same plant can be used for making dyestuffs and the like in time of peace, for explosives and poison gas when war comes." This argument, according to Taussig, was "pushed to the hilt . . . with little endeavor to ascertain just how far the military needs went, or whether each and every kind of coal tar product had to be bolstered up at home in order to meet these needs." [6]

In the 1922 Act the duties on both intermediates and dyes were raised, but much more significant was the introduction of a new basis for assessing the duties. Hitherto, the general rule of American customs law had been that the dutiable value of imports should be determined by the selling price in the country of exportation. For imports of coal tar products only, the new act substituted two alternative bases of valuation: for "competitive imports," [7] American selling price; for "noncompetitive," United States value. American selling price was defined as the price at which a *comparable domestic article* is freely offered to all purchasers in the principal market of the United States. United States value was the price at which the *imported merchandise* is offered for sale in the principal market in the United States, less duty, transportation costs, insurance, commissions and other expenses and an allowance for profit.

Calculated by either of the two new methods, the dutiable value of dyes and intermediates, in all but a few exceptional cases, has been considerably higher than the foreign value, the usual basis of assessment. A 60 percent duty assessed on the selling price of a comparable American chemical product in New York, or on its United States value, will almost in-

[6] F. W. Taussig, *The Tariff History of the United States* (8th ed.; New York: Putnam's, 1931), p. 474.

[7] An imported coal tar product is considered "competitive" if it "accomplishes results substantially equal to those accomplished by the domestic product when used in substantially the same manner." See Tariff Act of 1922, sec. 402(f); Tariff Act of 1930, sec. 402(g).

variably cost the importer more dollars in duty than the same rate assessed on the price of the goods in Frankfurt or Basle. In general, the change doubled the actual impact of the duties. That is, a rate of 60 percent calculated on the new basis—American selling price—was equivalent to 120 percent on the old basis. Thus the shift to the new basis of valuation concealed the actual amount of protection which the chemical industry derived from the tariff.[8]

Various protected industries in 1922 had demanded American valuation as a defense against postwar currency depreciation and, as in the case of coal tar chemicals, against fraudulent undervaluation of imports. The Senate Finance Committee, after an exhaustive investigation (the so-called Reynolds Investigation), rejected American valuation as a general rule,[9] but accepted it for coal tar products. Senator Smoot, the Committee's chairman, in explaining this action, admitted that it was a means of concealing the extraordinarily high protection which the bill was giving to the chemical industry.[10] The Act of 1930 retained, in general, the earlier rates on both dyes and intermediates.[11] It also retained American selling price and United States value as the bases for assessing duties.

Administrative difficulties connected with the new system

[8] An analogy can be found in the taxation of real estate. An increase in the assessed value of a piece of property will cost the owner more dollars in taxes, even if the rate of taxation is constant.

[9] Section 315 of the Act, reenacted as Section 336 of the Act of 1930, authorized the President to raise import duties, in order to "equalize" foreign and domestic costs of production. The increase was limited to 50 percent of the statutory rate, but if this proved insufficient to bridge the gap in costs the President might shift the basis of valuation of the imports to American selling price. As the result of actions taken under this provision the following commodities are now valued at American selling price: rubber-soled and rubber footwear, canned clams, and wool-knit gloves.

[10] See interchange between Senators Smoot and Jones, *Congressional Record*, 67th Cong., 2d sess., v. 62, pt. 4 (April 24, 1922), p. 5884; cited in R. Elberton Smith, *Customs Valuation in the United States* (Chicago: University of Chicago Press, 1948), p. 141.

[11] The 1922 Act had specified that the ad valorem part of the duty on intermediates was to remain at 55 percent for two years and in September 1924 to be lowered to 40 percent. Similarly, the duty on dyes and other finished products was to be reduced from 60 percent to 45 percent. The lowered rates which became effective in 1924 were maintained in the 1930 Act.

of valuation have added an element of "invisible" protection. According to the Tariff Commission:

The customs authorities have had much difficulty not only in determining whether domestic production of a given dye has reached a point where it can be considered competitive but also in determining the actual American selling price on which to base the duty. The uncertainty involved has in itself been a deterrent to imports. Moreover, in some instances, when an American selling price has once been established as a basis for the duty, that basis has tended to remain constant for a long period of time.[12]

Importers are disturbed by frequent transfers from the noncompetitive to the competitive classifications with consequent increases in duties. This process the Tariff Commission has described as follows:

The category into which an imported dye falls is changeable. For example, an imported noncompetitive dye may have a United States value of $1, on which (under the agreement with Switzerland) a 40-percent duty would be levied. When a domestic manufacturer produces and offers for sale a product that accomplishes substantially the same results as the imported product, he may have the latter declared competitive (upon application to the customs authorities) and thus made dutiable on the basis of the selling price of the corresponding domestic article. If the price of the domestic dye is $1.50 per pound, the imported dye, which has been declared competitive, would then be dutiable at 40 percent of $1.50. The new duty would be equal to 60 percent of the United States value of the imported dye. In many cases the difference between the two valuations is much greater than that mentioned in this illustration.[13]

The Commission in another report said:

Largely on account of the rules of valuation, the duties provided for by paragraphs 27 and 28 have in fact been practically prohibitive of imports of "competitive" products of lower or medium unit value and have held imports of "competitive" products of high unit value to small volume.[14]

[12] U. S. Tariff Commission, *Dyes*, War Changes in Industry Series, Report No. 19 (Washington: GPO, 1946), p. 19.
[13] Same, p. 39.
[14] U. S. Tariff Commission, *Summaries of Tariff Information*, v. 1, pt. 2 (Washington: GPO, 1948), p. 46.

In postwar years the production by domestic firms of a larger number of specalized dyes has brought them in direct competition with the importers over a wider range of products. The result has been to raise the proportion of dyes classified as competitive from less than 10 percent, by value, in 1947 to 23 percent in 1954.

Reductions in Tariffs under the Trade Agreements Program

Reductions in duties on synthetic organic chemicals were made in bilateral trade agreements with Belgium (1935), Switzerland (1936) and the United Kingdom (1939), and also in the multilateral negotiations under the General Agreement on Tariffs and Trade at Geneva (1947) and at Torquay (1951). Altogether, 88 out of the 116 major classifications were reduced, 32 in more than one agreement.

Various reductions in the duties on intermediates have

Table 34

U. S. Rates of Duty on Major Synthetic Organic Intermediates and Dyes, 1930 and 1955

(percent ad valorem; cents per pound)

Pars. 27 and 28	1930 rate	1955 rate
Intermediates:		
Phthalic anhydride	40% + 7¢	20% + 3½¢
Anthracene, refined	40% + 7¢	20% + 3½¢
Phenol	20% + 3½¢	20% + 3½¢
Cresols:		
75% to 90% pure	40% + 7¢	10% + 1¾¢
Ortho-, meta- and paracresol, 90% or more pure	20% + 3½¢	10% + 1¾¢
Naphthalene, refined	40% + 7¢	10% + 1¾¢
Styrene	45% + 7¢	22½% + 3½¢
Azo and fast color salts and bases	40% + 7¢	20% + 3½¢
Textile assistants	40% + 7¢	40% + 7¢
Naphthol AS and derivatives	40% + 7¢	20% + 3½¢
Other coal tar intermediates	40% + 7¢	25% + 3½¢
Dyes:		
Colors, dyes and stains, except synthetic indigo and sulphur black	45% + 7¢	40%[a] (min., 22½% + 3½¢)
Color acids, bases, lakes, compounds	45% + 7¢	45% + 7¢
Synthetic indigo and sulphur black	20% + 3¢	20% + 3¢

[a] The preferential rate to Cuba is 32% (min., 18% + 2.8¢).

brought the rates on some items down to half the 1930 level and on some to one-quarter. (See Table 34.) The only change in the dye tariff occurred in 1936 when the agreement with Switzerland reduced duties from 45 percent plus 7 cents per pound to a simple ad valorem rate of 40 percent. The effect on imports of this moderate concession, however, was considerably diminished by the fact that it did not apply to trade with Germany, the country which in prewar years supplied half of the dyes imported into the United States. Germany, because of her discrimination against American goods, had been deprived of most-favored-nation treatment in October 1935. Ironically, her most-favored-nation status was restored in 1942, during World War II, in order to facilitate the withdrawal of German goods from customs warehouses.

Attempts to Abolish American Valuation

Only Congress can change the basis of valuation; this is a matter which lies outside the scope of trade agreements. Attempts to secure Congressional action on this subject have proved unsuccessful.

The Customs Simplification Act of 1951 (H. R. 1535, 82d Congress, 1st session), in Section 14, eliminated American valuation[15] and provided that all import duties should be assessed on export values. The Treasury Department, which sponsored the bill, urged the adoption of Section 14 in order to insure uniform practice in determining the value of imports. The legislation was desirable also, the Treasury pointed out, in order to carry out a line of policy to which the United States had subscribed when, at Geneva in 1947, its representatives signed the General Agreement on Tariffs and Trade. In Article VII, Par. 2(a) of GATT, they had agreed that:

> The value for customs purposes of imported merchandise should be based on the actual value of the imported merchandise on which duty is assessed, or of like merchandise, and should not be based on the value of merchandise of national origin or on arbitrary or fictitious values.[16]

[15] In order that the change should not decrease the amount of protection afforded to any domestic industry, the bill directed the Tariff Commission to establish equivalent rates on the new basis.

[16] General Agreement on Tariffs and Trade, *Basic Instruments and Selected Documents*, v. 1 (revised) (Geneva: Author, 1955), p. 18.

They undertook to recommend to Congress the revision of customs laws which were in conflict with this Article. In a statement to the Ways and Means Committee, the Treasury's representative contended that the American selling price was an "arbitrary basis of valuation" because there was "no semblance of any relationship between the value of domestic competitive products and the value of the imported article." [17]

H. R. 1535 was voted by the House but failed of passage in the Senate. Later attempts, in 1953 and 1955, to amend the customs administrative laws so as to eliminate American valuation proved unsuccessful.[18]

Table 35

U. S. IMPORTS OF SYNTHETIC ORGANIC CHEMICALS, 1947 AND 1954

	1947		1954	
	Quantity (1000 pounds)	Dutiable value (1000 dollars)	Quantity (1000 pounds)	Dutiable value (1000 dollars)
Intermediates	2,177	567	5,779	3,758
Dyes	838	2,185	2,996	7,910
Lakes and toners	1	3	410	269
Medicinals	94	1,418	1,600	15,472
Flavor and perfume materials	463	3,031	1,175	3,317
Plastics and resin materials	543	278	14,998	3,464
Rubber-processing chemicals	1	1	127	86
Elastomers	3,010	470	38,098	9,897
Plasticizers	40	54	118	47
Surface-active agents	103	116	1,227	506
Pesticides and other organic agricultural chemicals	20	13	851	349
Miscellaneous chemicals	17,115	1,205	99,474	17,333
Total, synthetic organic chemicals	24,405	9,340	166,853	62,411

Source: Synthetic Organic Chemical Manufacturers Association, *Trade, Strength and Security* (New York: Author, 1953); U. S. Bureau of the Census

[17] Statement of William R. Johnson, Assistant to the U. S. Commissioner of Customs, before the House Ways and Means Committee, *Simplification of Customs Administration*, Hearings, 82d Cong., 1st sess., on H. R. 1535 (Washington: GPO, 1951), p. 148.
[18] For an excellent outline of the history of American valuation and a discussion of its merits and defects, see Smith, *Customs Valuation in the United States,* cited, pp. 139-142, 218-248.

Imports

The 1947 and 1954 imports of synthetic organic chemicals are shown in Table 35, divided into 12 groups as in Table 32. It is evident that the imports, despite their rapid gains in post-war years, are still inconspicuous, either when compared in the aggregate with total sales of domestic firms (about $4 billion in 1954), or when taken group by group. Domestic manufacturers are chiefly concerned with imports of dyes, which were valued at $2.2 million in 1947 and $7.9 million in 1954, and intermediates, which rose from $567,000 to $3.8 million in the same years. The rapid rate of growth is impressive, but the absolute amounts of foreign dyes and intermediates entering the United States still remain small when compared with domestic production.[19]

Dyes. The development of foreign competition in dyes in postwar years is shown in Table 36 below, together with fig-

Table 36
DYES: U. S. SALES, EXPORTS, IMPORTS AND APPARENT CONSUMPTION, 1929, 1937, 1947-1954

Year	Total sales (including exports)	Exports	Imports (dutiable value)	Apparent consumption	Ratio of imports to apparent consumption (percent)
			(in millions of dollars)		
1929	45.8	7.3	8.2	46.7	17.6
1937	64.6	6.3	5.2	63.5	8.2
1947	148.2	77.5	2.2	72.9	3.0
1948	163.8	58.8	2.8	107.8	2.6
1949	142.5	44.8	2.2	99.9	2.2
1950	190.8	29.1	4.8	166.5	2.9
1951	176.7	27.8	7.0	155.9	4.5
1952	170.7	14.2	5.8	162.3	3.6
1953	167.5	15.9	6.0	157.6	3.8
1954	160.3	19.7	7.9	148.5	5.3

Source: U. S. Tariff Commission, U. S. Bureau of the Census, Synthetic Organic Chemical Manufacturers Association

[19] Comparing the 1954 data in Tables 32 and 35, we get a quantity ratio of total imports of synthetic organic chemicals to production of 1 to 170. The ratio of dye imports to dye production was 1 to 48; of intermediates, 1 to 795.

ures for 1937, a representative prewar year, and 1929. (See also Chart J.) The postwar years, taken by themselves, present a somewhat discouraging picture to the 45 domestic firms which produce dyestuffs. Both domestic sales and exports have fallen while imports have increased. But in the longer view the postwar decline is seen to be a process of contraction from the boom generated by the war, which in 1950 had carried sales of domestic dyes to over three times the prewar level. Exports in the peak year of 1947 were 12 times the prewar level, but most of this increase was owing to the rise in prices. Measured in pounds, the 1947 exports were only four times the 1937 figure.

The postwar increase in imports of dyes, from $2.2 million in 1947 to $7.9 million in 1954, also must be viewed in perspective. If one looks back to 1929, it is apparent that in the past 25 years foreign competition in dyes has lost much of its force. Table 36 shows that in 1929 imported dyes supplied 17.6 percent of the domestic market. Since then the trend has been downward. By 1937 the importers' share had been cut in half, and during the war it fell almost to zero. In this perspective, the postwar recovery, which in 1954 brought imports up to about 5.3 percent of American consumption, seems much less menacing. Furthermore, even the 1954 percentage exaggerates the real impact of the foreign competition since it covers imports of noncompetitive as well as competitive dyes. The latter, according to the Tariff Commission, accounted in 1954 for only 23 percent of total imports:

	Foreign invoice value
Imports of dyes: competitive	$1,321,656
noncompetitive	4,493,429

Eliminating imports which are not like, or similar to, any domestic product, we find that the 1954 share of domestic consumption supplied by competitive imports was less than 2 percent.

More real sources of anxiety for producers of dyes appear to be (1) the decline in exports and (2) the stagnant condition of the domestic market. The wartime boom in exports, which raised them from $6.3 million in 1937 to $77.5 million in 1947, was largely the result of the disappearance of German dyes from world markets. The inability of Switzerland and the United Kingdom to fill the gap created a rare opportunity for American dye makers. After 1947, however, they were not able to hold their new markets against the revived German and other European industries. Within the eight-year period, 1947-1954, their export sales had declined by nearly $60 million. In 1947 over one-half of all sales of American dyes had gone abroad; in 1954 only one-eighth.

The dye manufacturers found no compensation in the domestic market for the loss of exports. The American market for dyes, in fact, appears to be shrinking, owing principally to changes in the textile industry which takes about 80 percent of the dye output. New fashions, like the shift from heavier to lighter apparel (see Chapter 6, p. 150), have called for less coloring matter per yard of cloth.

Intermediates. Imports of intermediates, semimanufactures which form a link between the primary products and the more valuable finished products such as dyes, have also shown a substantial increase in postwar years, from 2 million pounds valued at $567,000 in 1947 to 5.8 million pounds valued at $3.8 million in 1954. But here again the imports are inconsiderable, compared with the output of the American chemical industry. Domestic production of all intermediates in 1954 amounted to 4.6 billion pounds, of which 1.8 billion pounds were sold and the balance consumed by the producing companies in their own operations. The value of the sales was $320 million, 85 times the value of the imports. The market for intermediates, unlike that for dyes, has shown rapid expansion over the past 25 years. Postwar production and domestic consumption show a steady upward trend and the prospects for further growth are good.

A detailed comparison of production and imports of the various intermediates, item by item, is impracticable because of their number, more than one thousand, and also because of the lack of adequate statistical information.[20] Enough information is available, however, to show that only a few inter-

[20] The classifications of the import data collected by the Department of Commerce do not agree with the classifications of production data collected by the Tariff Commission. Moreover, many of the intermediates are produced by only a few firms—often by a single firm—and hence production figures are not disclosed.

CHART J

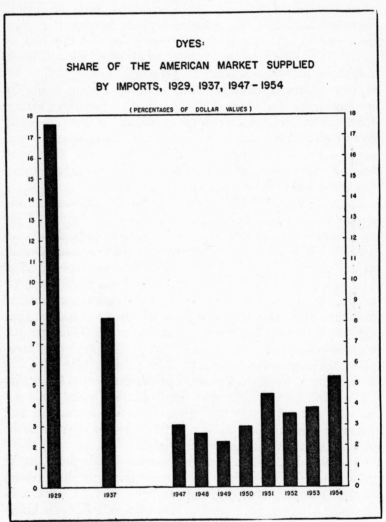

DYES:

SHARE OF THE AMERICAN MARKET SUPPLIED

BY IMPORTS, 1929, 1937, 1947 - 1954

(PERCENTAGES OF DOLLAR VALUES)

Source: Table 36

mediates are imported in amounts at all comparable to the sales of the competitive products of American chemical factories. Even in such cases the imports are usually sporadic, arriving to take advantage of some unusual condition in the American market.

The Case of Phthalic Anhydride

Phthalic anhydride, which has been cited at Congressional hearings and in trade papers as an example of a chemical that needs tariff protection,[21] at first was used principally in dye manufacture. Recently a flood of new uses—as a basis for plasticizers, in paints, in surface coatings for refrigerators and automobiles, in insect repellents—has greatly enlarged the demand.

Phthalic anhydride, a "tonnage item," is produced by a continuous process by only a few firms, nine in 1955. In response to the growing demand for new uses, domestic suppliers more than doubled their output between 1946 and 1951, raising it from 113 million pounds to 250 million. At this point the capacity of existing American facilities seems to have been reached. New construction, which had been undertaken, however, made possible additional production of almost 100 million pounds in 1955. The four-year record of production is shown below:

1952	228,576,000 pounds
1953	226,646,000 "
1954	253,847,000 "
1955	347,311,000 "

The Geneva trade agreement, effective January 1948, cut the duty on phthalic anhydride in half, from 7 cents a pound plus 40 percent (calculated on the American selling price) to 3½ cents plus 20 percent. Subsequent imports followed an erratic course (see Table 37).

[21] See U. S. House, Committee on Ways and Means, *Trade Agreements Extension Act of 1953*, Hearings, 83rd Cong., 1st sess., on H. R. 4294 (Washington: GPO, 1953), pp. 235-236. Much of the information in the following paragraphs has been drawn from articles by James E. Sayre in *Chemical and Engineering News*, v. 30 (December 8, 1952), pp. 5138-5142, and v. 32 (May 17, 1954), pp. 2052-2060.

Table 37

U. S. IMPORTS OF PHTHALIC ANHYDRIDE, 1948-1954

Year	Quantity (pounds)	Dutiable value (dollars)
1948	806,939	341,894
1949	2,319,169	428,637
1950	1,368,508	279,447
1951	203,210	38,137
1952	231,572	50,378
1953	18,370,076	3,987,329
1954	738,518	150,446

Source: U. S. Bureau of the Census. The 1955 imports have been estimated at about one-half the 1954 quantity. See U. S. Department of Commerce, *Chemical and Rubber Industry Report*, v. 3, no. 3 (March 1956), p. 14.

Because of the insistent demand in the American market for phthalic anhydride, the 1948 reduction in duty and the increased imports did not depress market prices. On the contrary, they rose, from 14½ cents a pound in 1947 to 22 cents two years later. The unusually large imports of 1953, at a time when new domestic facilities were coming into operation, explains the slight drop in prices in 1953-1954.

There seems at present no prospect of damaging competition in this product from abroad. Foreign plants have a production capacity of about 200 million pounds annually, less than one-half the foreseeable American capacity, including plants now under construction. All signs point to the further expansion of the American market for phthalic anhydride. Chemical engineers in 1954 predicted a 35 percent expansion in demand within five years, and the Paley Commission, looking further ahead, has estimated the 1975 demand at 2.2 billion pounds, almost five times the capacity of American plants now in operation and under construction.

Factors in Import Competition

Our survey of tariff history (pp. 192-193) indicates that the State Department, in the trade agreements thus far negotiated, has dealt gently with synthetic organic chemicals. The number of items on which duties have been cut is impressive, but judging from import statistics the cuts have been ineffective. The important fact to keep in mind is that the trade agreements made no change in the system of American valuation. Hence, even after the reductions, the duties on dyes, intermediates and other important synthetic organic products dutiable under paragraphs 27 and 28 remain high enough to block all but a few million dollars worth of imports, and those which succeed in surmounting the tariff barrier are largely noncompetitive.

Manufacturers agree that their business has not suffered injury as the result of tariff reductions made in trade agreements. Mr. Samuel Lenher, a vice president of du Pont and president of the Synthetic Organic Chemical Manufacturers Association, told the House Ways and Means Committee in January 1955: "We have not yet been seriously hurt, and we make no such claim. We are sure of, and are very earnestly bringing to your attention, the fact that we are going to be hurt. We do not say we are going to be driven out of business, but I am here to tell you for our trade association that bits and pieces of our business will disappear in the future under the present level of tariffs." [22]

Are the fears of future competition well founded, or have the American manufacturers underestimated their ability to meet foreign competition? What are the elements of strength and weakness in their position?

The lower wages paid to workers in chemical plants in Germany, Switzerland and other competing countries are often cited as affording a decisive advantage to foreign producers. At the end of 1954 average hourly earnings in American chemical plants were reported to be $1.90; in Switzerland $.76; in Germany, $.50, and in the United Kingdom, $.46.[23] But differences in wages, as we have pointed out in earlier chapters, do not always cause corresponding across-the-board differences in production costs. Over a wide range of products, American firms, although paying wages three or four times those paid by their German, Swiss and English com-

[22] *Trade Agreements Extension*, Hearings, 84th Cong., 1st sess., on H. R. 1 (Washington: GPO, 1955), p. 1140; see also similar statements by Dr. Lloyd of Dow Chemical Co., p. 1117, and Mr. Ernest M. May, p. 1142.
[23] *Chemical Week* (October 8, 1955), p. 32.

petitors, have been able to undersell them. The explanation is found, as in the electrical manufacturing industry, the automobile industry and many others, in the much larger investment of capital in American plants and in the use of mass-production techniques which raise hourly outputs per worker far above those prevailing in foreign factories.

Continuous and Batch Processes

This generally accepted principle explains why American firms can export synthetic organic chemicals at the rate of several hundred million dollars a year. Mechanization, however, is not applicable in the same degree to all products. Some organic products are made by continuous processes in which raw materials are added to the stream and final products removed without interruption. Predetermined operating conditions, temperatures, pressures, etc. are maintained by controlling and recording instruments. Thus, little human supervision is needed and a large volume of product emerges with the aid of only a few workers. Relatively few of the "fine" organic chemicals, however, are turned out by any single plant in quantities sufficient to justify the heavy investment in automatic and semiautomatic machinery which the continuous method requires. Instead they are made by the "batch process," which has been described as follows: "Quantities of chemicals . . . are carried through an entire step in a tank, vat, pressure chamber, or mixing vessel, then transferred to the next step. Complete processing may require tens or even hundreds of separate steps before completion. The chemicals which begin the processing stage may remain in process for months before emerging in finished form." [24] Even in the production of dyes by this process, instrumentation has proved an efficient means of controlling chemical reactions. In the production run of a particular dye some manufacturers have introduced an almost automatic process, but none of them has yet been able to take the next step, to switch equipment automatically from one type of dye to another. One difficulty is the need of cleaning the vessels (in which the reactions take

[24] Synthetic Organic Chemical Manufacturers Association, *Trade, Strength and Security* (New York: Author, 1953), p. 1.

place) after each production run so as to avoid contamination of the next batch.

To avoid the high costs of batch processing, manufacturers, as soon as prospective demand seems to justify the step, have begun to make some of their organic chemicals in a continuous stream—phthalic anhydride, for example. The new petrochemical plants make all their intermediates by a continuous process. For example, styrene, used in the production of plastics, can be produced at the rate of 2 million pounds a month in a continuous-process plant in which 250 instruments insure automatic operation and only 35 employees are needed.

Access to the American Market

In the production of low-volume specialties American manufacturers are handicapped by their high wage scale; in other respects they have important advantages. Their access to cheap and abundant supplies of basic raw materials, coal, petroleum and natural gas, is unequalled in European countries. American producers of synthetic organics profit also by their nearness to, and close association with, producers of heavy chemicals. In addition, their direct access to customers in the American market, particularly in the textile and paper industries, constitutes an important competitive advantage. No importer of fine chemicals can hope to penetrate the American market effectively without the aid of a sales organization capable of furnishing customers with services comparable to those supplied by the big domestic manufacturers. In selling high-grade dyes the service factor is all-important. It may mean sending chemical engineers or other experts to textile mills or paper factories to correct mistakes and to instruct operators in the proper methods of utilizing dyes and colors. The need of maintaining sales and service organizations in this country has been one reason why foreign dye manufacturers have set up American factories.

Leadership in Research

American chemical manufacturers were at first handicapped in competition with Germany by the lack of trained chemists.

This handicap no longer exists. The rapid development of the American chemical industry in the past 40 years has been made possible by scientific research, well organized and generously financed, both in pure chemistry and in its application. In chemical engineering the United States has now assumed the leadership formerly held by Germany. The number of trained chemists and chemical engineers has shown rapid increase. The colleges and universities have greatly improved the quality of their training. Leading chemical companies have supplemented this work by the appropriation of large sums for the maintenance of well-equipped research laboratories staffed with highly paid scientists.

It is true that a number of important new chemical products had their origin in European laboratories, e.g., the insecticide DDT and penicillin. But in both cases their successful development on a commercial scale was owing to American engineering skills. A group of European experts in 1952 reported that "practically all important developments in chemical engineering, such as the fluidizing technique, extractive distillation, hypersorption, and the centrifugal extractor, have been evolved in America although most of them were foreshadowed in Europe." It is "highly significant," continues this report, "that practically all the important correlations constituting the working tools of the chemical engineer have been established in America." [25]

Foreign manufacturers of dyes are sending promising young men each year to American technical schools. The influx of young European scientists to American institutions has been so great as to raise the fear in some quarters that such training constitutes a subsidy to our foreign competitors.

Research workers command higher salaries in the United States than in European countries. On this account, rather than because of the quality of the work done abroad, some of the American companies have "farmed out" research projects in European countries. The Union Carbide and Carbon Corporation, for example, is assigning a substantial amount of research work to European Associates, S. A., of Brussels.

[25] OEEC, Technical Assistance Mission No. 23, *Chemical Apparatus in the U. S. A.* (Paris: Author, 1952), p. 35.

Imports and Prices

American producers of organic chemicals are not so much concerned about the occasional loss to importers of sales of this or that chemical, as with the influence of imports on prices. When manufacturers have idle capacity, as many had in 1954, they may find it more economical to meet the low prices of imported chemicals than to let their facilities remain idle, or to operate them at a low rate. Chemical concerns reduce prices occasionally in order to broaden the market for a product, as in the case of nylon and other synthetic fibers. A firm, when it has made a large investment in research and engineering to develop a new product, may use price-cutting as a weapon to scare off potential competitors. But as a means of winning trade away from competitors, price-cutting is regarded as old-fashioned and ineffective. The larger firms do not usually depart from standard price lists. In general, they try to hold their customers and gain new ones by giving them unusually effective "service," or by introducing some slight modification in their product which will differentiate it from that of competitors.

Many circumstances produce situations of imperfect competition in chemical markets. "The complexity of chemical processes . . . the exceptional importance of joint products and byproducts, the large scale of production required to get the most economical results, and the extremely specialized character of plant equipment, all tend to impede competitive adjustments." [26] Often one finds that a certain product is made exclusively, or predominantly, by a single firm. It may be protected by patent rights, or it may require specialized and costly investment in plants and unusual technical knowledge and experience. Potential sales, even at lower prices, may be narrowly limited. Hence, once a single firm has undertaken production, other firms would hesitate to compete.

The Sources of Foreign Competition

Total exports of chemicals from West Germany, the United Kingdom and Switzerland in 1954 were as follows:

[26] George W. Stocking and Myron W. Watkins, *Cartels in Action* (New York: Twentieth Century Fund, 1946), p. 377n.

	Dyestuffs	Organic chemicals	All chemicals
		(in thousands of dollars)	
West Germany	65,724	146,418	604,857
United Kingdom	31,867	76,492	570,755
Switzerland	68,923	n.a.	208,149

Source: OEEC, Chemical Products Committee, *The Chemical Industry in Europe* (Paris: Author, 1955); U. S. Bureau of Foreign Commerce, *Foreign Trade of Switzerland*, World Trade Information Service, pt. 3, no. 55-46 (November 1955)

In the principal competing countries, West Germany, Switzerland and the United Kingdom, the manufacture of chemicals shows a high degree of concentration. But comparison of the chemical industries of the United States and Germany no longer shows an American David pitted against a foreign Goliath. The sales of synthetic organic chemicals produced in American plants in 1954 exceeded the combined sales of all chemicals, both organic and inorganic, in West Germany in that year by $1 billion. In fact, the combined sales of two American firms, du Pont and Union Carbide and Carbon, were nearly as large as those of the entire West German chemical industry.

The German chemical industry was badly damaged by wartime bombing and by postwar dismantling operations. The severance of East and West Germany left one-third of the productive facilities under Russian control, including the largest German nitrogen plant, the largest European plant for the manufacture of synthetic rubber and many others. Important raw materials, brown coal and potash, were in the Russian zone of occupation. The breakdown of trade with the areas under Russian control, in Germany and in Eastern Europe, made necessary radical changes in the structure of the West German chemical industry. In addition, the war and postwar disturbances deprived Germany temporarily, at least, of its leading position in chemical research. Large numbers of scientists lost their lives in battle or in concentration camps; many were deported or left the country voluntarily.

Aided by $40 million of Marshall Plan money and profiting by the remarkable recovery of the national economy, the West German chemical industry surmounted its handicaps and by 1954 had raised production to about double the prewar level (i.e., the level of production, not of the prewar Reich

but of the area now included in the German Federal Re-
public). Total sales of all chemicals in 1954 amounted to about
DM 12 billion, the equivalent of nearly $2.85 billion. In the
years 1951-1953 about 8 percent of exports of German chemicals were sold in the United States and 2 percent of all exports
of dyestuffs.

The great trust, I. G. Farbenindustrie, which before World
War II dominated the German chemical industry, was split
up in 1953 into three principal successor companies. Together
they employ about 100,000 workers and account for 30 percent of the West German output. It is possible that they may
reunite if the Bonn government should see fit to remove the
restrictions on cartelization imposed by the Allied governments. Or each may expand independently of the others either
by absorbing smaller units or by joining American or other
foreign interests.

The British chemical industry is dominated by Imperial
Chemical Industries which in 1954 had total sales of £352
million ($986 million). Its sales in foreign markets were £67.5
million (about $190 million) or 33 percent of all British ex-
ports of chemicals. ICI accounted for 60 percent, by value, of
the dyestuffs manufactured in the United Kingdom.

The Swiss chemical industry comprises about 200 firms,
but the bulk of the business is in the hands of a dozen large
and middle-sized companies. Switzerland has no deposits of
oil, coal or natural gas; hence its chemical industry is engaged
principally in converting imported intermediates and other
semimanufactures into fine chemicals, such as pharmaceuticals and dyestuffs. About 90 percent of the products are
exported. Swiss exports of dyes to all countries in 1954 were
valued at $69 million. Of these exports somewhat less than 10
percent went to the United States. The three principal companies, Ciba, Sandoz, A. G. and J. R. Geigy, A. G., are members of a "community of interest agreement." All have subsidiaries in foreign countries. In prewar years the leading
Swiss firms were associated with the I. G. Farben combine.

Interrelation of American and Foreign Firms

A popular concept of competition in foreign trade pictures
American firms lined up shoulder to shoulder, in serried ranks,

to repel the invading foreign manufacturers and importers. In appearances before Congressional committees, when tariff rates are under discussion, the opposing interests, foreign versus domestic, solidify, but no such clear-cut separation appears in the conduct of business affairs. There we find evidence of cooperation as well as conflict.

The absence of competition has been made, on occasion, the grounds for government action. In 1942, the Department of Justice procured an indictment against five leading dye manufacturing companies, including two which were controlled by foreign capital, charging violation of the Sherman Antitrust Act. The Department also charged that understandings existed between American dye manufacturers, including foreign-owned concerns, and the International Dyestuffs Cartel affecting competition in domestic and foreign markets. In early 1946 the case was settled by a plea of nolo contendere and payment of fines aggregating $110,000.

In commenting on this case the U. S. Tariff Commission observed "The plea of nolo contendere . . . and the imposition of fines, can scarcely, by themselves, assure effective competition in the future. The multiplicity of dyes produced, the complexity of the processes involved, and the great number and complexity of the patents on dyes make it difficult for government authorities and courts to determine how far competition actually exists or to enforce measures to assure effective competition. Nevertheless, it should be possible to safeguard competition in at least the major kinds of dyes, especially those on which patents have expired." [27]

For a long time the American chemical industry, particularly the coal tar industry, has not been exclusively American. High import duties after World War I encouraged German and Swiss dye manufacturers to establish branch plants on the American side of the tariff wall. A German company, Friedrich Bayer, had begun manufacturing dyes at Rensselaer, New York, as early as 1882. Its American properties were sequestered in World War I, but the Bayer firm reacquired control in 1924.

By 1928, German interests, now represented by I. G. Farbenindustrie, had regained control of the dye factories which

[27] U. S. Tariff Commission, *Dyes*, cited, p. 18.

they had owned before World War I and, in addition, many of the confiscated patents. The American I. G. Farben, organized in 1929, purchased the General Aniline works and in 1939 was reorganized as the General Aniline and Film Corporation. In 1942, the U. S. government took possession of the company's dye plant at Linden, New Jersey, and other physical assets.[28] It also seized many patents which the German owners had never licensed. (The dye patents were released for general industrial use in 1948.)

In November 1953 the General Dyestuffs Corporation, formerly a German-controlled marketing organization, was merged with General Aniline by exchange of stock. The latter is operated under a board of directors appointed by the Alien Property Custodian. Under government management it has become one of the leading American producers of dyes; its sales of all products in 1954 were $104 million. The eventual disposition of the firm is still uncertain. A Swiss holding company, Interhandel, maintained that it, not the German I. G. Farbenindustrie, was the real owner and sued, unsuccessfully, in United States courts for restoration of the property. The failure of this litigation may open the way for direct negotiations between the American and Swiss governments.

In 1920 the three largest Swiss dye manufacturers, Sandoz, Geigy and Ciba, set up an American branch plant, the Cincinnati Chemical Works, under joint ownership and operation, but each company retained its own American sales organization to handle imports, as well as products of the Cincinnati plant. Ciba (originally Gesellschaft für Chemische Industrie Basle) now produces pharmaceuticals in Summit, New Jersey, plastics and textile assistants in Kimberton, Pennsylvania, and dyes at Toms River, New Jersey, in an $18 million plant completed in 1953.

Leading American concerns have established branch plants in foreign countries or have invested funds in foreign enterprises. For example, du Pont has wholly owned foreign sub-

[28] Six other German-owned chemical companies seized during World War II have been sold to United States citizens, viz., American Potash and Chemical Corporation; Buffalo Electro-Chemical Corporation; Jasco, Inc.; Rare Chemicals, Inc. and Boehringer Corporation; Rohm & Haas Company; and Schering Corporation.

sidiaries in Canada, Mexico, Brazil, Cuba and Peru and partly owned enterprises in Argentina and Chile. Union Carbide has several branch plants in Canada and numerous wholly owned subsidiaries in other foreign countries. Monsanto has major interests in ten foreign countries.

Domestic firms have made arrangements with foreign producers for the exchange of technical information. Many domestic producers handle foreign dyes which they either import directly or through an importing firm. By thus supplementing their own products they are able to offer their customers a fuller selection.

Chemicals and National Security

Forty years ago, the manufacture of synthetic organic chemicals was a defense industry, *par excellence*. In World War I the United States discovered the need for a strong chemical industry and provided the restrictions on imports necessary to give it a start. During World War II, the chemical industry rendered invaluable services to the cause of national defense.

The Synthetic Organic Chemical Manufacturers Association has stated that "all chemical production in World War II was essential to the war program. All important basic chemicals were under allocation, and their thousands of chemical derivatives could not be made unless some war or essential civilian use demanded their production. On this basis *all* of the *15 billion pounds* of synthetic organic chemicals produced in 1944—at the peak of World War II production —were essential to our national defense." [29]

Explosives, rocket propellants, airplane fuels, medicinals and pharmaceuticals (penicillin, sulfa drugs, atabrine), DDT and other insect repellents, protective clothing and synthetic rubber are listed among the essential products that are made by, or are dependent on, the chemical industry. To satisfy the requirements of the armed services in wartime, chemical production would have to be rapidly expanded. But because of its great flexibility the American chemical industry, so its spokesmen state, could readily supply the new demands.

Representatives of the industry emphasize the importance

[29] *Trade, Strength and Security*, cited, p. 18.

of having adequate facilities available for the production of intermediates, particularly styrene, phenol and aniline. Chemicals such as these, it is argued, cannot be stockpiled. The only economical way to be sure that production facilities will be adequate for any emergency is to protect these products—and their derivatives (e.g., dyes)—from foreign competition.

Three Questions

A strong chemical industry is undeniably essential to national security, and it is clear that many of its products are of critical importance in wartime. These facts in themselves, however, do not prove that tariff protection is necessary, or advisable. Before that conclusion can be reached, three questions must be answered: (1) Is the American chemical industry really vulnerable to foreign competition? (2) Is it probable that with lower import duties domestic production would fall to a point where the country would be dangerously dependent on overseas sources? (3) Even should this danger exist, is continued tariff protection at the present high levels the best way to ward it off?

In heavy chemicals the American producers, without any tariff protection or with only low rates of duty, dominate the domestic market. The menace of foreign competition, if it exists at all, is found in the field of coal tar products and other synthetic organic chemicals. But even in this more sensitive area the United States, because of 40 years of progress, has little cause for anxiety.

In raw materials and crude products we are better off than any foreign country, thanks to our great coal, oil and iron and steel industries.[30] Through the development of its petrochemical industry the United States has freed itself from dependence on foreign supplies of intermediates, and in this field the American position appears impregnable. Domestic firms, with a production of 4.6 billion pounds of intermediates in 1954, supplied over 99 percent of domestic consumption.

Production of intermediates has been built up on the broad base of a rapidly expanding and widely diversified civilian

[30] Coal tar crudes are by-products of coal carbonization. Their supply is determined by the demand for coke which is used primarily as fuel in blast furnaces.

demand for synthetic rubber, synthetic fibers, plastics, dyes, insecticides, medicinals, etc. Since few of these end-products are at all troubled by foreign competition, no special safe-guarding measures are needed for intermediates. Their great peacetime domestic market guarantees that extensive produc-tion facilities will be available to supply a mobilization base in time of national emergency. Canada, it should be noted, has a growing chemical industry which would be able in an emergency to supply a part of our requirements.

The temptation to think of the defense issue in terms of 1914-1918, or even 1941-1945, must be avoided. The Tariff Commission reported in 1946 that the defense argument for dyes was losing its validity.[31] It is true that the equipment and skilled personnel of a dye plant can be readily turned to the production of TNT and other explosives, as well as many medicinals, and many of the products which regularly come from dye plants are needed in war. It is also true that inter-mediates are easily diverted into a great variety of chemicals for defense. But after World War I the raw material base for organic chemicals was greatly broadened by the rise of the fermentation industry (methanol, ethanol, butanol, glycerol, acetone, citric acid), and after World War II by the still more spectacular rise of petrochemicals. Thus products and proc-esses based on coal tar have become relatively less important. Technical progress, also, in the wide field of organic chemistry is now largely independent of research in dyes.

Dye production, moreover, is now a small and decreasing segment of the organic chemical industry. Its output in 1954 was only five-tenths of one percent, by quantity, of the total output of synthetic organic chemicals. (In value, sales of dyes accounted for 4 percent of all sales.) Because of the great expansion of other branches of the industry, intermediates would still be produced in large quantities and research would still continue, even were domestic production of dyes greatly curtailed.

Among medicinals and pharmaceuticals, certain products have proved of great value in wartime, penicillin and other antibiotics, atabrine and the various sulfa drugs. But the pro-duction of antibiotics is now firmly established in this country.

[31] *Dyes*, cited, p. 18.

The United States is the world's largest producer of penicillin and exports it in large quantities. Sulfa drugs are imported to some extent but not in sufficient quantities to endanger the domestic industry. Internal competition and the rapid fluctuations in demand for widely advertised cure-alls seem to be more significant than imports in affecting the fortunes of domestic producers of pharmaceuticals.

Alternatives to Tariff Protection

The Department of Defense keeps under close scrutiny the conditions of supply of all chemicals used directly in military operations, rocket fuels, primers, detonators and explosives, as well as chemical products essential to the health and efficiency of men and women in the services. If at any time the Department should decide that increasing imports threatened the continued production in this country of essential chemical products, it has a choice of several remedies. It may accumulate stockpiles of such products as may be stored without deterioration; it may recommend that Congress encourage production by direct subsidies; or, as in the case of synthetic rubber, it may, with Congressional approval, set up production in government plants. The President, if he finds that increased imports of any article are impairing or threatening to impair the national security, may take whatever action he deems necessary to "adjust" the imports. This broad grant of authority would permit him to raise import duties or to impose quotas or absolute embargoes.

Each of these alternatives has its merits and its defects. Government ownership of manufacturing plants in peacetime, an invasion of a field traditionally reserved for private business enterprise, is a measure of last resort. In the chemical industry particularly, where important new developments occur almost daily, there is danger that government operation would stifle research and retard technical progress. Stockpiling operations almost inevitably have disturbing effects on market conditions. Furthermore, stockpiling is not an effective means for continuously maintaining manufacturing operations at a minimum level. Once the government has accumulated an adequate supply of the material in question its activity ceases.

Businessmen dislike subsidies because they involve periodic

reports and the inspection of their records by government officials. Nevertheless, from the point of view of the public interest, subsidies, as we have pointed out on page 129, are effective and economical. In comparison, tariff protection is a clumsy instrument; its effects in stimulating production are uncertain, and the burden it imposes on consumers, and on the national economy, can only be estimated.

Chapter 9

THE ELECTRICAL MANUFACTURERS AND THE BUY AMERICAN ACT

THE 1953 AWARD by the U. S. Corps of Engineers of contracts for four generators and ten main transformers for installation at the Chief Joseph Dam on the Columbia River attracted nation-wide attention. When, early in December 1952, the bids on this contract were opened, the lowest was found to be that of the English Electric Company, $5,556,000. The lowest domestic bid, a combined tender of two companies, Westinghouse and Moloney Electric Company, was $7,170,161. The Army, had it purchased the English equipment, would have paid $682,000 to the U. S. Treasury in import duties. But the duties, although reckoned in the total price of the foreign equipment, would not actually have represented an additional cost to the federal government, being taken out of one pocket and paid into another. Hence the total saving to the American taxpayer would have been actually the difference between the lowest domestic bid and the lowest foreign bid, something over $1,600,000.

The Buy American Act, however, required that federal agencies should purchase commodities *of domestic manufacture,* unless the price was "unreasonable" or unless such purchases were "not consistent with the national interest." According to the Army procurement regulations the $7 million price asked by the two American firms was not unreasonable, since it did not exceed 125 percent of the foreign price, including import duties. But at this point the State Department intervened. It held out for the award to the foreign firm, on the ground that by so doing the United States would be substituting trade for aid, assisting the economic recovery of a friendly nation, and thus promoting the national interest. The matter was deemed of sufficient importance to be considered at meetings of the President's Cabinet (March 27 and April 3,

1953) where, after much discussion, it was decided to reject all bids and call for new tenders.

In explaining this unusual procedure, Secretary of Defense Wilson stated that there was nothing in the original specifications to show that there was equal and comparable quality in the bids submitted by the competing firms. His action brought editorial protests from newspapers across the country. The *Salem Capitol Journal* (Ore.) said: "If a wall should be erected against foreign electric equipment, the tariff is the place to erect it, not by discrimination in the awarding of Government contracts." [1] The *Chicago Tribune*, a paper not noted for an international point of view, pointed out that there was no unemployment in electrical manufacturing. Instead, the industry was enjoying the largest volume of sales and the highest profits in its history. The *Tribune* concluded: "The contract for the hydroelectric project at a needlessly high cost to the American taxpayer cannot be justified. . . . The Buy America [sic] Act should be repealed if it cannot be held in reserve for application in time of economic distress." [2] The *New York Times*, and other Eastern newspapers, stressed the inconsistency between President Eisenhower's pledge to work for the highest possible level of international trade and the Defense Department's rejection of the English bid.

The *Times* of London (April 22, 1953) said that in England there was "deep disappointment at the United States' failure to live up to the 'good creditor policy'. . . ." In the House of Commons, Mr. Peter Thorneycroft, President of the Board of Trade, spoke of the decision as a "bad omen for the future. . . ." He said: "Whatever the reasons why all bids have been rejected . . . the effect will be to give all or at least some of the American firms a second chance, as they failed at first, to beat their British competitor on price." [3] This prediction proved true; for the result of the second round of bidding was a compromise award. English Electric, which had cut its original bid by about four percent, got the contract for the transformers. The contract for the generators

[1] Quoted by Representative Walter Norblad in *Congressional Record*, 83rd Cong., 1st sess., v. 99, pt. 10 (May 5, 1953), p. A2557.
[2] Quoted by Representative Frank E. Smith, same, p. A2378.
[3] House of Commons, *Parliamentary Debates*, v. 514 (April 20, 1953), col. 679.

went to Westinghouse for $4,249,601, a reduction of $717,-000 or 14 percent from its earlier bid. British sentiment was appeased somewhat several months later by the award to an English firm, Ferranti, of a contract for transformers for the McNary Dam. In November 1954, also, the English Electric Company was awarded a million dollar contract for two hydraulic turbines to be installed at the Table Rock Dam in Arkansas. These purchases, however, seem to have indicated only a temporary relaxation of the Buy American policy. In August 1955, Secretary of Defense Wilson directed the Army to award contracts for six generators and three transformers for the Chief Joseph Dam to the Westinghouse Electric Corporation and the Pennsylvania Transformer Company. The sum of the American bids, about $7 million, was almost $1 million in excess of the bid of the English Electric Company. The Secretary cited the substantial unemployment in the Pittsburgh area, where the American plants are situated, as justification for his decision. In an editorial criticizing this award the *Wall Street Journal* said that the government pretended to have a competitive bidding policy but squeezed out the low bidder because it was a foreign manufacturer. The editorial continued:

Now this latest award means, of course, that the American taxpayers, the truly forgotten, will have to fork up an extra million dollars just so a domestic firm can get the business. And this at a time when American business is booming as never before.

It also means that the Government is working at cross purposes. With one hand we pour out billions of dollars to help build up the economies of our friends abroad and provide them with needed U. S. dollars, while with the other hand we prevent them from earning those dollars for themselves and in a way that would save us dollars.

It must be a considerable puzzlement for our friends. We make what is, presumably, a bona fide request for bids. A foreign firm makes a bona fide bid that is the lowest of the lot. But comes award day the foreign entry finds he's playing under a movable handicap.[4]

* * *

As regards the bulk of its products, the American electrical manufacturing industry is not vulnerable to competition from

[4] *Wall Street Journal*, August 31, 1955.

abroad. Industrial equipment and household appliances are standardized items which the American firms produce in great quantities for sale all over the world. Since about 1950, however, foreign competition has developed in heavy electric power equipment[5] (generators, transformers, switchgear, etc.), and the American industry has seen with dismay the award of valuable federal contracts to English, Swiss and other foreign firms. In this kind of custom-made equipment, the lower labor costs of the foreign firms constitute a decisive advantage. A huge generator capable of developing 200,000 horsepower is not bought off the shelf or from a catalog. It is not made on an assembly line, but is constructed to detailed specifications. Each of these giant machines is a unique product; no exact duplicate may ever be made. (See illustrations facing pp. 224 and 225.) The same is true to a large extent of the accessory equipment, transformers, circuit breakers, etc., which must have correspondingly large capacity.

Only a few American firms are equipped to produce the heaviest types of electrical equipment, and the total amount of their business in this field seems insignificant when compared with their sales of all products. Nevertheless, they have strongly opposed the entrance of foreign firms into this sector of the home market. Their demand for rigorous restriction of federal purchases of foreign-made equipment is based partly on economic grounds; they argue that because of higher costs they cannot compete with the foreign producers. But their major argument is political, or strategic. They contend that the installation of foreign equipment in large power projects endangers national security. (For a fuller discussion, see pp. 241-242.)

Consistent with this position they have not asked for increased import duties but rather for the more rigorous application of the Buy American Act, to prevent the purchase of

---

[5] The Edison Electric Institute defines heavy electric power equipment as follows:

Large steam turbine-generators—10,000 kilowatts and larger.
Small steam turbine-generators—4,000 to 9,999 kilowatts.
Generators for hydraulic turbines—4,000 kilowatts and larger.
Steam generators—450 pounds per square inch pressure and higher.
Hydraulic turbines—5,000 horsepower and larger.
Power transformers—501 kilovolt-amperes and larger.

foreign-made electrical equipment for use in power installations critical for national defense. Their argument has not been accepted by the procurement officers of the U. S. Corps of Engineers or by the Bureau of Reclamation. Both agencies have continued to award contracts to qualified foreign bidders.

Dimensions of the Domestic Industry

Electrical manufacturing is one of the country's largest industries, and the American industry is larger than that of any other country. In 1953, 4,400 firms, with close to one million employees, turned out products worth more than $16 billion. Of this amount, $4.7 billion, nearly one-third, was accounted for by the sales of two concerns, the General Electric Company and the Westinghouse Electric Corporation. Their employees, 222,000 in General Electric and 112,700 in Westinghouse, made up one-third of the industry's total. The third largest firm, Allis-Chalmers, with sales of $514 million, employed 36,700 workers.

Even aside from the three largest firms, the industry was characterized by large-scale operations. Twelve companies had sales in excess of $100 million in 1953, and seven others exceeded $50 million. The combined sales of the 25 largest companies were $8,551 million, over 50 percent of the industry's total sales. In 1952 more than 200 firms employed 1,000 persons and over; 73 had as many as 2,500 workers. At the other end of the scale were some 3,000 firms, each of whom employed less than 100 persons.

It has been said with some truth that there is no American electrical manufacturing industry; instead there are four industries whose products may be grouped as follows: (1) power-producing equipment—generators for hydro and thermal plants, motor turbines, transformers, electric locomotives and diesel engines; (2) producers' goods—small apparatus, industrial lighting and heating equipment, motors, wire and cable, meters and electrical instruments, railway signal equipment, diesel engines; (3) consumers' goods—refrigerators, vacuum cleaners, clothes washers, dish washers and smaller appliances, and radio and television sets; (4) defense items—jet engines, guided missiles, aircraft armament systems. Most of the firms make only a few products; only two, Westinghouse and General Electric, cover the entire field.

The history of the industry from small beginnings at the end of the last century is one of rapid growth. Total shipments in the years 1935-1939 averaged $2.2 billion and in 1946-1950 $10.0 billion. They rose to $14.2 billion in 1951, $14.9 billion in 1952, $16.3 billion in 1953 and $15.6 billion

Table 38

U. S. SHIPMENTS OF ELECTRICAL MACHINERY AND ALLIED PRODUCTS, 1939, 1947, 1950-1954

(in millions of dollars)

	1939	1947	1950	1951	1952	1953	1954
Generating, transmission and distribution equipment	248	912	1,096	1,437	1,710	1,780	1,829
Signal and communication equipment	115	703	536	732	890	961	1,053
Insulated wire and cable	204	895	880	1,097	1,266	1,311	1,250
Insulating materials	42	155	193	249	237	274	245
Illuminating equipment	113	461	582	667	648	670	674
Industrial apparatus	229	1,235	1,422	1,986	2,214	2,351	2,108
Building equipment and supplies	109	378	404	534	475	478	442
Appliances	608	2,531	4,217	3,791	3,689	4,155	3,812
Other electrical products[a]	787	2,780	3,739	3,675	3,756	4,330	4,182
Total	2,454	10,048	13,069	14,168	14,884	16,310	15,595

[a] Including radio, electronic and television equipment, specialty capacitors and transformers, X-ray equipment, land transportation motors and controls, electric lamps, air conditioning and commercial refrigeration equipment, radio receiving-type and cathode ray tubes, recording devices.
Source: National Electrical Manufacturers Association

in 1954. Allowing for the intervening rise in prices, the physical output of the industry was then about five times that of prewar years.

The gains in shipments of some of the largest groups of products are shown in Table 38. The table understates the real growth since, for security reasons, certain products, such as electrically controlled gun-fire systems, guided missiles and detection devices, have been omitted in recent years from published statistics.

The Expansion of the Domestic Market

In 1954, almost 45 million American homes and farms were classified by the Bureau of the Census as "wired for electricity"; in 1939 the number had been less than 25 million. This development has gone hand in hand with the increase in the generation of electric power from somewhat over 100 billion kilowatt hours in 1939 to an estimated 472 billion in 1954. For the electrical manufacturing industry, the expansion has furnished a rapidly growing market for generators, turbines, transformers and other distributing and transmission equipment.

Extension of power lines, falling prices of electric power and the rise in national income help to explain the great expansion in the sales of household appliances of all sorts. The constant improvement in these appliances has been the result of vigorous programs of research and progress in engineering and design. The growing use of electric equipment in factories for the generation of power, and its transmission to individual machines, furnished a new market for industrial equipment. At present about 85 percent of the power used in American factories is furnished by electric motors.

Defense orders provided an important new market. Sales of electrical products to the defense departments alone amounted to $2.8 billion in 1953. In that year about 30 percent of General Electric's sales were military items. Approximately 24 percent of Westinghouse's sales in 1953 were for government account, including both defense items and goods for normal peacetime uses.

Defense spending, although still huge, measured by any previous peacetime experience, in 1955 had passed its peak. Further expansion of the civilian market for electrical manufactures, like that of all large manufacturing industries, depended principally on the general level of industrial activity and of national income, but this, in turn, was somewhat dependent on the volume of defense spending. With these qualifications in mind, producers of electrical equipment and appliances looked forward confidently to future growth in sales. The expansion programs of the public utilities and of public bodies, the Department of the Army, the Bureau of

Reclamation, T.V.A., the Atomic Energy Commission and the New York State Power Authority, supported their optimistic view. According to a 1954 estimate, the investor-owned power companies and the public agencies would have to double their capacity by 1963. This would require an expenditure of some $50 billion for equipment and facilities.

A Prosperous Industry

The combined net income of ten electrical manufacturing companies, 1947-1954, is shown in Table 39, in comparison with net income of 378 industrial companies. In general, the makers of heavy electrical equipment, including the three largest companies, had a better record of earnings than companies which make principally household appliances.

In assessing the future prospects of firms engaged in electrical manufacturing, a 1954 Standard & Poor's survey estimated that the development of new household appliances will continue "at least at the same rapid rate as has prevailed in the past few decades. Prospects for industrial use of electrical equipment are enhanced by the growing trend toward factory automation." [6]

Table 39

COMPARATIVE NET INCOME OF ELECTRICAL COMPANIES, 1947-1954

(1947-49 = 100)

	1947	1948	1949	1950	1951	1952	1953	1954
10 electric companies[a]								
Before taxes and after reserves	86	108	106	181	183	102	217	192
After taxes and reserves	85	104	110	155	125	132	146	171
378 industrial companies								
Before taxes and after reserves	90	112	99	147	162	141	156	141
After taxes and reserves	89	111	101	129	119	110	120	126

[a] Including Black & Decker, Cutler-Hammer, General Electric, McGraw Electric, Philco Corp., Radio Corp. of America, Square D, Sylvania Electric Products, Westinghouse Electric, Zenith Radio.
Source: *Electrical Products*, Standard & Poor's Industry Surveys, v. 123, no. 38, sec. 2 (September 22, 1955), p. 20

[6] *Electrical Products*, Standard & Poor's Industry Surveys, v. 122, no. 28, sec. 2 (July 15, 1954), p. 2.

Noting that the use of electrical equipment by the armed forces had grown to "huge proportions," the survey concluded: "Long-term growth prospects of all segments of the industry are favorable." A year-end statement of the National Electrical Manufacturers Association predicted that the industry's 1955 sales, after a slight decline in 1954, would equal or exceed the record year 1953.

Electrical manufacturers had little difficulty in postwar adjustment to peacetime conditions. Sales for the industry as a whole, and for companies whose financial reports are available, declined sharply in 1946 but recovered rapidly in 1947 and later years. In most cases, sales showed no falling off after the 1951 rearmament boom. At the end of 1954 none of General Electric's 147 plants was working less than 40 hours a week;[7] some plants were still on a two-shift, 80-hour weekly schedule. Owing to a falling off in defense business, the company's 1954 net sales were five percent below the $3.1 billion record established in 1953. Earnings rose, however, because of the elimination of the excess profits tax. In 1954 they were 7.2 percent of sales. Both earnings and sales showed improvement in the first six months of 1955, the continued decline in government business being more than offset by civilian sales, particularly in the field of heavy equipment.

Westinghouse's sales in 1954, despite a decline in the early months of the year in orders for power generating equipment, were slightly better than in 1953, a record year. In early 1955 the company reported a "very considerable" rise in orders for steam turbines. That year it completed a $300 million expansion program, the second launched since the war, which enlarged by 50 percent its productive capacity.

Allis-Chalmers, the third largest firm, earned $26.1 million in 1954, compared with $21.9 million in 1953. In order to increase production of electrical transformers and switchgear, this company was planning to spend $9.5 million in two of its plants.

Sales in Foreign Markets

In 1954, American manufacturers sold $876 million of electrical products, about five and one-half percent of their total

[7] Statement of President Ralph J. Cordiner, as quoted in the New York Times, December 16, 1954.

shipments, in foreign countries. The relation of exports to total shipments in previous years is shown below.

Table 40

DOMESTIC SHIPMENTS AND EXPORTS OF ELECTRICAL
MACHINERY AND ALLIED PRODUCTS,
1937, 1947, 1950-1954

Year	Exports	Total shipments	Percent exported
	(million dollars)		
1939	105.6	2,454	4.3
1947	573.9	10,048	5.7
1950	444.3	13,069	3.4
1951	640.1	14,168	4.5
1952	759.8	14,884	5.1
1953	902.2	16,300	5.5
1954	876.0	15,600	5.6

Source: U. S. Bureau of the Census, National Electrical Manufacturers Association

Two of the leading firms sold a somewhat higher proportion of their goods abroad than the average for the industry. Westinghouse's 1953 exports were about seven percent of total billings; Allis-Chalmers exported approximately nine percent; General Electric's sales were about five percent. Table 41 shows in some detail exports of heavy equipment, with which this chapter is principally concerned. Canada, as the table indicates, for the last 15 years has been the chief foreign customer for American electrical products. Before World War II, our northern neighbor bought about 18 percent of the total exports. Since 1947 the proportion has increased steadily, until in 1953 and 1954 it reached one-third.

The active trade in both directions between the United States and Canada in electrical manufactures consists in part of intercompany transfers between American firms and their Canadian subsidiaries.[8] (See Tables 41 and 43.) In selling generators, transformers and other heavy equipment in the

[8] General Electric has 12 branch factories in Canada; Westinghouse has three, and Allis-Chalmers has two. Three smaller American companies, Moloney Electric, S. Morgan Smith and Square D, also have Canadian factories.

Vertical shaft generator, 49,500 KVA, fitted with a thrust bearing designed for a maximum load of 1,550 metric tons; runway speed, 345 RPM. Manufactured by Brown, Boveri & Company.

Power house with nine hydraulic generators, 108,000 KVA each; Bureau of Reclamation project. Each generator weighs approximately 1,000 tons; diameter, 45 feet; height above the floor, 32 feet. Manufactured by Westinghouse Electric Corporation.

Table 41

U. S. EXPORTS OF ELECTRICAL MACHINERY AND ALLIED PRODUCTS, TOTAL AND TO CANADA, 1939, 1947, 1950-1954

(values in millions of dollars)

	1939	1947	1950	1951	1952	1953	1954
All electrical exports:							
Grand total	105.6	573.9	444.3	640.1	759.8	902.2	876.0
Total[a]	105.6	551.5	388.3	537.8	615.4	657.5	608.5
To Canada	18.8	93.4	77.0	122.4	166.7	222.2	198.7
Percent to Canada	*17.8*	*16.9*	*19.8*	*22.8*	*27.1*	*33.8*	*32.7*
Generators:							
Total	4.9	52.3	19.8	31.9	35.5	24.7	22.6
To Canada	0.3	2.7	2.5	4.2	4.7	5.5	3.0
Percent to Canada	*6.1*	*5.2*	*12.6*	*13.2*	*13.2*	*22.3*	*13.1*
Transforming and converting apparatus:							
Total	2.8	20.9	23.5	25.8	32.2	30.7	27.1
To Canada	0.2	1.3	1.8	3.0	5.4	7.1	5.7
Percent to Canada	*7.1*	*6.2*	*7.7*	*11.6*	*16.8*	*23.1*	*21.2*
Motors and controls:							
Total	7.4	45.7	41.1	47.5	57.1	49.4	44.6
To Canada	1.6	8.8	10.3	17.2	17.8	16.3	17.2
Percent to Canada	*21.6*	*19.3*	*25.1*	*36.2*	*31.2*	*33.0*	*38.5*
Turbines, steam engines, water wheels:							
Total	0.3	11.2	8.6	10.2	11.4	18.0	15.3
To Canada	0.1	1.2	1.6	2.0	1.8	3.5	1.8
Percent to Canada	*33.3*	*10.7*	*18.6*	*19.6*	*15.8*	*19.4*	*12.5*

[a] Excluding "Special Category" commodities which, for security reasons, are not given by countries.
Source: U. S. Bureau of the Census

Canadian market, American manufacturers are successfully meeting competition, on even terms with Swiss, Italian and other European firms, and on less than even terms with English firms, whose products benefit by preferential tariff rates. In less industrialized countries, also, Venezuela, Mexico, Brazil, Cuba and Colombia, American electrical manufacturers sell their products in competition with European firms. Some European countries, American manufacturers have complained, have barred their markets by requirements for import licenses. These requirements no longer exist in Germany and Switzerland, but are still retained by the United Kingdom.

Relations with Manufacturers Abroad

The high degree of concentration in the manufacture of heavy equipment, both in the United States[9] and in foreign countries, facilitated close cooperation. Leading American companies acquired a financial interest in the principal competing firms abroad, and made agreements with them for the exchange of patent rights and technical information. These early agreements, which in effect allocated markets among the participants, were supplemented in 1930 by the International Notification and Compensation Agreement which provided for similar cooperation in the remaining markets of the world. Warned by their legal advisers that the latter agreement violated the antitrust laws, General Electric and Westinghouse in 1931 organized under the Webb-Pomerene Act the Electrical Apparatus Export Association, using it as an instrument for participation in the international cartel. The Association, later joined by other American firms, continued in operation until 1947 when it was dissolved, as the result of a complaint by the Department of Justice of violation of the Sherman Antitrust Act. Under a consent decree, the Association and its member companies were enjoined from making any agreements with foreign competitors for notification of inquiries for bids, price fixing or division of sales territories.[10]

In October 1953, Judge Phillip Forman (of the U. S. District Court, District of New Jersey) entered a judgment in a case against the General Electric Company. He found that the company had been a party to illegal agreements with manufacturers in the United Kingdom, France, Belgium, Germany, Italy and Japan, some going back to 1892, to allo-

[9] As early as 1928, General Electric and Westinghouse produced together over 70 percent of the entire American output of heavy equipment.
[10] *Report of the Federal Trade Commission on International Electrical Equipment Cartels* (Washington: GPO, 1948), pp. 6-21.

cate world sales territories and to pool patents and knowledge relating to the manufacture of incandescent lamps. The decision required the elimination of restrictive provisions in the agreements and prohibited any similar agreements in the future. A few months earlier the Westinghouse Electric Corporation and two German concerns, Siemens and Halske and Siemens-Schuckert-Werke, signed a consent decree in a federal antitrust suit dating from 1945. The government had charged that in a cartel agreement the companies had split up territories on a world-wide basis and had agreed to the exchange of patents and know-how on an exclusive basis. Westinghouse was barred from making further restrictive agreements with the two German concerns.

Import Competition

Before World War II the American industry experienced practically no competition from abroad. The German firm, Siemens and Halske, established a branch office in Chicago in 1892 but sold out to General Electric in 1900. Brown Boveri, the leading Swiss manufacturer, first established an American connection in 1925,[11] and Ferranti, an English firm, set up an office in New York in 1936. But none of these enterprises had made a significant dent in the American market when World War II intervened.

In industrial equipment and household appliances, the absence of foreign competition can be explained by the low costs of American firms in producing articles of mass consumption. But in custom-made heavy equipment, the cost advantage has been on the side of the foreign firms. Nevertheless, until recently they seemed to have been unable to sell their equipment in competition with the domestic product in the American market. This situation may have a number of explanations. In prewar years cartel agreements, which provided that each participating company would not invade the domestic territory of the others, were a factor of considerable

[11] After a few years, the parent company lost control, and the American branch was liquidated soon after. Between 1931 and 1943 U. S. manufacturing and servicing rights were assigned to Allis-Chalmers. In 1946 a new American subsidiary was established. See *Business Week* (June 13, 1953).

importance.[12] After 1933 the Buy American Act constituted a formidable obstacle. During World War II and in the immediate postwar years, foreign companies were in no position to export heavy equipment of any kind to the United States.

In official statistics, the imports of heavy equipment are included with other types of foreign-made electrical machinery which have always been small, compared with the sales of domestic manufacturers. In 1954, a record year, the foreign goods supplied about three-tenths of one percent of the domestic market. (See Table 42.) In reading the table one should note that much of the heavy equipment already bought by federal agencies had not arrived in U. S. ports and hence did not appear in the import statistics.

Table 42

DOMESTIC SALES AND IMPORTS OF ELECTRICAL MACHINERY AND ALLIED PRODUCTS, 1939, 1947, 1950-1954

(in millions of dollars)

Year	Imports	Total sales of domestic manufacturers
1939	2.1	2,454
1947	3.5	10,048
1950	9.5	13,069
1951	18.8	14,168
1952	27.4	14,884
1953	44.1	16,300
1954	46.8	15,600

Source: U. S. Bureau of the Census, National Electrical Manufacturers Association

Canada is the principal supplier of electrical manufactures to the United States, as well as the principal market for U. S. exports of these products. Imports from Canada in 1954 were 22 percent of all electrical goods purchased from foreign countries. (See Table 43.) Canada supplied 29 percent, by value, of all the generators imported, 50 percent of the trans-

[12] U. S. Senate, *Electric Power Industry. Supply of Electrical Equipment and Competitive Conditions*, 70th Cong., 1st sess., S. Doc. 46 on S. Res. 329 (Washington: GPO, 1928), p. 138.

Table 43

U. S. Imports of Electrical Machinery and Allied Products, Total and from Canada, 1939, 1947, 1950-1954

(values in thousands of dollars)

	1939	1947	1950	1951	1952	1953	1954[b]
All electrical imports:							
Total	2,091	3,537	9,499	18,823	27,443	44,105	46,789
From Canada	47	1,924	3,141	5,660	12,814	15,570	10,463
Percent from Canada	2.2	54.4	33.1	30.1	46.7	35.3	22.4
Generators:							
Total	46	92	93	399	330	346	628
From Canada	a	79	36	119	188	309	179
Percent from Canada	.2	85.5	38.8	29.9	56.8	89.2	28.6
Transformers and converters:							
Total	17	63	183	279	565	8,744	5,041
From Canada	2	15	39	35	245	5,906	2,525
Percent from Canada	10.0	24.0	21.1	12.5	43.3	67.5	50.1
Motors:							
Total	34	422	811	2,334	2,527	2,114	2,731
From Canada	5	386	383	496	791	467	697
Percent from Canada	14.7	91.4	47.3	21.2	31.3	22.1	25.5
Turbines, steam engines, water wheels:							
Total	101	50	56	791	306	306	885
From Canada	1	8	1	25	14	23	246
Percent from Canada	.6	15.6	1.8	3.1	4.6	7.6	27.8

a Less than $500.
b The total for 1954 includes $1.1 million of imports which cannot be allocated by countries; thus country totals are slightly understated.
Source: U. S. Bureau of the Census

formers and converters, 22 percent of radio apparatus, and over 60 percent of telephone and telegraph apparatus. The trade with Canada, as we remarked above, is unique because it includes exchanges between American firms and their Canadian subsidiaries. Engineering equipment and household appliances both figure in these exchanges.

Ranking next in importance to Canada as a source of 1954

imports were the United Kingdom, West Germany, Switzerland, Japan and Italy. (See Table 44.)

Table 44

U. S. IMPORTS OF ELECTRICAL MACHINERY AND ALLIED
PRODUCTS, BY COUNTRY OF ORIGIN, 1939, 1947,
1950-1954

(in thousands of dollars)

Country	1939	1947	1950	1951	1952	1953	1954
Canada	47	1,924	3,141	5,660	12,814	15,570	10,463
United Kingdom	203	863	2,578	4,140	5,573	9,787	10,380
West Germany	585	11	595	1,356	1,612	3,906	8,336
Switzerland	102	89	381	1,478	1,297	2,964	4,498
Italy	3	11	27	203	324	342	324
Japan	809	123	402	785	645	1,013	2,209

Source: U. S. Bureau of the Census

Bidding on Federal Contracts

Bidding by foreign firms on federal contracts dates from the revival of the English electrical manufacturing industry, and that of other European countries, after World War II. Devaluation of sterling in 1949 helped English exports to the United States. Then, even before the "trade not aid" policy was announced, officials of the Mutual Security Administration encouraged British firms to compete for federal contracts. In effect, they were told "if you blighters want dollars, come over and earn them." Encouraged by this invitation, the English Electric Company began operations in the United States in 1951 and secured its first contract in 1952. In 1950 English and other foreign firms had been awarded about 10 percent of all federal contracts for electrical equipment. In 1952 out of 187 awards of $25,000, and over, with a value of $42,623,000, foreign bidders secured 19 jobs valued at $2,632,-800, or six percent of the total. In 1953 the foreign bidders had still greater success. Out of 107 awards they again received only 19, but these were worth $10,283,000, or 39 percent of total.[13] A comparison of foreign and domestic bids on certain federal contracts awarded in the years 1952-1954 is shown in Tables 45 and 46.

[13] Foreign firms did not bid on all contracts but only when they felt they had some chance of winning. In 1952 they entered bids on 36 contracts and in 1953 on 40.

Table 45

CERTAIN U. S. ARMY CONTRACTS FOR HYDROELECTRIC EQUIPMENT

Awarded to Foreign Firms

	Opening date	Low bidders (* — Bid awarded to)	Evaluated bid price (inc. duty)	Evaluated differential (percent)
Garrison (North Dakota) 9 (33,333 KVA) transformers	17 Apr 52	Ferranti Elect. (Eng.)* Allis-Chalmers (U. S.)	$1,137,605 1,357,500	19.33
McNary (Oregon) 6 (56,500 KVA) transformers	5 May 53	Ferranti Elect. (Eng.)* English Elect. (Eng.) Moloney Elect. (U. S.)	1,007,420 1,074,307 1,189,740	17.20
Gavins Point 3 (31,500/42,000 KVA) transformers	22 May 53	Industrie Elettriche (Italy)* Penn Transformer (U. S.)	390,147 464,742	19.10
Chief Joseph (Washington) 10 (103,000 KVA) transformers	27 May 53	English Elect. (Eng.)* Moloney Elect. (U. S.)	1,928,014 2,311,428	19.88
McNary (Oregon) 2 (73,684 KVA) generators	27 Oct 53	English Elect. (Eng.)* General Elect. (U. S.)	3,984,051 4,771,517	19.77
Table Rock (Arkansas) 2 (68,000 HP) turbines	29 Sept 54	English Elect. (Eng.)* Newport News (U. S.)	1,066,662 1,192,715	11.82
Awarded to Domestic Firms				
Dalles (Oregon) 2 (14,210 KVA) generators	10 Feb 54	Westinghouse (U. S.)* English Elect. (Eng.)	865,134 804,727	7.5
Chief Joseph (Washington) 2 (67,368 KVA) generators	15 Apr 54	Westinghouse (U. S.)* English Elect. (Eng.)	2,076,200 1,842,294	12.69
Dalles (Oregon) 8 (82,105 KVA) generators	1 Oct 54	General Electric (U. S.)* English Elect. (Eng.)	9,076,220 10,654,398	17.39

Source: U. S. Department of the Army

Table 46

Certain U. S. Bureau of Reclamation Contracts for Hydroelectric Equipment

Awarded to Foreign Firms

	Award date	Low bidders (* — Bid awarded to)	Amount for comparison[a]	Difference[b]
Eklutna (Alaska) 2 (16,667 KVA) generators	3 Jan 52	Pacific Oerlikon (Swiss)*	$ 639,005	$162,893
		English Elect. (Eng.)	692,570	
		Elliott (U. S.)	801,898	
		Westinghouse (U. S.)	829,254	
Folsom (California) 1 (80,000 KVA) autotransformer	11 Mar 52	English Elect. (Eng.)*	532,813	24,198
		Ferranti Elect. (Eng.)	536,600	
		Westinghouse (U. S.)	557,011	
		Allis-Chalmers (U. S.)	577,865	
Palisades (Idaho) 4 (30,000 KVA) generators	26 May 53	Pacific Oerlikon (Swiss)*	2,204,174	75,964
		American Elin (Austrian)	2,212,500	
		Westinghouse (U. S.)	2,280,138	
		Elliott (U. S.)	2,362,731	
Sioux City (Iowa) 3 (20,000 KVA) autotransformers	16 Oct 53	American Elin (Austrian)*	439,915	238,164
		Brown Boveri (Swiss)	508,975	
		Industrie Elettriche (Italy)	533,376	
		English Elect. (Eng.)	625,875	
		General Elect. (U. S.)	678,079	
Jamestown (North Dakota) 3 (33,000 KVA) autotransformers	29 Jan 54	American Elin (Austrian)*	531,099	182,469
		Industrie Elettriche (Italy)	537,115	
		English Elect. (Eng.)	678,301	
		Penn Transformer (U. S.)	713,568	

[a] Amount for comparison includes duty, evaluation for efficiency, 25% differential for cost of foreign manufactured component, and maximum price increase (escalation) stipulated by bidder.
[b] Excess of lowest domestic bid over lowest foreign bid, after inclusion of duty, evaluation for efficiency and 25% differential in foreign bid, and after inclusion of evaluation for efficiency and maximum price increase (escalation) in domestic bid.
Source: U. S. Department of the Interior

Markets in the United States for Heavy Equipment

Estimated sales of large generators, motors, transformers and other heavy electrical equipment were about $800 million in 1953 and around $1 billion in 1954.[14] It is generally calculated that 80 percent of this business is furnished by the power companies and industrial enterprises, and the remainder by public bodies, including municipal, state and power district systems, and federal agencies. It is only in the relatively small public sector of the American market that foreign suppliers have been able to make any inroads. Thus far, they have had little success in selling to industrial enterprises or to privately owned public utilities.

Manufacturing companies, factories, mines and other industrial enterprises usually buy their electrical power; hence, they are not in the market for generators. Their purchases consist of motors, transformers and other items, most of which are standardized products which domestic electrical manufacturers turn out in large volume. In supplying these products the English, Swiss, Austrian and other foreign concerns have no cost advantage.

But the large generators and other machines of great capacity, which the big utility companies are installing in their power stations, are custom-made. These can be supplied by English, Swiss and Italian engineering firms at a considerably lower price than the most efficient American firms. Foreign firms, because of the limited size of their domestic markets, export the bulk of their output. They make various pieces of equipment to order, to suit the wide variations in the demands of foreign purchasers. In this type of manufacturing, where mass-production techniques cannot be employed, wages are a decisive factor in costs. Largely on this account, English, Swiss and Italian companies have been able to install their heavy electrical machinery in Europe, Latin America, Australia, India and elsewhere in competition with American manufacturers. The latter contend that the foreign equipment is inferior to that which they supply.

[14] These estimates are based on annual additions to electrical generating capacity as reported in the *Electrical World* (January 25, 1954) and on opinions of electrical engineers. In estimating costs of equipment the conservative factor of $60 per kilowatt has been used.

Why the Public Utilities Do not Buy Foreign-made Equipment

The lower prices which English, Swiss and other foreign firms can quote do not attract the purchasing agents of American public utilities. Thus far, with few exceptions, they have bought only American-made electrical machinery and equipment. To some extent this preference is based on custom and tradition. More than 50 years ago, when the electrical industries were in their infancy, a close relationship developed between Westinghouse and General Electric, the two largest American manufacturers of electrical equipment, and the newly organized electric street railway and lighting companies. These local enterprises in a new field found difficulty in raising capital. The manufacturers, seeking to widen their markets, came to the rescue. They took the local companies' bonds and stocks in part payment for generators, motors and other equipment. Later General Electric, in order to turn its holdings into cash, organized in 1905 the Electric Bond and Share Corporation and held the majority of its voting stock. Until 1924, when this relationship was dissolved, the companies affiliated with Electric Bond and Share continued to buy practically all their equipment from General Electric.[15] Although its legal and financial basis has disappeared, the situation established a half-century ago still obtains. The private power companies, now greatly expanded and consolidated, still buy their heavy equipment from a few domestic suppliers.

Besides the force of habit, there are other possible explanations. A public utility sells its electrical energy in a market which is largely free from competition. Its rates are fixed by public service commissions which for the most part emphasize improvement of service rather than reduction of costs. The higher cost of the domestic equipment becomes a part of the capital investment which is the basis for the fixing of rates. Under these circumstances, public utility officials responsible for letting contracts for new equipment do not go out of their way to invite bids from foreign firms. Unlike the purchasing

[15] U. S. Senate, *Electric Power Industry* . . . , S. Doc. 46 (1928), cited, pp. 98, 100, 112.

officials of federal, state and local bodies, they are not required by law to do so.

Account must also be taken of human factors. The engineers in the private utilities and in the manufacturing companies are often well acquainted; they may have worked together. Many engineers now employed by the power companies received their practical training in the shops of the manufacturers, for whose equipment they have a high regard. They know they can rely on the domestic firms for technical services and for prompt repairs in case of breakdown. These considerations, taken all together, have outweighed possible savings from purchasing foreign machines.

The Public Sector: State and Municipal Projects

Foreign manufacturers of heavy electrical equipment, unable to make any impression on the private enterprise market, have concentrated their attention on public bodies, federal, state and municipal. Usually these bodies must open the bidding on their contracts to qualified foreign firms, although in many states Buy American legislation authorizes purchasing agents to favor domestic sources of supply.

Only a few cities in the United States own their electric power plants, and foreign firms have not as yet had much success in entering this market. The Swiss firm, Brown Boveri, sold two turbogenerators to the city of Cleveland, at a reported saving of $570,000; it has also filled smaller orders from municipally owned and cooperative power stations. In June 1953, it failed to obtain a contract for supplying the city of Detroit with a 50,000-kilowatt steam turbine generator although its bid, $1,296,000, was $650,000 less than that of the successful American firm. Rejection of this bid seemed in strange contrast to the previous pronouncement of the Detroit Board of Commerce, in which it termed the Buy American Act "illogical" and "indefensible." The Board, however, said that the Buy American policy was not involved in the award. It defended the action of the city's Public Lighting Commission on two grounds: (1) that the Swiss company did not meet the Commission's specifications, and (2) that the company had not met the city's requirement that it should be licensed to do business in the state of Michigan. The city of Seattle in 1950 rejected a low bid of an English company for generators to be installed in its municipal power plant. Three years later, the city awarded a $100,000 contract for cables to an English firm, at a saving of $50,000 over the lowest American bid.

The St. Lawrence Power Project of the New York State Power Authority with its initial 700,000-kilowatt capacity will be the second largest hydroelectric development in the world. Naturally, the contracts for the generators, water wheels and other equipment for this project were eagerly sought by foreign and domestic manufacturers. Announcing the purchasing policy of the Authority, Mr. Robert Moses, its chairman, stated that in awarding contracts he would apply to bids of foreign firms a differential in favor of United States bidders generally similar to that used by federal agencies and departments. He insisted that the Authority would not be "swayed by pressure from manufacturers . . . to force the exclusion of foreign competitors." [16] The award to the General Electric Company, in early 1955, of the entire contract for 16 large generators (60,000 KVA each), involving an expenditure of $13 million, appeared in conflict with this statement of policy, since the bid of a Swiss firm, Brown Boveri, on four of the machines was lower than that of the American company. (The Swiss firm, because of its more limited manufacturing facilities, was unable to bid on the entire contract.) The Authority rejected the bid because the expense of maintaining spare parts for only four generators seemed excessive. The Swiss firm accepted the decision as reasonable and made no protest. In June 1955 the English Electric Company, the lowest of six bidders, was awarded a contract for two 120,000 KVA, three-phase auto-transformers.

Federal Power Projects

With the exception of the St. Lawrence Project, the principal area of competition between foreign and domestic firms has been in federal power developments. The shortage of nitrogen in World War I was responsible for the building by the U. S. War Department of the Wilson Dam, although

[16] New York Times, December 16, 1954.

work was not actually begun until 1925. The beginning of a sustained federal program for the development of the nation's hydro resources dates from the depression years in the early 1930's. In 1933-1939 more than $1.25 billion went into some 1,450 projects for the establishment, or improvement, of public power undertakings. At the end of this period the installed capacity, federally owned, was between two and four percent of the national total. In 1953 federal power plants had a capacity of 15,000,000 horsepower or 12 percent of the national total. They included such well-known undertakings as Hoover Dam (Boulder Dam), Grand Coulee, Bonneville, McNary Dams, and the numerous projects of the Tennessee Valley Authority.

The activities of federal agencies in the field of hydroelectric power were stepped up during World War II to meet demands for additional electric power from defense industries. The new projects were situated principally in the Pacific Northwest, in the states of Washington, Oregon and Idaho, where the Columbia River and its tributaries have great hydroelectric generating capacity. During the war a number of strategic industries requiring large amounts of power, such as the reduction of aluminum and other metals and the manufacture of aircraft, were established in the area.

In the foreseeable future, federal agencies will continue to be the principal purchasers of hydroelectric equipment. Planned additions to hydroelectric capacity, as reported to the *Electrical World*, are shown below:

Table 47

PLANNED ADDITIONS TO HYDROELECTRIC CAPACITY

(in kilowatts)

	1956	*1957*	*After 1957*
Power companies	378,700	35,000	2,737,500
Municipal, state and power district systems	138,850	30,000	1,660,000[a]
Cooperatives	1,500	1,000	500
Federal agencies	792,833	763,066	3,669,450
Total	1,311,883	829,066	8,067,450

[a] Including 940,000 kilowatts for the St. Lawrence River Project.
Source: "Electrical Industry Statistics," *Electrical World* (January 24, 1955)

Manufacturers Urge Restriction of Imports

The electrical manufacturing industry grew to maturity without much assistance from tariff protection. Competition from abroad being insignificant, moderate rates of duty, 30 percent in 1922 raised to 35 percent in 1930, satisfied the domestic producers. They raised no public outcry when trade agreements with the United Kingdom, Switzerland and Sweden, and subsequent multilateral agreements, cut the 1930 rates approximately in half. In these agreements the duty on vacuum cleaners was reduced from 40 to 20 percent ad valorem, on washing machines and electric fans from 35 to 17½ percent, on radio and television apparatus from 35 to 12½ percent, and on cooking stoves from 35 to 10 percent. No reduction was made in the 20 percent duty on incandescent light bulbs with metal filaments, the usual type. On imports of heavy equipment the following changes were made:

	1930 rate	1955 rate
	(percent ad valorem)	
Transformers	35	12½
Generators	35	15
Turbines: Steam	20	15
Hydraulic	27½	15
Switches and switchgear	35	17½

For many years, electrical manufacturers as a group took no position, publicly, in tariff matters. Their trade association, the National Electrical Manufacturers Association, neither opposed nor advocated the extension of the Trade Agreements Act on the many occasions when this matter came before Congress. The industry, because it included so many and such varied undertakings, was subjected to the pull of conflicting forces which left it on dead center in the tariff dispute. Small and medium-sized companies, manufacturing household appliances (washing machines, refrigerators, vacuum cleaners) and industrial equipment (small and medium-sized generators, motors and transformers), have taken little or no interest in tariff matters. The well-established reputation of American brands, their excellence of design and workmanship and the availability of repair service and replacements constituted decisive competitive advantages. Periodical complaints were heard of imports of Japanese Christmas tree lights and other small incandescent bulbs; certain domestic manufacturers protested against any reduction in tariff rates on these items. Makers of radio and television apparatus objected to increasing imports of competing products from West Germany and the United Kingdom. Foreign competition, measured quantitatively, was insignificant (domestic shipments in 1954 were about $1.7 billion; imports were only $3.0 million). But the protesting domestic manufacturers were being forehanded. Mr. James D. Secrest, executive vice president of the Radio-Electronics-Television Manufacturers' Association, is reported to have declared: "We will try to put out the flame while it is still a small brush fire." [17]

Unified action by the entire industry looking toward increased tariff protection dates from November 1953, when the National Electrical Manufacturers Association (NEMA) submitted to the Randall Commission an elaborate memorandum. It included an analysis of international trade in electrical apparatus and equipment, an examination of U. S. legislation, treaties and customs regulations, especially with regard to the Buy American Act, and a report by the Stone and Webster Engineering Corporation which compared unfavorably the "capability and reliability" of foreign-made heavy electrical equipment with that produced in the United States. With these reports the Association submitted to the Commission an "economic appraisal and interpretations" of the data prepared by Professor O. Glenn Saxon of Yale University. He found American tariffs inadequate to protect the electrical manufacturing industry's domestic market and urged "the elimination of the importation into the United States of all those custom-built items, having high labor content, such as heavy electrical machinery and equipment which are vital to the U. S. economy and national security." [18] This purpose, he suggested, might be accomplished by tariffs or quotas, or by broadening the philosophy of the Buy American Act and strengthening its administration to prohibit all federal imports of the undesirable items.

[17] *New York Times*, December 5, 1954.
[18] *The Foreign Trade Position of the United States and the Electrical Manufacturing Industry of the United States* (New Haven, 1953), p. 17.

Attitudes on Trade Agreements Act

At the 1955 hearings on the extension of the Trade Agreements Act, the two leading firms were found on opposite sides of the tariff fence. The chairman of the board of General Electric, Mr. Philip D. Reed, appeared as a proponent of the bill, H. R. 1. "In broad effect," he stated, "the General Electric Company favors . . . the extension of the Trade Agreements Act." [19] He qualified his favorable attitude only with respect to federal procurement of heavy electrical equipment. This area of foreign trade, he contended, because of its relation to national security should constitute an exception to the President's program of foreign aid and tariff reduction.

The Westinghouse Electric Corporation took its stand among the opponents of H. R. 1. Mr. Gwilym Price, president of the company, based his opposition to further reduction primarily on economic grounds. The American electrical manufacturing industry, he contended, was in a far worse competitive position vis-à-vis foreign firms than before World War II, because of increased productivity abroad and low wages, one-third to one-tenth the American rate. Mr. Price recognized that Westinghouse had a large stake in export trade but rejected the argument that imports paid for exports. "If we attempt to increase our exports by lowering tariffs on products which we make competitively here, we are simply giving benefits to certain industries at the expense of other American industries. . . ." [20] The lowering of tariffs in this country, he found, had not resulted in a liberalization of trade throughout the free world. "It is harder today to sell American-made electrical equipment in foreign countries that manufacture such equipment than it was either in the 1930's or just after the war." He criticized the State Department for having brought about reductions in our tariffs "in an unsuccessful effort to influence foreign governments, without obtaining comparable reciprocal action . . . and without ade-

[19] U. S. House, Committee on Ways and Means, *Trade Agreements Extension*, Hearings, 84th Cong., 1st sess., on H. R. 1 (Washington: GPO, 1955), p. 883.
[20] Same, p. 1058.

quate consideration of the impact of those tariff cuts on the domestic economy." [21]

Reference to national security came in the concluding portion of Mr. Price's statement. He criticized federal bidding techniques for failing to take into account "lower maintenance and repair, better service, better assurance of consistent power supply, and the vital defense aspect of the power industry. . . ." "The American industrial plant," he said, "is the keystone of our national defense. In turn this plant relies upon dependable sources of electric power. Therefore, our electric-power installations are as vital as tanks, battleships, and atomic bombs. As such they should no more be built and serviced by foreign suppliers than any other major weapons of war." Accordingly, he recommended that "no imports of power equipment should be permitted for use in critical installations." [22]

The Defense Argument

Spelled out in more detail, the "defense argument" as advanced by American manufacturers runs as follows:

(1) From the point of view of national defense, heavy electrical equipment is a critical commodity because of the need of maintaining at all times a supply of electric power adequate for defense industries and for the continued operation of the civilian economy.

(2) It is essential that federal agencies should buy their electrical equipment from domestic suppliers, since foreign suppliers are not in a position to furnish an adequate supply of qualified products. They operate on a smaller scale than do the large American firms,[23] and they have had little experience

---

[21] Same, pp. 1058, 1059.

[22] Same, p. 1060.

[23] The consolidated balance sheet of the principal British manufacturer, English Electric, covering operations in the United Kingdom, Canada, Australia and South Africa, showed assets of £70 million (about $200 million) in 1953. In that year, the Westinghouse balance sheet showed assets of $1,265 million; General Electric's assets were $1,697 million. No comparable figures are available for Brown Boveri, the leading electrical manufacturing firm in continental Europe. In its 27 manufacturing plants in eight European countries, Brown Boveri employed about 50,000 workers. The English Electric group of companies employed 65,000; Westinghouse, 113,000; and General Electric, 222,000.

in producing the largest types of equipment. For example, the largest generator built, before 1954, by the principal English firm was only one-third the size of the generators required at the McNary Dam. Giant electrical generators "defy extrapolation." Their construction involves totally new design and new principles of construction. Moreover, if war interfered with shipments of vital equipment from Europe, foreign manufacturers would be unable to make good on their commitments.

(3) Foreign-made equipment, it has been alleged, does not have the "capability or reliability" of equipment furnished by the American manufacturers. According to the Stone and Webster Engineering Corporation, in a survey prepared for NEMA, this is the "generally accepted opinion" of American engineers. But many qualified engineers do not share the opinion attributed to them, and some American manufacturers are not altogether satisfied with this statement issued in their behalf. As regards "capability" they agree. American equipment, they say, is designed to carry a 15 percent overload, while foreign equipment usually will carry the load specified in the contract, but no more. American firms admit that their own generators and other equipment have occasionally broken down, and they do not assert that the record of the foreign firms in this respect is any worse than theirs.

(4) In case of breakdown, foreign equipment cannot be promptly repaired. The foreign firms, they say, are not in a position to do the job. American firms would be handicapped if they attempted to set the foreign-made machinery in running order, because of fundamental differences in designs and materials, the unavailability of drawings and specifications, differences in units of measurement, and the lack of standardization of parts. Patterns and dies, they state, would be lacking for the construction of new parts for damaged machinery.

(5) When buying foreign electrical machinery, the U. S. government is taking the risk that essential parts might have been deliberately weakened by saboteurs inspired by Communist propaganda. Also, enemy agents in foreign countries might be able to get access to blueprints giving precise details of strategic installations. This knowledge would facilitate the bombing of American hydroelectric projects.

The Reply

Foreign firms deny these contentions. Their engineers, they assert, are as competent as the American to design the largest types of machines. They point to their long experience in equipping power plants in many parts of the world. They admit occasional failures of their equipment, as do American firms, but deny that their record is any worse than that of American manufacturers.

Two large foreign firms, English Electric and Brown Boveri, have factories in Canada which stock parts and have facilities adequate for many types of repairs. Repairs which they are not equipped to take care of could be handled by the American engineering firms with whom they have established connections. These firms the American electrical manufacturers often employ for rewinding coils and other repairs.

Repairs to their equipment, foreign firms say, will not be delayed by lack of detailed drawings and specifications. For every piece of heavy electrical equipment which it sells in the United States, the leading English firm claims that it keeps duplicate detailed drawings on microfilm in its New York and Toronto offices.

Confronted with the contradictory statements of the domestic and foreign parties at interest, the federal procurement authorities have favored the latter. American manufacturers have not been able to convince the U. S. Corps of Engineers, or other federal agencies, that purchases of the English, Swiss and other foreign equipment endanger national security. Responsible officials deny that in awarding contracts to foreign firms they have failed to properly safeguard the public interest. They assert that they have entertained bids only from firms, both foreign and domestic, whose experience had demonstrated their ability to furnish reliable products and to service them satisfactorily.

They point out that all federal power projects, with the possible exception of one hydroelectric plant in Alaska, are interconnected in networks with other hydro or steam plants. In the Pacific Northwest, for example, all the major utilities are connected in the Northwest Power Pool, with the federal transmission grid as the backbone. In such a network the failure of a single generating unit, even the largest, would cause the loss of only a small fraction, perhaps one percent, of the total power output, and stand-by thermal equipment is regularly available to take up the extra load until repairs can be made. Engineers in government employ recognize that a breakdown of any equipment, foreign or domestic, *if it resulted in prolonged interruption of service*, would be a serious matter, particularly in wartime. But, in their judgment, the chances that the foreign-made generators or transformers, etc. would be liable to failure and could not promptly be repaired are not great enough to justify refusing to purchase them.

The Buy American Act—Its History and Purpose

The policy of the federal government with respect to purchases of foreign-made goods is based on the Buy American Act of 1933 (Title III, Act of March 3, 47 Stat. 1520; 41 U. S. C. 10a-10c). It is a matter of some interest, in view of recent controversies, that manufacturers in Pennsylvania and California had urged Senator Hiram Johnson of California to introduce this legislation. Interested in obtaining contracts for supplying turbines and other equipment for the power plant at Boulder Dam (later renamed Hoover Dam), they feared they might be underbid by German or other foreign firms. But a reading of Senator Johnson's statement and of the ensuing debate does not reveal any mention of considerations of national security. Besides economic considerations, the Senator had in mind only retaliation against the Buy British policy introduced after World War I.[24]

The act of 1933 lays down the general principle that only goods produced in the United States shall be acquired for public use. Manufactured goods must be produced "substantially all from articles, materials, or supplies mined, produced, or manufactured . . . in the United States. . . ." Four important exceptions are provided: Purchasing officials may buy goods of foreign origin,

(1) When the purchase of domestic goods is inconsistent with the public interest;

[24] *Congressional Record*, 72d Cong., 2d sess., v. 3 (February 2, 1933), p. 3175.

(2) When the "articles, materials, or supplies," or their component materials, are not produced in the United States "in sufficient and reasonably available commercial quantities and of a satisfactory quality";

(3) When the cost of the domestic goods is unreasonable; or

(4) When the articles, etc., are to be used outside the United States.[25]

Over the past 20 years various federal agencies, for the guidance of their purchasing officers, have issued administrative orders, including comprehensive lists of articles not produced in the United States. The critical phrase, "unreasonable cost," was defined by the Procurement Division of the Treasury Department, in its circular of June 20, 1934, as a cost of 25 percent in excess of the foreign cost, except that on purchases where the foreign bid is less than $100, a differential of 100 percent should apply. Later, other government agencies adopted the 25 percent differential so that it became a standard formula.

The Act gave full discretion to heads of departments and other federal establishments to determine the circumstances under which purchases of domestic goods would be "inconsistent with the public interest." But for many years this provision was a dead letter. No agency seems to have justified its purchases of goods made abroad on the ground that it would have been contrary to the public interest to have procured them at home. But with the development of the Marshall Plan and later policies of aid to Western Europe, the public interest aspects of foreign procurement acquired new and growing significance. Since 1952, in Defense Department purchases, which are 80 percent of the federal total, the public interest clause has had top priority, overshadowing the calculations of price differentials.

The Department of Defense took the initiative in broadening the interpretation of the Buy American Act in its directive of May 27, 1952. It provided that in any case involving foreign bids where the differential was less than 25 percent, and the total amount involved was more than $25,000, the pro-

[25] Originally applying only to purchases for use of foreign missions and naval vessels visiting foreign ports, this exception has become of considerable importance in connection with "off-shore" procurement.

curement officers should refer the matter for consideration at the Secretarial level. In a second directive of June 19, 1952, William C. Foster, then Acting Secretary of Defense, was more explicit. The stated purpose of his directive was to assure that in making awards "due weight" would be given to the "objectives of the Mutual Security Program." Mr. Foster said:

For the Department of Defense adequately to support the Mutual Security Program and promote the mutual security of the United States and other friendly countries, it is requested that competitive bids from sources in the United States and friendly foreign countries be considered on a common basis, this being consonant with the public interest.[26]

The Acting Secretary did not define his ambiguous phrase, "on a common basis," but his directive went far in giving specific content to the public interest clause. He instructed purchasing agents to take into account both "strategic considerations" and "domestic economic considerations." Under the first heading they had to examine the reliability of foreign sources of supply, depending (a) on their productive capacity and (b) on their possible location "in an area where political or economic instability might hinder production or delivery." On the other hand he called their attention, in somewhat indirect fashion, to the possible logistical advantage of maintaining or increasing production capacity in a friendly foreign country. To harmonize these objectives was a formidable task. The procurement officers were required, also, to consider, before making their recommendations, whether the "articles, materials, supplies or their related U. S. production facilities are of such strategic importance that domestic self-sufficiency must be fostered." [27]

Under "domestic economic considerations," purchasing officials were directed to inquire whether buying scarce materials from domestic sources would unduly interfere with U. S. military production. They were to consider whether domestic bidders were entitled to special consideration as "small businesses," and also whether their plants were situated

[26] U. S. Department of Defense, Directive No. 4105.22.
[27] Same.

in an area of substantial labor surplus, and finally whether their industry was in a depressed condition or was characterized by "widespread open capacity." Obviously, this comprehensive directive, which governed only the Defense Department's purchases, was susceptible to a wide variety of interpretations. It remained in effect until December 1954 when it was superseded by a Presidential Executive Order, to be discussed later.

The Bureau of Reclamation (Department of the Interior) in its purchases of heavy electrical equipment adhered to the regulations of the General Services Administration which governed also the buying of all other civilian departments and establishments. The G.S.A. regulations specified that a differential of 25 percent should be applied in favor of domestic products, except when the cost of the product was less than $100. Then the differential should be 100 percent. The Bureau required that the U. S. import duty should be excluded from the foreign price before computing the differential, whereas the practice of the Defense Department had been to include the duty. The latter procedure favored domestic bidders by lessening the disparity between their bids and those of the foreign competitors.

The G.S.A. regulations gave purchasing agents of the Bureau of Reclamation no guidance in interpreting the phrase, "the public interest." Hence, in its awards, the Bureau adhered rigidly to economic factors. Its treatment of foreign bidders, consequently, was somewhat less liberal than that of the U. S. Corps of Engineers. Taking into account the public interest, the latter at times awarded contracts to foreign firms whose bids were only 19 to 17 percent less than those of domestic manufacturers.

Dissatisfaction with the Buy American Policy

In several years of controversy over the Buy American Act, particularly in 1952-1954, it would be difficult to detect a single note of approval. On grounds of economy, advocates of freer trade have condemned the Act's basic principle, i.e., discrimination in favor of domestic producers in the purchase of supplies for government use. But the domestic suppliers themselves were not satisfied. They complained, especially

those who lost federal business to foreign firms which underbid them, that federal procurement officers had not discrimi-
nated enough in their favor. British manufacturers complained
that the Buy American Act had kept them out of a profitable
American market. They contrasted their exports to the
United States with sales to Canada where they encountered
no similar handicap.[28] They were confused by the divergent
procurement policies of various federal agencies. Even within
a single agency they found a lack of consistent practices. Administrative officials, they asserted, were influenced by changes
in the political climate in Washington and were amenable
to pressures exerted indirectly by domestic manufacturers
through their Congressmen.

The Buy American Act has been condemned from the
point of view of general foreign economic policy. The American Farm Bureau Federation has called it "one of the major
stumbling blocks thwarting a sound two-way trade between
this country and its allies." [29] President Gordon Gray of the
University of North Carolina, in his 1950 Report to the President, found the Buy American principle "in direct conflict
with the basic foreign economic policies of the United States.
. . ." [30] On this ground, and because the Act of 1933 prevented military procurement officers and government contractors from buying goods where they could be obtained
most quickly and most cheaply, his Report urged Congress to
repeal the legislation. The Bell report (1953) found that Buy
American restrictions raised government costs by establishing
a "super tariff" on goods purchased for public use, and recommended that the necessity for the restrictions should be considered.[31]

The staff of the Randall Commission estimated that the Buy
American policy was costing American taxpayers as much as
$100 million each year, in higher prices paid by government

[28] See *The Banker* (December 1953), p. 358.
[29] In *The Nation's Agriculture*, as reprinted in *Congressional Record*, 83rd
Cong., 1st sess., v. 99, pt. 12 (August 3, 1953), p. A5077.
[30] *Report to the President on Foreign Economic Policies* (Washington:
GPO, 1950), p. 84.
[31] Public Advisory Board for Mutual Security, *A Trade and Tariff Policy
in the National Interest* (Washington: Author, 1953), p. 5.

purchasing agents for domestic goods, plus an additional $100 million in loss of customs revenue which would have been collected had the goods been imported. The Commission, in its majority report, advised that the Buy American Act, and similar provisions of other acts, be amended so as to permit the President to apply the legislation on a reciprocal basis, exempting from its provisions "bidders from other nations that treat our bidders on an equal basis with their own nationals."[32] The Commission recommended that, meanwhile, a more liberal policy be adopted in the administration of the 1933 Act.

The application of Buy American policies to government purchases of heavy electrical equipment occasioned critical comment both at home and abroad. American legislators denounced administrative officers for having favored foreign bidders too much. Senator Malone of Nevada found that federal awards of electrical equipment to English and Swiss firms had been responsible, in part at least, for 136,500 employees in American electrical manufacturing factories being out of work. On the grounds of public interest he saw no justification for awarding contracts to Swiss firms. Switzerland, he pointed out, was not threatened by Communism.[33]

Congressman Shelley, of California, complained that the State Department applied pressure on administrators to award a contract for hydraulic governors to a Japanese firm. On this contract the successful Japanese bid was $1,073,522, about $250,000 under the lowest American bid. To prevent the recurrence of such an award, the Congressman introduced a bill which would have prohibited any federal agency from purchasing from foreign firms any equipment used in producing, controlling, distributing, modifying or rectifying electrical energy.[34] The bill allowed only one exception. When the material desired could not be readily obtained in satisfactory quality from domestic sources, it might be bought from for-

[32] Commission on Foreign Economic Policy, *Report to the President and the Congress* (Washington: GPO, 1954), p. 45.

[33] *Congressional Record*, 83rd Cong., 2d sess., v. 100, pt. 5 (May 18, 1954), p. 6758.

[34] H. R. 9696, 83rd Cong., 2d sess. See *Congressional Record*, 83rd Cong., 2d sess., v. 100, pt. 7 (June 28, 1954), p. 9098.

eign firms. No provision was made for the comparison of domestic and foreign prices.

Congressman Hays of Ohio introduced a letter from a constituent (R. Thomas & Sons of Lisbon, Ohio) protesting against the award of a contract of 100,000 suspension insulators for the Bonneville Dam to a Japanese firm. The contract, the Ohio firm complained, would establish a dangerous precedent. "Up to this time the Japanese have not successfully invaded our American market." [35] The firm said that the United States government should not break this barrier with its purchases.

Representative Smith of Mississippi, on the other hand, complained that the Buy American Act protects excessive profits of domestic manufacturers of electrical equipment. The Act, he said, imposed a super duty on top of the import duty, thus depriving the American consumer of the "traditional benefits of competition that have made our economy strong." [36]

Economic considerations, not national defense, formed the basis of the protest of a vice president of Westinghouse. In a letter introduced by Senator Malone in the *Congressional Record* [37] he argued as follows: The purchase by a federal agency of a large transformer from the English Electric Company for the Folsom Dam in California meant the loss of $1 million in wages and salaries to Westinghouse employees and officers. The government lost $600,000 in taxes which the company would have paid had it won the award. The stockholders lost prospective dividends. From these facts he concluded that the U. S. government, and the national economy, suffered a net loss from buying the cheaper foreign equipment. His reasoning, however, neglected two important considerations: (1) Westinghouse's export sales, as well as its domestic business, generate taxable income; and (2) foreigners cannot buy American goods unless they can sell their products for dollars. The apparent gain in taxable income through the award of federal contracts to American bidders was offset,

[35] *Congressional Record*, 83rd Cong., 1st sess., v. 99, pt. 12 (July 30, 1953), p. A4841.

[36] Same, 83rd Cong., 1st sess., v. 99, pt. 5 (June 4, 1953), p. 6087; *New York Times*, July 23, 1953.

[37] 83rd Cong., 2d sess., v. 100, pt. 5 (May 18, 1954), p. 6757.

and probably more than offset, by the loss of taxes on income which would have been produced by export business.

The President's New Directive

The 1953 Chief Joseph awards, which we discussed at the beginning of this chapter, brought to a climax the mounting demand for reform of Buy American practices. The President, however, took no action until December 17, 1954, when he issued his Executive Order No. 10582. To ensure uniformity he made the order applicable to all executive agencies, including executive departments, independent establishments and other instrumentalities of the executive branch of the government. It superseded all previous directives of these agencies relating to the interpretation of the Buy American Act.

The President, it seems, had intended not only to bring order out of the chaos of conflicting directives but also to liberalize the administration of the Act, making it somewhat easier for foreign bidders to secure federal contracts. Previously, procurement officials, in determining whether the price of a domestic article was unreasonable, had added a 25 percent differential to the foreign price. In other words, if the domestic price was less than 125 percent of the foreign price there was a prima facie case for buying from the domestic source. The new directive cut this margin to 6 percent of the foreign price, inclusive of the estimated import duty and costs, or 10 percent, excluding the duty and all costs incurred after arrival in the United States.[38]

If purchasing agents had been authorized to make their decisions on price differences alone, the new order would have given foreign firms cause to rejoice. But Section 3 of the Executive Order opened a wide door for rejection of foreign bids on grounds of national interest and national security. It authorized awards to a domestic bidder in order that "a fair proportion of the total purchases" may be placed with small business, or because he (being the lowest domestic bidder) offers to produce practically all of the desired materials in areas of substantial unemployment. Prices may not be entirely disregarded. The directive provides that nothing in this section (i.e., that dealing with the public interest) "shall prevent

[38] On bids of less than $25,000, only the duty is excluded.

the rejection of a bid . . . which is excessive. . . ." But it did not define "excessive."

In the final section of his directive (Section 5), the President gave notice that he intended to concentrate in his office responsibility for awards which, on grounds either of public interest or of national security, disregarded price differences. He required all procurement officers who award or reject bids on these grounds to submit the pertinent facts to him within 30 days.

The President failed to include, among the grounds for the rejection of a domestic bid, the promotion of "the mutual security" of friendly countries. In this respect, the new order seems a retreat from the Foster memorandum of June 19, 1952.

Whether or not the Executive Order will prove a significant move in the direction of lowering trade barriers will depend in large measure on the President. If his subordinates are convinced that he will back them up, they will interpret the Act in accordance with their best judgment, independent of outside pressures. This may not mean, however, an increase in the number of large awards of federal contracts to foreign firms. Instead, we may find that domestic bidders, feeling the spur of foreign competition, may lower their prices. For example, in 1954 General Electric underbid all competitors, domestic and foreign, on one of the biggest of recent federal contracts, for equipment for the Dalles Dam hydroelectric project in Oregon. For eight generators to be delivered in 1959, the General Electric bid was $11 million, which was more than $2 million under the lowest foreign bid, that of English Electric. The Allis-Chalmers Manufacturing Company was the low bidder on two turbines for the Dalles Dam, and Westinghouse on two generators for Table Rock Dam, when their bids were, respectively, 16 and 3 percent lower than the lowest foreign bid. For the St. Lawrence River Project, Allis-Chalmers' bid on 13 transformers was more than $200,000 below the lowest foreign bid.

What the Federal Business Means to the American Industry

Of the 4,000 American manufacturers of electrical machinery and equipment, not more than 25, including the three leading firms, General Electric, Westinghouse and Allis-Chalmers, have recently entered bids for federal contracts. Compared with the annual total sales of the larger group, in the neighborhood of $16 billion, the amount of federal purchases of heavy electrical equipment in recent years—$43 million in 1952 and $26 million in 1953—seems inconsiderable. Moreover, the biggest slice of the market lost to foreign firms in any recent year was only $10.3 million in 1953. Viewing these figures in their relation to the total operations of the 25 American firms, one wonders why they have shown such concern over the award of a few contracts to English, Swiss and other foreign manufacturers.

The importance of the federal contracts appears more clearly when the industry is broken down into individual concerns. Except for the Big Three, the firms which have bid on federal contracts are specialists. Some make only transformers, others water wheels, etc. For one of these firms, whose annual sales may not exceed $20 or $30 million, a million-dollar contract, or even a half-million-dollar job, is worth fighting for. Even for one of the big diversified firms, whose total annual sales may exceed $1,000 million, federal contracts are important. The large firms are really aggregations of many divisions, each of which has its own accounting system. The division which makes hydraulic generators, for example, is expected to pay its own way. Since each piece of equipment of this size requires many months for its production, a continuous flow of orders is essential.

The Threat of Excess Capacity

In late 1953 and early 1954, when domestic manufacturers were registering strong complaints against federal awards to foreign firms, they either had excess capacity in the plants making heavy equipment, or were threatened with this condition. They had enlarged their facilities in order to take care of the postwar buying spree of the public utilities, but the end of that spree seemed in sight. In November 1953 the Edison Electric Institute reported: "Orders for new equipment are falling off rapidly and backlogs are being reduced." [39] Six

[39] Edison Electric Institute, *Fourteenth Semi-Annual Electric Power Survey* (New York: Author, November 1953), p. 1.

months later the situation was still worse. At a time when the equipment manufacturing industry was geared for the highest production rate in history, it was faced with an "almost complete drop-off in new orders." "During the six-month period ending April 1, 1954, the total capacity of large steam turbine-generators ordered was about 10 percent of the capacity shipped during the same period. In the case of generators for hydraulic turbines, the ratio was about 3 percent, and for hydraulic turbines 6 percent." [40]

Beginning about the middle of 1954, the rate of ordering new equipment moved sharply upwards. As of April 1955, the Edison Electric Institute reported that the capacity of generators for hydraulic turbines placed on order during the past six months exceeded that ordered during the previous two and one-half years. The gains, however, were not sufficient to absorb total manufacturing capacity in this and other types of heavy equipment. Manufacturers can now produce generators for hydraulic turbines at the rate of 3,000,000 kilowatts per year. Their 1955 business occupied about half their productive facilities, and the outlook for 1956 was not much better. In this situation it is natural that they should be eager to obtain federal contracts to help them carry their heavy burden of overhead costs.

Impact of Imports on Prices

The impact of imports of heavy equipment, like other imports, on domestic business cannot be measured merely by the quantity of goods brought into the domestic market. One must take account also of the effect on prices. In the case of government purchases of heavy electrical equipment, foreign competition exerts a maximum effect on domestic prices. The bids of both the foreign and domestic companies on identical items are public property. Domestic firms, in order to obtain the federal business, are occasionally forced to cut prices to the bone. The effects of price-cutting on federal contracts, manufacturers fear, will not be limited to that sector alone of their domestic market; it may result in weakening the price structure in the vastly more important private enterprise sec-

[40] *Fifteenth Semi-Annual Electric Power Survey* (New York: Author, May 1954), p. 13.

tor. In this sector, made up very largely of sales of heavy equipment to privately owned power plants, prices have long displayed remarkable stability, as is to be expected in a branch of industry where a few large firms do a large proportion of the total business. They compete, normally, not by under-bidding each other's prices, but by offering their customers better service and additional "gadgets." The lean business of 1954, however, seems to have been responsible for the short-lived price war which broke out in early 1955. In this "January white sale" the three complete-line companies slashed their prices on major items, generators, transformers, etc., in some cases as much as 35 percent. Purchasing agents for public utilities across the country were able for a few weeks to pick up amazing bargains.[41]

The Outlook for Hydroelectric Power

In 1953 the power systems brought into service 118 thermal units with a capacity of 8.6 million kilowatts. In that year 54 hydro plants were added with a capacity of only 1.6 million. Prospects for a large expansion in the American market for hydroelectric equipment over the next 20 or 30 years are not bright. A substantial increase in the demand for electric energy is predicted over the next 20 years, from installations developing atomic power for military and civilian use, from the rapidly expanding chemical industry, from the metal industries and for air conditioning and space heating. But the sources of this new power will be thermal stations, not hydroelectric plants.

Optimistic estimates of the potential water power resources of the United States must be received with caution. The development of many sites, where physical conditions appear favorable, would be uneconomic, because of distance from population centers and other markets for electric energy. When allowance is made for the loss of energy in transmission, the cost of hydroelectric power from these sources would exceed that generated from coal or oil. Finally, power from atomic fission, we are told, is just around the corner. Considerations such as these probably inspired the estimate

[41] See *Business Week* (February 19, 1955); *Wall Street Journal*, March 17, 1955.

of the Edison Electric Institute which stated: "It is almost certain that thermal generating units will constitute upwards of 90 per cent of the generating capacity to be installed in the next quarter century. This is because practically all the economic hydro sites have been developed in areas reasonably close to the heavy population centers, and particularly in the eastern part of the country." [42]

*   *   *

A small group of American firms have made large investments in specialized facilities for the production of hydroelectric equipment of giant capacity. The market for this equipment, which has never been extensive, is now seen to have only limited possibilities for future expansion. This fact is fundamental in explaining the manufacturers' strong protests against federal purchases of foreign equipment, and their demand for strict enforcement of Buy American policies.

[42] Edison Electric Institute, *Looking Ahead to the Last Quarter of the First Century of Electric Power in the United States,* 22nd Annual Convention (June 1-3, 1954), pp. 9-10.

Chapter 10

INJURY AND ADJUSTMENT

THE Trade Agreements Act sponsored by Cordell Hull has been regarded at home and abroad as a turning point in American tariff policy. The bilateral and multilateral agreements concluded with foreign governments under its authority have reduced American import duties on thousands of commodities. Statistical measurements of the height of tariffs are particularly imperfect, but it is probably safe to say that in 20 years tariff bargaining has cut the average level of the American tariff in half. In view of a long protectionist tradition reaching back for almost a century this is a remarkable accomplishment. Equally remarkable is the lack of resistance offered until recently by protected interests.

A number of circumstances rendered the tariff-cutting in this period practically painless. The State Department's negotiators, keeping in mind repeated assurances from the White House that no American industries would be injured, avoided cutting too deeply the duties on commodities known to be sensitive, politically. Also they have taken care, by various devices, to limit their concessions as far as possible to countries not regarded as dangerous competitors.

It should also be noted that domestic industries have retained practically intact the protection afforded by customs regulations and other features of our "invisible tariff." The Trade Agreements Act of 1934 gave the President no authority to simplify cumbersome procedures for entering foreign goods, or to change methods of valuation. In the Customs Administrative Act of 1938 and in the Customs Simplification Acts of 1953 and 1954, Congress made a number of changes designed to reduce the expense and delays in clearing merchandise through customs and in eliminating sources of inequity and annoyance to importers. The 1954 Act amended the Antidumping Act of 1921, removing some of the features which had proved burdensome to importers. The 1954 Act also directed the Tariff Commission to undertake a two-year study of the classification of imported merchandise. But on the major question, the valuation of imports, Congress has been unable, or unwilling, to legislate. Disputes over valuation and classification remain sources of delay and litigation which add to the importers' costs of doing business.

Postwar Opposition to Trade Agreements

The interruption of import trade during World War II acted as a super tariff which in effect nullified concessions made in trade agreements. The small quantities of imports which immediately after the war began to reappear in domestic markets caused little disturbance, for American manufacturers often were unable to satisfy the backlog of demand which had accumulated in the war years. But soon the situation changed. The industries of the United Kingdom, West Germany and other countries of Western Europe, having revived with the aid of Marshall Plan funds, began to send increased quantities of their goods to the United States. Imports of manufactured goods, in general, increased more rapidly than sales of domestic factory products. In some cases domestic production actually fell as the result of contraction from wartime expansion. Under these conditions the impact of foreign competition became noticeable, and complaints of injury were heard. The 1945 extension of the Trade Agreements Act occasioned practically no debate in Congress, but later renewals of the Act, beginning in 1947, met with progressively greater opposition from protectionist elements in both political parties. President Eisenhower, in 1953 and 1954, obtained with great difficulty one-year extensions of the program. In 1955 the alliance of producers of raw materials (oil, coal, copper, lead, zinc and wool) with textile producers and small manufacturing industries created a protectionist opposition stronger than any in the preceding 20 years. The President obtained a three-year extension of the Act, but had to accept curtailment of his tariff-reducing powers.

The rising tide of Congressional opposition to the Trade Agreements Act contrasted sharply with the trend in public opinion toward freer trade.

A 1953 survey conducted by the Council on Foreign Relations among leaders of opinion in 25 cities showed that a substantial majority of the 825 respondents believed that import duties should be reduced, even at the cost of injury to protected industries. The opinion of the 360 businessmen in the group did not diverge greatly from the rest of the sample. Similar results are shown by the Research Institute of America's recent poll of 500 business and labor leaders. Sixty percent favored further lowering of tariffs. When asked whether tariffs should be lowered "despite the possibility of injury to the particular American industries involved" 44 percent said "yes"; 35 percent "no"; and 21 percent were unsure.[1]

The study of business opinion conducted in 1954 by the Center for International Studies of the Massachusetts Institute of Technology and the National Opinion Research Center[2] confirms the findings of earlier, less systematic inquiries. Of the 903 business executives interviewed in the M.I.T. survey:

    5 percent favored raising tariffs;
    38 percent would lower them;
    31 percent would leave them at present levels;
    22 percent answered "don't know"; and
    4 percent refused to generalize.

Some 300 executives said that they had changed their minds about tariffs during or since World War II; more than three-fourths of them had changed in the direction of freer trade. "Businessmen," according to this survey, "are today less inclined to want increased tariff protection for American products than are the general run of their fellow citizens." [3] The interviewers reported that the business community, *in general*, viewed the tariff as one of its less pressing problems, rating it lower in importance than taxes, labor relations and political stability abroad. But the tariff is a local issue. Some business firms feel strongly that imports threaten their existence. Congressmen and Senators are more sensitive to their wishes than to the results of public opinion polls.

[1] Percy W. Bidwell, "The Tariff in Transition," *Foreign Affairs*, v. 32, no. 3 (April 1954), p. 465.
[2] Raymond A. Bauer, Susanne Keller and Ithiel de Sola Pool, *What Foreign Trade Policy Does American Business Want?* (Cambridge: M.I.T. Center for International Studies, 1955).
[3] Same, p. 3.

Concern for protected industries is not the sole reason why Senators and Representatives have opposed the trade agreements program. Some have long been committed in principle to protectionism. Others object to tariff-making by an administrative agency, in this case the State Department. They have never been reconciled to the fact that changes in tariff rates can now be made without Congressional approval.

Since 1948 the escape clause provisions in the Trade Agreements Act have provided a procedure by which firms or industries injured by tariff reduction can voice their complaints and demand relief. Yet the Tariff Commission has not been swamped with applications. It has found cause for action in only a few cases. The record from April 1948 through March 1956 was as follows:

Total number of escape clause applications 74
Number of applications withdrawn or dismissed 21

Tariff Commission action:
   No increase recommended 26
   Increased duty recommended 17
   Quotas recommended 3

Presidential action:
   Tariff Commission recommendation rejected 12
   Tariff Commission recommendation accepted 7

Cases pending:
   Before the Commission 7
   Before the President 8

Undoubtedly the expense of preparing an application and presenting it effectively before the Commission deterred many potential complainants. Many also must have been discouraged by the small proportion of successful applications.

Tests of Injury

To demonstrate that any industry has actually suffered as the result of import competition is not an easy task. The mere fact that imports have been increasing is not conclusive. When the domestic market expands, both imports and domestic production rise and American firms prosper. Automobile manufacturers, for example, do not complain of the rapid increase in imports of foreign-made automobiles. Where the magnitudes are more nearly equal, and growth of the imports exceeds that of the domestic industry, the latter may allege that it has suffered injury because its share of the domestic market is less.

Jeweled-lever watches furnish an illustration. The American market has taken, on the average, about 10 million watches per year in the last five years; in prewar years the annual average was about 3.6 million. The increase has been very largely supplied by watches with Swiss movements. Over the 20 years the output of American manufacturers did not decline, but their share of the market fell considerably. Does this constitute injury? On this question the Tariff Commission disagreed. A minority held that the Swiss had created a new market in the United States and that American firms could not have been injured by failing to get something which they had never possessed. The majority decided otherwise, and Congress, in an amendment to the 1955 act extending the trade agreements legislation, supported it.

The determination whether an industry has been damaged by imports involves a comparison of its present state with its condition in some previous period. But what period? During World War II, and even in 1946 and 1947 before foreign competition revived, some American industries, household china, for example, supplied the bulk of the domestic market, whereas in prewar years they had had only a small share. Then, with the return of more normal conditions abroad, imports reappeared in the American market, displacing the domestic product. If one considers only the postwar years, a case may be made for injury, but in the longer view it is clear that the foreign producers were only regaining a position established in the years before the war.

The administrator and the legislator have to distinguish, also, between injury caused by imports and injury arising from changes in domestic conditions of supply and demand. When business is bad, American firms are tempted to make a scapegoat of foreign competition, although their difficulties may have arisen primarily from domestic causes. Our case studies abound in illustrations of this truth. We found that advances in the methods of blowing glass tableware by machinery robbed the hand plants of a large share of their domestic market. The makers of household chinaware suffered from the inroads of attractively designed earthenware of domestic origin. The introduction of new synthetic fibers and blends of wool and synthetics, together with revolutionary changes in techniques of spinning, has upset the woolen and worsted industry far more than the revival of imports from the United Kingdom and other foreign sources. Changing American habits of living and working have reduced the sales of glassware, chinaware and woolens and worsteds.

Let us assume that an industry has passed all the tests of real injury. The tariff has been reduced, imports have increased, and domestic production and employment are falling. Profits, as far as can be ascertained, are below the level of other manufacturing industries. But an economist would want to inquire further. He would ask whether the various firms in the industry were conducting their affairs efficiently. He would want to know what efforts they were making to reduce costs or otherwise to improve their position vis-à-vis their foreign competitors. In other words, he would be curious about the possibilities of economic adjustment without tariff help.

The Experience of Individual Firms

Injury and adjustment, although for the sake of convenience we deal with them separately, are in fact interdependent. For the degree of injury sustained by any firm depends upon its success or failure in adjustment. The reader should note the emphasis on the individual business enterprise. In exceptional cases, for reasons of national defense, the purpose of tariff protection may be to guarantee the production in this country of specific commodities. But usually the policy is directed to maintaining the prosperity of a group of business firms. It is important to note that within an industry each firm differs from another in its ability to cope with new developments, whether in domestic or foreign competition. Within the scope of this study it has been impossible to analyze in detail the operations of giant corporations, comparing one with another. But our studies of import-sensitive industries, in which small firms are typical, have revealed striking differences in the capacity of business enterprises to survive, and even to prosper, in the face of import competition.

In woolens and worsteds, some companies in postwar years continued to earn profits and enlarged their operations while others went into liquidation. While the Waltham Watch Company was undergoing a series of reorganizations, Elgin, Hamilton and Bulova showed increased earnings. Among ten manufacturers of bicycles, five were operating profitably in 1954, one of the worst years in the history of the industry; two of the smaller firms were doing exceptionally well. In the branch of the glassware industry which makes hand-fashioned articles, five or six substantial concerns did not suffer from the depression which affected other firms. The Tariff Commission found wide variation in profits earned in postwar years by ten manufacturers of household china; half of them at least had no unsatisfactory profit experience, and two regularly made substantial profits.

The Process of Economic Adjustment

Economic adjustment is a new note among the familiar themes of tariff controversy. But the process is not new in American economic history. The building of the Erie Canal and later the railroads forced New England farmers to abandon wheat and wool growing and to migrate westward, or to seek industrial employment in the expanding urban communities nearer home. All the great labor-saving inventions, from the spinning jenny to electronic computers, have forced some employers to seek new products and some workers to find new jobs. Changes in methods of production and the introduction of new products have changed the economy of whole regions. Shifts of population have left some communities stranded (ghost towns) while boom towns have sprung up in new locations. The conversion of large sectors of American industry from civilian to defense production in 1918, and again in 1941, and the reconversions which followed in postwar years are illustrations on a monumental scale of adjustments to economic change.

With this dynamic background, Americans have come to regard economic change—even rapid change—as normal. The resulting disturbances and injuries suffered by firms and industries we accept as necessary features of our system of free, competitive enterprise. We rely on the mobility of our labor force and the ingenuity of our businessmen to minimize the transitional losses. Unavoidable losses we regard as far outbalanced by the gains to the community from cheaper and better services and commodities.

Compared with the disturbances in the home market which have been brought about and are still in process—by technological change and by the shift of industries to new areas—increased competition from abroad is a small matter. Would, for example, the effects of freer international trade be as revolutionary as the advent of the automobile? According to one estimate, less than one million jobs in the United States are clearly dependent on continued tariff protection. Yet every month, "in the great churning of our industrial process, some two million workers change their jobs, mostly of their own volition." [4]

Nevertheless, the individual manufacturer and his employees who are threatened, or feel threatened, with foreign competition fail to be impressed by this general reasoning. Invasion of their markets by producers *in other regions in the United States*, although unwelcome, is unavoidable, but competition from abroad is a horse of an entirely different color. Foreign manufacturers are not subject to domestic labor legislation, or to our antitrust laws. They are suspected, in addition, of receiving subsidies from their governments in one form or another. Hence, their competition is often labeled "unfair."

Against foreign competition, also, there is available a defense, viz., the tariff, which cannot be employed within the United States. No matter how much a New England manufacturer may resent the competition of cheap cotton goods from South Carolina, there is little he can do about it, as long as the constitutional guarantee of free trade among the states of the Union remains in force. His only remedy[5] is to reduce his costs in manufacturing and marketing, to diversify his products or, as a last resort, to transfer his capital and managerial ability to some less vulnerable line of business.

[4] John K. Jessup and Michael A. Heilperin, "A New, Daring Plan to Unshackle Trade and Enrich the Free World," *Life* (January 4, 1954), p. 59.
[5] Aside from federal minimum-wage legislation.

Economic disturbances usually have multiple causes. It would be difficult to find any industry, or branch of industry, which is suffering solely from foreign competition. Changed conditions of domestic demand or new sources of domestic supply often bear a considerable measure of responsibility. But, in general, the problems of adjustment are similar, whether the causes of dislocation are to be found in changed conditions of foreign or domestic competition.

Methods of adjustment fall into two main groups: (1) self-help, i.e., methods by which firms, or groups of firms, adapt their business operations so as to deal effectively with new competitive situations; (2) activities of state and local bodies, public and private, and federal agencies in assisting business firms and communities to deal with economic dislocation.

Opportunities for Cost Reduction

In a free economy, such as the United States, the forces of competition continuously operate to bring about more efficient methods of production and market distribution. American manufacturers throughout our history have been famous for their ingenuity in reducing costs by substituting power-driven machinery for hand labor. In electrical manufacturing, in chemicals, in iron and steel, success has been achieved in the low-cost production of standardized commodities for a wide market. And even in small-scale manufacturing there are opportunities for cost reduction; for example, in making hand-fashioned glass one firm has achieved substantial economies in labor costs through time and motion studies. But, in general, import-sensitive industries of this type will find the best prospects for economic adjustment in increased attention to analysis of consumers' demand, to the study of the changing characteristics of the market, in an attempt to discover effective ways of exploiting its possibilities in competition with foreign firms. Thus success in developing new designs explains why some chinaware firms, particularly on the west coast, were building up their business while others were going downhill.

Diversification

Diversification of products into lines not subject to import competition was urged by the staff of the Randall Commission as the "most satisfactory form of adjustment." This recommendation has received support from the Committee for Economic Development and from other advocates of freer trade. Specialists in market research advise that business firms threatened by fluctuations in the business cycle, changes in demand and technological innovations should explore systematically the possibilities of product diversification. A firm may undertake the manufacture of new items which it can produce with its present facilities and market with its established organization, or it may invest surplus funds in an entirely new field. Our case studies show that both types of diversification have been introduced by firms subject to import competition. Their experience, however, and that of other firms engaged in domestic business, indicates that diversification cannot be considered a "sure-fire" remedy for all cases of injury arising from a changing market situation. The successful selection of new products requires elaborate studies of market possibilities as well as of production techniques. Not all injured firms will be able to command the necessary financial resources and managerial skills.

The recent difficulties of American bicycle manufacturers were in some measure due to their tardiness in recognizing the new trend toward the lightweight machine. Somewhat earlier the manufacturers of jeweled-lever watches suffered because they were slower than the Swiss in grasping the potentialities of the American market for new types of watches in the medium-price range. American firms making labor-intensive commodities, unable to reduce their costs *on identical products* to the level of competitors in low-wage countries, found their only recourse was to avoid head-on collision with imports, offering their customers something distinctive, which usually has meant something more expensive. Thus the Steuben firm, by concentrating on glass of the highest quality, has become immune to foreign competition. The manufacturers of Lenox china are in a similarly happy situation.

Practically all manufacturers of bicycles use their facilities in the off-season to make other products—lawn mowers, air conditioning appartus, equipment for gasoline service stations, etc. Some woolen and worsted mills make automobile fabrics as well as apparel cloths; others are weaving synthetic and blended fabrics. Makers of hand-fashioned glass are experimenting with fiber glass. Some manufacturers of fine household china also make hotel ware, a product less vulnerable to import competition. In addition to defense items, the watch companies are engaged in making watch cases and bracelets, men's jewelry and electronic apparatus. But "divergent" diversification of this sort, although it may enable bicycle manufacturers or watch makers to survive when menaced by foreign competition, does not guarantee the continued production of bicycles or watches in this country.

Some Manufacturers Are Also Importers

The same observation applies to the combination of importing with manufacturing, another kind of adjustment adopted by various firms under pressure from imports. Congressmen are sometimes surprised in tariff hearings to learn that the manufacturer who is complaining of injury from imports is himself engaged in importing. All four American manufacturers of jeweled-lever watches are now importing Swiss watch movements, which they put in cases and sell either under their own or another trade name. Several domestic bicycle manufacturers have made arrangements with English or other foreign firms to market their machines in this country. American producers of dyestuffs are also engaged in importing.

Logically, it may seem difficult to reconcile importing with manufacturing and the advocacy of higher import duties, but it nevertheless can make sense from the point of view of practical business. As a rule the manufacturer is principally interested in manufacturing. Importing is a side line which enables him to offer his customers a more complete line of products, including items which he can acquire abroad more cheaply than he could make in his American factory. This device enables him to keep his marketing organization fully occupied. It is obvious, however, that importing, if carried far, adversely affects the interests of factory workers.

Assisted Adjustment: Needs and Objectives

Methods of self-help such as we have described will not always provide adequate remedies for injury from foreign competition.

While American industry in general had extensive experience in diversifying its products to meet economic dislocation from various sources, there is little doubt that many marginal firms in import-sensitive industries would have trouble adjusting to increased imports. Most of these industries have been in a long-term decline, and are characterized by weak financial situations, severe seasonal or cyclical unemployment, and wages below national levels that obtain in growing industries. The smaller firms would find it particularly difficult to adjust to further dislocation from import competition. If they were to follow the example of the larger companies which have successfully met the same problems, many of them would probably need technical assistance—marketing analysts and production engineers—to aid in determining what new products to manufacture. Excellent assistance is available from private sources, but generally proves too expensive for small companies to bear without assistance. Many would also need additional financing to help pay for the new machinery that any conversion would require. Many would not have the background of earnings to qualify for financing entirely from private sources. Therefore, Government help aimed at assisting with adaptation to future needs, not at compensating for past losses, might be useful.[6]

When an import-sensitive industry, such as woolens and worsteds, fine china or hand-fashioned glass, furnishes the sole, or the predominant, source of employment in a community, tariff reduction may threaten economic dislocation. This, however, is not peculiarly a tariff problem. Overspecialization in one product renders a community vulnerable to any sudden change, no matter whether it originates abroad or at home. And in both cases the same remedy may be applied, viz., industrial diversification, the creation of new opportunities for employment by broadening the community's industrial base.

New England in the past 25 years has furnished a striking example of economic dislocation and adjustment on a regional scale. The decline of the textile industry and the failure of other manufacturing to keep pace with national growth have been the subjects of much discussion, with differing interpre-

[6] Commission on Foreign Economic Policy, *Staff Papers* (Washington: GPO, 1954), pp. 386-387. An early suggestion for government aid to injured industries will be found in Eugene Staley's *World Economic Development* (Montreal: International Labour Office, 1944), ch. 11.

tations and suggested remedies.[7] Recent developments in this region seem to have disproved the prophets of doom. Dr. Alfred C. Neal, a capable and well-informed observer, has concluded that "the surface manifestations that have been interpreted as evidence of long-term deterioration in the New England economy are actually evidences of the movement of the economy to a higher level of productivity and income." [8] In other words, New England is well on the way to successful adjustment owing largely to the resourcefulness and initiative of business firms. In critical local situations much valuable assistance has been furnished by community development programs and by state development commissions.

In a few New England towns and cities groups of business-men and bankers, after surveying their local resources, have raised money, advertised their advantages as industrial loca-tions, purchased real estate and built plants for prospective new manufacturing enterprises. Such campaigns have brought substantial results in Nashua and Manchester, New Hamp-shire. In these cities diversification of industry has brought a more stable business situation and has checked the decline in employment. In the Massachusetts textile cities of Lawrence, Lowell, New Bedford and Fall River, however, similar efforts have been less successful; in these cities unemployment, par-ticularly of textile workers, is still a troublesome problem.[9]

[7] See particularly Seymour E. Harris, *The Economics of New England* (Cambridge: Harvard University Press, 1952); Committee on the New England Economy of the Council of Economic Advisers, *The New Eng-land Economy* (Washington: GPO, 1951); *The Economic State of New England*, Report of the Committee of New England of the National Plan-ning Association (New Haven: Yale University Press, 1954).

[8] *The Transition in the Economy of New England*, lecture by Alfred C. Neal at Trinity College, Hartford, Conn., December 15, 1954. As vice presi-dent of the Federal Reserve Bank of Boston, Dr. Neal has been in a position to become intimately acquainted with shifts in the economy of the region. See also "Employment in New England" in the Bank's *Monthly Review* (January and February 1954).

[9] *The Staff Papers* presented to the Randall Commission, cited, contain (pp. 411-426) detailed accounts of community development programs in eight New England cities (Danbury and Danielson, Connecticut; Lawrence, Lowell and New Bedford, Massachusetts; Manchester and Nashua, New Hampshire), and also in Auburn, Hornell and Utica, New York; Altoona, Pottsville, Scranton and York, Pennsylvania. The story of redevelopment in Iron Mountain, Michigan was told by John S. Coleman in *Hearings be-fore the Commission on Foreign Economic Policy* (Washington, October 28, 1953), pp. 282ff. (Stenographic transcript.)

The few really successful instances of adjustment to economic dislocation through organized community effort have attracted widespread attention, but little is known about the large number of one-industry communities which have undertaken no effort of this kind, or have been only partially successful. Manufacturers are sometimes reluctant to establish new enterprises in mature communities which are declining or where labor is strongly organized. They prefer "industrially virginal areas." Hence the search for new industries may be an extended process. In Lawrence, Massachusetts, although 39 new companies were settled in the five-year period of 1948-1953, the process of economic readjustment at the end of that time remained unfinished.

From the point of view of the workers, even the more successful diversification programs have involved considerable hardship. Labor is far from being perfectly mobile. Displaced workers do not immediately or automatically fit into new occupations. In a recent survey of 1,700 displaced textile workers in Massachusetts,[10] Professor Miernyk found that about half had failed to find new jobs. The older workers, particularly, lacked both the inclination and the ability to find employment in another industry. Workers who did move to other jobs usually suffered losses in earnings because of downgrading in skill classification. On this account, and for other reasons, about half the workers in Dr. Miernyk's sample found the new jobs less satisfactory than the old. The limitations on labor mobility, disclosed in his study of textile workers, are confirmed by other more general studies.

Federal Responsibility

The case for federal aid to firms adversely affected by tariff reductions rests in part on the inadequacy of state and local assistance. Moreover, the federal government has a unique responsibility. It was federal legislation—the protective tariff —which years ago encouraged firms to invest in the woolen and worsted business, in making chinaware, glassware and coal tar chemicals and in other industries vulnerable to foreign

[10] William H. Miernyk, *Inter-Industry Labor Mobility* (Boston: Northeastern University Press, 1955).

competition. And it was a shift in federal economic policy which reduced tariffs, exposing some of the protected industries to injury from imports. Hence it would seem logical that the federal government share with the injured industries, and communities, the burden of adjustment. Stanley H. Ruttenberg has said: ". . . as long as the federal government is going to be responsible for the development of international trade policy, it must be also responsible for finding solutions to problems which grow out of such policy." [11]

Payment of compensation from the federal treasury to injured firms and their employees has been advocated on grounds of political expediency, as well as justice. But how should fair compensation be determined? Increased imports, or falling prices, seldom if ever constitute the sole causes of injury. Instead, as we have seen in our case studies, they are usually accompanied by changes of domestic origin. These extraneous factors would have to be eliminated in some fashion or other before the proper amount of compensation could be determined. Furthermore, payments from the federal treasury to victims of tariff reduction might set a dangerous precedent. Many kinds of federal legislation would be found to injure some industry, business or economic interest, all of which would not fail to urge their claims.[12]

In any case, compensation should not be paid to enable firms injured by tariff reduction to continue in their original line of business. The purpose, rather, should be to enable them to transfer their resources to some line less vulnerable to foreign competition.

The McDonald Plan

A comprehensive plan for federal assistance, not involving direct payments of money, was presented to the Randall Commission by one of its members, Mr. David J. McDonald, president of the United Steel Workers of America. Its principal features were:

[11] *Hearings before the Commission on Foreign Economic Policy* (October 28, 1953), cited, p. 175.
[12] Clair Wilcox has presented convincingly these and other arguments against compensation in his article, "Relief for Victims of Tariff Cuts," *American Economic Review*, v. 40, no. 5 (December 1950), pp. 884-889.

1. *Eligibility for assistance.* Only companies, employees and communities affected by action of the President in (a) lowering an import duty below a peril point[13] or (b) in rejecting a recommendation of the Tariff Commission for an increase in duty would be eligible.

2. *Assistance to injured companies and communities.* Technical assistance needed by companies and communities in carrying out diversification programs would be paid for from federal funds. This assistance might cover the cost of services of consulting engineers, experts in market research and other technicians. Financing required for expansion or diversification might be provided by the Small Business Administration[14] with enlarged authority and appropriations if needed. Accelerated tax amortization should be granted on new plant and equipment introduced to diversify or expand production into lines not affected by tariff change. Similar privileges should be accorded to new firms established in injured communities.

3. *Assistance to displaced workers.* Diversification, either by companies or by communities, Mr. McDonald recognizes, may not be successful in restoring prosperous conditions. Consequently, employees in companies eligible for federal assistance might not be able to secure alternative employment promptly. "Present unemployment insurance benefits," Mr. McDonald argues, "are inadequate to meet this need. Since this displacement would be the result of our national trade policy, Federal responsibility is clear. States where the impact happens to fall heaviest should not be penalized in a program designed to benefit the na-

[13] The "peril points" are rates of duty determined by the Tariff Commission below which the President cannot, in the Commission's judgment, reduce tariffs without injury to American industry or business. The President may reduce duties below the peril points, but if he does so he must explain his action to the Congress. The peril point amendment, attached to the Trade Agreements Act when it was extended in 1948, was repealed the following year, but was reenacted in 1951.

[14] Established July 30, 1953, the S.B.A. succeeded the Small Defense Plants Administration in activities relating to government procurement. The purposes of the S.B.A. are to obtain for small business concerns "a fair share" of government orders; to help these concerns to obtain adequate capital and credit, competent management and expert technical advice. A "small" firm for government procurement purposes is defined as one with 500 or fewer employees; for other purposes the limit may be raised to 1,000 employees. Most of the firms which have suffered, or would suffer, serious injury through tariff reduction probably employ less than 1,000 employees each. Here, the S.B.A. would seem to be a particularly appropriate agency to administer federal aid.

tional interest." [15] Extension of the present unemployment benefits is the remedy proposed, and also supplemental benefits to be
paid for a limited duration to workers forced to take new jobs at
substantially lower rates of pay. Counseling and placement programs to enable displaced workers to find alternative employment,
retraining allowances and allowances for expenses of moving to
new locations are also recommended. Older workers who may
be unemployable might be made eligible for O.A.S.I. retire-
ment benefits before the age of 65.

The Commission decided it could not recommend the Mc-
Donald proposals to the government "for the reason that no
matter how great our sympathy may be for the problems of a
displaced worker, or those of a business with a shrinking volume, this is but one phase of a much broader problem. . . .
In a free economy, some displacement of workers and some
injury to institutions is unavoidable. It may come about
through technological change, alterations in consumer preferences, exhaustion of a mineral resource, new inventions, new
taxes, or many other causes. Since it has never been seriously
proposed that the burden of all such injury arising in a free
economy should be assumed by the Government, the Commission felt that it was not appropriate to propose such a plan
in the tariff area only." [16]

In concurring with the Commission's rejection of the proposed adjustment assistance program, three of its members
pointed out that various forms of government aid were already available to industries threatened with injury from
technological advancement, style changes, or other causes. For
unemployment insurance benefits, displaced workers may turn
to the state and federal agencies. Employment information,
placement and training are available from the Department of
Labor. Employers may obtain technical advice from the Department of Commerce. From the Small Business Administration they may get preferential treatment in federal procurement and loans. These Commissioners objected to the creation
of a new federal bureau to grant relief from tariff injury. "A

[15] Commission on Foreign Economic Policy, *Report to the President and
the Congress,* Statement of David J. McDonald (Washington: GPO, 1954),
pp. 57-58.
[16] Same, p. 54.

tariff rate would become a vested right. Accurate determination of damage to this right would be extremely difficult, and would be certain to involve political pressures and favoritism." [17]

Commissioners who dissented from the majority's recommendation for lowering tariffs also rejected the McDonald adjustment proposals. Senator Millikin said:

It strikes me as an infringement on human dignity and our conception of individual freedom to set up in this country a system of central planning which would remove workers out of their home communities, their home jobs, their churches, recreations, and away from lifelong friendships.[18]

Transfer of resources is the guiding purpose of the McDonald plan. It aims to help investors, management and workers to shift their capital and their skills out of industries injured or threatened by foreign competition and into branches of manufacturing or other economic activities where they would be more effective and less vulnerable. Thus the plan would supplement and reinforce a basic purpose of tariff reduction, viz., to raise the general level of productivity of the American economy.

Proposed Legislation

Transfer of resources is also the purpose of a bill, incorporating many features of the McDonald Plan, introduced in the 83rd Congress by Representative Harrison A. Williams, Jr., of New Jersey (H. R. 9652). Similar legislation was proposed in 1955 by Representatives Williams, Eberharter of Pennsylvania and Donohue of Massachusetts, and in the Senate by Senators Kennedy of Massachusetts and Humphrey of Minnesota, but in Congress no substantial support was forthcoming for any of the bills. In urging his bill in the Senate Senator Humphrey said:

We should be concerned about those industries or communities that are suffering cutbacks in production or localized depression. There will be differences of opinion as to whether these problems are always brought about directly by tariff concessions. But the

---

[17] Statement of Commissioners Bush, Parker and Vorys, same, p. 59.
[18] Same, p. 84.

problems are there. Even if they are not always directly attributable to tariff cuts and imports, they are sometimes thought to be; and what people think to be the truth has a very controlling influence on their decisions. This is a political fact that many of us have to live with. We cannot ignore the pleas of a stricken industry or community for tariff protection, whether the injury from imports is real or merely imagined.[19]

Political Aspects

Practical politics furnishes a strong argument for federal assistance. Legislation of this type would make it easier for many Congressmen and Senators, who, although convinced that freer trade is in the national interest, nevertheless have protected industries in their districts, to vote for tariff reduction. They would be able to defend their action by referring to programs of federal assistance.

Legislators with protectionist leanings and businessmen who fear foreign competition have shown no enthusiasm for adjustment programs. Opposed to tariff reduction, they logically reject remedies for injuries resulting therefrom. For them the only acceptable remedy for insufficient protection is more protection.

The proposed legislation has failed to obtain much support from advocates of lower tariffs, many of whom consider that the assistance for distressed industries already provided in federal legislation should be adequate to take care of firms injured by tariff cuts. Specific legislation in their behalf would only substitute for the tariff a new kind of paternalism, adding new agencies to Washington's all too prolific bureaucracy.

A General Program for Distressed Areas

Some economists have urged that aid to industries suffering from tariff reduction should be made part of a general program for the relief of distressed industries.[20] Economic dislocation, they point out, usually arises from a variety of causes.

---

[19] *Congressional Record*, 84th Cong., 1st sess. (May 4, 1955), p. 4767. (Daily edition.)

[20] See *A Critique of the Randall Commission Report*, prepared by Klaus Knorr and Gardner Patterson on the basis of a conference held at Princeton University, February 4-5, 1954 (Princeton: International Finance Section, 1954), pp. 29-33.

It is always difficult, and often impossible, to distinguish the impact of import competition from influences of domestic origin. Rather than the establishment of a separate agency to assist industries injured by tariff reduction, it would be preferable to provide for them in a general federal program for aid to distressed areas.

Federal efforts to aid industrial communities suffering chronic depression date from 1949. Technical assistance has been provided and tax favors have been granted to induce companies to construct plants in communities suffering from unemployment. Employers in the depressed areas have been given preferences in bidding on government contracts. The failure of these measures to significantly reduce unemployment in the labor surplus areas led the President's Council of Economic Advisers to recommend, in January 1956, a new and far-reaching program. Based on its recommendations, the Area Assistance Act of 1956 (S. 2892) provides for loans to finance, in part, the cost of new industrial plants in distressed areas. The Act would make grants for technical assistance and would give priority to applications for needed public facilities. A bill introduced by Senator Paul Douglas (S. 2663) is considerably broader in scope, embracing expanded unemployment compensation to retrain workers and tax amortization aid; it would also authorize a program of public works projects.

* * *

In the ten years following World War II, tariff reduction, for the reasons set forth earlier in this chapter, caused no disaster. Would further progress in the direction of free trade be equally painless? In the following, final chapter, after some general considerations, we shall take up this question with reference to each of our case study industries.

Chapter 11

SOME CONCLUDING OBSERVATIONS

IT HAS BEEN SAID of the tariff that "its existence alone creates the conditions that make it indispensable." How much truth is there in this statement? How important is the tariff today? For what industries is it indispensable? What circumstances prevent American firms from competing on even terms with foreigners? Are high wages a real handicap? Does national security require that certain industries essential to national defense be safeguarded by restrictions on competing imports? These are questions which constantly recur in discussions of tariff policy. Each of the eight case studies supplies information and opinion which help to answer them. The pertinent material is brought together and summarized in this concluding chapter.

The Tariff and National Defense

For the past 20 years political considerations have exercised strong and pervasive effects on American commercial policy. Even before World War II we were employing trade controls in an attempt to persuade Germany and Japan to abandon their aggressive policies. During that war we used trade controls as a "hidden weapon" to supplement the military effort. After the surrender of Germany and Japan, a state of tension in our relations with Soviet Russia led to controls over export and import trade as measures of national security. Exports to Russia and satellite countries were restricted, and imports from these countries were discouraged by denying to them the tariff reductions extended to other countries in trade agreements. All trade with Communist China was forbidden. The desire, for political reasons, to strengthen the economic position of England and other friendly European countries brought about a relaxation in the administration of the Buy American Act. But some American manufacturers still urge that defense considerations demand more rigorous restrictions on government purchases from foreign firms.

Since 1945, Congressional hearings and debates over the continuation of the policy of tariff reduction through trade agreements have given increasing attention to political and strategic factors. Presidents, Secretaries of State and other high administrative officials, on the one hand, have persistently argued that cutting our import duties would build up the power, and the willingness, of our European allies to resist Communist aggression, both from within and without.

Protectionists, on the other hand, in Congress and in industry, have argued that the critical state of international affairs called for higher, not lower, tariffs. This sentiment was responsible for Section 2 of the 1954 extension of the Trade Agreements Act, which provided that the President might disapprove any reduction in duty made in a trade agreement if he found "that such reduction would threaten domestic production needed for projected national defense requirements."

The section was unnecessary for the President already had full discretion in this matter. A year later, however, Congress granted the Executive a real and important enlargement of his tariff powers. The 1955 Act gave the Office of Defense Mobilization authority to determine whether there is reason to believe that imports of any commodity threaten the national security. If the ODM advises the President to that effect, and if he upon investigation finds this to be a fact, he shall "adjust" the imports so as to remove the threat. Thus, the Office of Defense Mobilization "has come to play a vital role in foreign economic policy" by establishing precedents for determining the essentiality of domestic industries to the national security. Numerous industries have filed applications with the ODM for increased protection—including some which failed to obtain relief from the Tariff Commission under escape clause procedures. Commenting on this development a Senate committee warned that the concept of defense essentiality might "dominate over other necessary factors in trade policy." [1]

---

[1] U. S. Congress, Joint Committee on the Economic Report, *Foreign Economic Policy*, Report No. 1312, 84th Cong., 2d sess. (Washington: GPO, 1956), p. 31.

Preparing for What Kind of War?

Usually those who present the "defense argument" assume that the next war will resemble World Wars I and II, that it will be a long, drawn-out struggle fought with conventional weapons for unlimited objectives. In those wars the ability of American industry to convert rapidly to defense production proved decisive. But if the largest nuclear or thermonuclear weapons are used in the next war, the military decision may be reached, not in years, but in weeks. "A mobilization base," a military expert has pointed out, "is virtually valueless in such a war. The outcome will depend on military forces in fighting readiness at the outset. Those built from a broad mobilization base, however efficiently organized, and shipped across oceans, will not be available until long after the whole issue has been decided. A mobilization base, although the key strategic element in a non-atomic world war, is actually a useless millstone around our necks in preparing to fight a modern nuclear war. It is incompatible with a strategy of instant, massive retaliation." [2]

But all military experts do not agree that the next war will be a general, world-wide conflict in which nuclear weapons will bring a quick decision. Some maintain that warfare on the Korean model, fought with conventional weapons in the pursuit of a limited objective, is still a possibility which has to be considered. The use of atomic weapons might, or might not, cause a war of this kind to spread geographically until it became general. A third possibility is guerrilla warfare of considerable duration, fought without nuclear weapons but not requiring the production of large quantities of military "hardware." At present there seems no way of determining which of these alternatives has the highest degree of probability. If, however, a long, drawn-out struggle is one of the contingencies, it must be taken into account in defense plan-

[2] *The Defense Mobilization Base Concept and Foreign Economic Policy,* a statement by Richard S. Leghorn before the Subcommittee on Foreign Economic Policy of the Joint Committee on the Economic Report (Washington, November 14, 1955), p. 3. (Mimeographed.) Mr. Leghorn, a colonel in the U.S.A.F., Reserve, is the Manager of the Western European Department of the Eastman Kodak Company. See also "Foreign Trade and National Defense" by Raymond Vernon, in *Foreign Affairs,* v. 34, no. 1 (October 1955), pp. 77-88.

ning, and industrial mobilization therefore is still relevant.

But is the safeguarding of certain essential branches of manufacturing by import restrictions the best defense policy? Such restrictions are costly; they involve directing productive resources from more effective to less effective uses, and to that extent they weaken the national economy. On this account it has been argued that our best preparation for war of any kind would be the development of a flexible economy capable of rapid expansion and rapid conversion from peacetime to wartime needs. In our labor force we would rely more on generalized than on special skills. We would give free rein to the ingenuity of our engineers and the alertness and enterprise of our business executives so that by unorthodox methods they could make use of generalized labor skills for specialized production. These qualities, it is said, are more likely to be developed by the encouragement, rather than by the restriction, of foreign competition.

The concept that a flexible economy is best suited to national defense has great value. It provides a better guide to policy than the notion that we must determine in advance the structure of production which will most effectively meet our needs when the emergency arises. For by that time our best-laid plans will almost certainly prove out of date. The acceptance of the principle of flexibility, however, does not rule out measures to preserve certain types of production and skills of peculiar value, if otherwise they might be lost.

What Industries Are Essential to Defense?

Our case studies of organic chemicals, electrical manufacturing and watches have shown how difficult it is to determine what industries are essential to national defense. The bare fact that certain products have been widely used in wartime, for military or essential civilian purposes, is in itself not significant. Cotton, coal, shirts and shoes would all fit this description of essentiality. To qualify for special consideration on grounds of national defense, the industry in question must supply commodities possessing certain unique qualities which make them practically indispensable. Or the workers in the industry must possess uniquely valuable skills. Furthermore, if the industry is asking for tariff protection, it must be vulnerable to foreign competition. It must show that, if present restrictions on imports were removed or relaxed, it could not continue operations at a level which defense authorities would consider an adequate base for wartime expansion.

Among the thousands of products of the synthetic organic chemical industry there are hundreds which could be called essential. Chemists and chemical engineers are admittedly indispensable. Chemical products enter into the manufacture of practically every kind of foodstuffs, clothing and other necessities for the fighting forces and the civilian population. But it is not at all clear that the continued manufacture of synthetic organic chemicals in this country at a safe level is threatened by imports.

In wartime a dependable supply of electric power, and one which can be rapidly expanded, is essential for defense industries and for the civilian economy. Thus the manufacture of power generating and distributing equipment becomes a legitimate concern of defense planning. In supplying steam turbines and other equipment for thermal stations, which supply more than 75 percent of the electric power now generated in this country, the domestic electrical manufacturers are not troubled by foreign competition. But in supplying hydroelectric equipment they are vulnerable.

In the United States at present only a few firms have special machine tools capable of producing and repairing generators, water wheels and other hydroelectric equipment of the largest capacity. To keep this division of their businesses in operation the American firms depend almost exclusively on federal contracts. In recent years, however, foreign firms have been able to underbid the American producers.

On defense grounds it would seem a prudent policy to maintain in this country minimum facilities for the production and repair of hydroelectric equipment. At present the American manufacturers are protected by import duties and by the provisions of the Buy American Act. Imports can be restricted by high duties or by quotas. But, for the present purpose, to effect a sharing of government purchases between foreign and domestic suppliers, the Buy American Act is more effective because it operates with more precision. The Act authorizes federal purchasing agents to award contracts to domestic manufacturers on grounds of national security, even when their bids are higher than those of foreign manufacturers. Preference of this sort is, of course, subject to abuse. The "protection" which it affords may enable the domestic firms to secure contracts at prices which yield more than normal profits. A wise administration of the Act, however, could guard against this danger and at the same time see to it that the American manufacturers received a share of the total federal business sufficient to keep essential facilities in operation. The Act, however, should be amended so as to apply only when security interests are involved. In its general application as a sort of super tariff it is indefensible.

Jeweled-lever watches present a test case on defense essentiality as applied to manufactured products. A series of official investigations have examined the manufacturers' contention that they are *uniquely* equipped to turn out the ultra-precise, miniature components of modern weapons. The facts, it seems, do not support these claims. Watch factories have excellent facilities for precision work, but they no longer have a monopoly position in this field. Nevertheless, their equipment and skilled workers would prove a valuable supplement to facilities in other industries.

Undoubtedly the armed services and civilians in key positions will need in wartime an adequate supply of reliable timepieces, but opinions differ on how many would be "adequate," and on what measures should be taken to make sure that a safe quantity would be available. The manufacturers are vulnerable to Swiss competition. This fact seems well established. Moreover, it is doubtful whether import duties at the present level will guarantee that watches will be produced in the United States at a level which defense authorities would consider adequate. But raising the tariff is not the only, or the best, means of accomplishing this result. From several points of view the payment of direct subsidies to manufacturers would be preferable.

Wages and Productivity

At tariff hearings manufacturers regularly contend that they need protection because the wages they pay are higher than those paid by competing firms in foreign countries. That

American wages actually are much higher is a matter of common knowledge. Our case studies afforded abundant illustrations. Advocates of freer trade often brush aside the high-wage argument with the remark that the higher American scale, since it reflects the higher productivity of American labor, is no indication of higher costs per unit of product. This holds true for standardized commodities which are turned out in quantity by mass-production methods. Under these circumstances heavy investments of capital make possible in American factories much larger output per employee per working hour than is possible in foreign plants which are not so well equipped.

For this reason electrical manufacturers and chemical companies are not, as respects the bulk of their products, troubled by imports. They are sensitive to competition from abroad only in a few specialties, such as batch-processed dyes, heavy hydroelectric equipment and other items which for technical reasons, or because of the limited market, could not be mass-produced and which consequently require large inputs of highly paid labor. In competing with foreign firms utilizing the same techniques and similar equipment, the high American wages constitute a real disadvantage.

High wages are a serious handicap to American producers of glassware, chinaware, watches, bicycles and woolens and worsteds. In American manufacturing, in general, labor costs make up 20 to 25 percent of factory sales price, but in woolens and worsteds it is 30-35 percent;[3] in chinaware, 60; in hand-fashioned glassware, 65; and in watches, 80 percent. In these industries the output per worker in some cases is higher than in foreign countries, but the difference is not sufficient to offset the higher wages. In at least one case, glassware, there is some evidence that output per worker may be higher abroad.

The fundamental difficulty of the import-sensitive industries is not the low wages paid abroad but the high wages paid by other American industries, based on their high labor

[3] Raw material, chiefly wool, constitutes the principal factor in the costs. On this account the proportion assigned to labor is only moderately high. In bicycles, the labor cost, according to one manufacturer, makes up 30 percent of total factory cost. This ratio would be higher if the firm made its own parts instead of purchasing them outside.

productivity. Manufacturers of hand-fashioned glass, we found, have to pay their workers wages which conform in general to the standard set by nearby glassware plants using automatic machinery. Household china factories have to compete for labor with those producing hotel ware by processes which are more mechanized. Manufacturers of watches, woolens and worsteds and bicycles have to pay going rates of wages based on the general high level of productivity in American industries, including those producing for export markets.[4]

The interdependence of wages in various sectors of American manufacturing is only one illustration of the need of relating the "tariff problem" in every industry to its domestic background. No industry stands by itself in competition with foreign suppliers. Each is an integral part of the entire American economy. Technological progress resulting in lower manufacturing costs, shifts in consumers' demand, owing to changes in living habits, and other influences of purely domestic origin, all have their influence on tariff-protected industries.

The impact of imports depends on the state of the domestic market, in general, and for the particular commodity. The stagnant or declining demand for hand-fashioned glassware, chinaware and woolens and worsteds makes foreign competition particularly troublesome. The general state of American business is just as important. Under conditions of full employment and rising incomes, increased imports may be absorbed without difficulty. Conversely, a business recession, as in 1953-1954, leads to complaints of injury. Fluctuations in national income and in the general level of business activity have usually been more important to the industries with which we are concerned than changes in import duties.

Manufacturing Costs May Not Be Decisive

Differences in manufacturing costs may not accurately measure the strength of import competition. Differences fav-

[4] Kravis has shown that export industries in the United States tend to pay higher wages than import-competing industries. See Irving B. Kravis, "Wages and Foreign Trade," *Review of Economics and Statistics*, v. 38, no. 1 (February 1956), pp. 14-30.

oring the foreign firms are often offset, in part or altogether, by a variety of competitive advantages favoring the domestic producers. Costs of inland transportation afford "natural" protection to American producers of bulky commodities such as iron and steel, plate glass and window glass.

Domestic firms have advantages in marketing. American bicycle factories can make deliveries in a few days; foreign suppliers require several weeks. Dye manufacturers render services to their customers which foreign producers can duplicate only if they are willing to set up elaborate and expensive distributive organizations in this country. Uncertainty regarding the trend of U. S. tariff policy makes such an investment somewhat speculative. Hence the decision of some foreign chemical concerns to undertake dye manufacturing in the United States.

Electrical manufacturers lay great emphasis on their superior facilities for making prompt repairs on heavy equipment and insist that in this respect English, Swiss and Italian firms are at a real disadvantage. Habit, tradition and personal relations help to explain why foreign electrical manufacturers have been unable to sell any significant amounts of their equipment to privately owned public utility companies.

The advantages are not all on the side of the domestic manufacturers. The prestige of some foreign goods, "snob appeal," if you like, helps their sales. Some Americans will buy British china and Swedish glassware even when priced higher than very similar domestic products.

Some imports compete with a wide range of the products of domestic firms, some only with commodities which are "like or similar." Obviously, imported hydroelectric generators do not compete with General Electric toasters, or with many other products of the American electrical manufacturing industry. It is not easy, however, to determine whether the imports of Japanese chinaware and glassware affect sales of all the corresponding American products or only those which are most nearly comparable in price. Our studies show that attempts at exact determination of comparability usually yield unsatisfactory results. Experts give conflicting testimony. When an administrator, a Tariff Commissioner, for example, has to decide, he will base his decision on his own best judgment, colored perhaps by his general attitude toward protection and free trade.

Changes in the volume of imports do not necessarily measure the force of foreign competition. Prices must also be considered. Import competition may actually increase while the quantity of imports remains stable, or even falls. For domestic producers under certain circumstances may decide to cut their prices in order to hold their customers. Chemical manufacturers with idle capacity in 1954 found it more economical to meet the low prices of imported chemicals than to let their facilities stand idle or to operate them at a low rate. A more striking illustration is to be found in the bidding on heavy electrical equipment for federal power projects. The Westinghouse company in April 1954 secured a contract for generators for the Chief Joseph Dam by cutting more than $700,000 (14 percent) from its original bid. Later, in October of that year, the General Electric Company, which had previously complained of inability to meet the low costs of foreign competitors, won a contract for eight generators for the Dalles Dam by a bid which was $2 million under that of English Electric, the lowest foreign bidder.

How Important Is the Tariff

What does the tariff mean to the eight industries selected as case studies? The question can best be answered by trying to estimate the effects of further tariff reduction. Much depends on how, and when, import duties are cut. In what follows we shall make what appear to be the most probable assumptions, viz., (1) that further reductions will be gradual, and (2) that they will not be undertaken in a period of general unemployment and falling national income. One further qualification: the predictions which follow are based on observation of present conditions and on recent developments, principally in the decade, 1945-1955. They may be falsified by changes which cannot now be foreseen, new trends in domestic demand and new developments in techniques of production at home and abroad.

For the three major industries, tariff protection has only marginal significance. The iron and steel industry, we found, had outgrown its need for tariff protection. Competition from abroad appears only sporadically and not in significant amounts. Manufacturers of synthetic organic chemicals feel the competition of certain special types of dyes and intermediates. If this protection were reduced, standardized dyes and intermediates would still be produced in the United States in large quantities by continuous processes, using large inputs of capital and small inputs of labor. Imports would increase of specialized products which can be economically produced only by the labor-intensive batch process. For the large chemical companies the sales of the sensitive items make up only a small percentage of total turnover. Increased import competition might cause them to shift production out of the profitable specialties into the less profitable "bread and butter" items, with consequent decline in profits. Smaller concerns which are less diversified would find it more difficult to adjust their business to increased foreign competition. Some of them might have to shut up shop.

For protection against foreign competition in hydroelectric equipment domestic firms rely not so much on import duties, which are moderate, as on the application of the Buy American Act. A more liberal administration of the Act (i.e., more generous treatment of foreign bidders) would either deprive American firms of certain contracts for generators, transformers, etc., or else force them to lower their prices and sacrifice a part of their profits.

Tariff reduction would prove a serious matter for some of the producers of hand-fashioned glassware and household china. The nature of the products and the limited extent of their markets narrowly restrict the economical use of labor-saving machinery. Hence, in competing with foreign firms the high American scale of wages is a serious handicap. The possibilities of economic adjustment are not promising. But even with reduced tariff protection these industries would not disappear. Some firms would survive because of superior management or because of the established reputation of their products. Others, in isolated communities, might continue in business by paying workers less than the union scale and by eliminating featherbedding practices. In both industries, total output and the number of firms would probably decline.

The postwar troubles of woolen and worsted mills have

been only distantly related to tariff reduction. Further cuts in import duties might lead to increased competition, affecting principally a small group of American firms which make fabrics in the highest price category. But the effect on the several hundred which account for the bulk of the American product would be negligible.

In the years, 1950-1955, competition from England and Germany cut deeply into the business of American bicycle manufacturers. Tariff reduction would in all probability be followed by the growth of imports at a faster rate than the expansion of the domestic bicycle market. Marginal firms would be eliminated, and the diminished domestic production would be concentrated in the more efficient enterprises.

The continued manufacture in the United States of jeweled-lever watches, in anything like the present volume, would seem impossible without substantial tariff protection. In postwar years, while imports of Swiss watches have been expanding, domestic production has showed little gain. The high wages paid by American manufacturers are not offset by higher output per worker. The Swiss industry, which turns out many times as many jeweled-lever movements as the American and sells them all over the world, is effectively organized for economical production and for marketing its products abroad. Cutting the tariff, particularly on watches of high jewel count, would cause American manufacturers to reduce their output of American-made movements, to increase their imports of Swiss movements, and to enlarge their investments in electronics and other outside industries.

The relation of the tariff and imports to American industries may be described in several ways. (1) Lower import duties would affect large-scale manufacturers only at the fringes of their business. (2) Certain small-scale industries, characterized by a high ratio of labor costs to total manufacturing costs and in some cases by declining markets, may themselves be considered marginal from the standpoint of American industry as a whole. (3) Within these so-called marginal industries increased imports would hit marginal firms the hardest.

Congressional committees are often told that, if the import duty on this or that commodity is reduced, the producing industry will be destroyed. But tariff changes usually do not determine whether or not an entire industry will survive or perish; they determine only the dimensions of the industry. Lowering tariff duties on commodities which are sensitive to import competition is a selective process. It cuts off the marginal firms, the fringes of the industry.

Balancing Gains and Losses

The effects of tariff change spread far beyond the industries immediately affected and the communities in which they are situated. From the national point of view import competition may bring gain or loss. If increased imports of bicycles cause an American factory to cut back production, or perhaps even to go out of business, firms which have supplied steel tubing, tires, wheels and other parts also suffer loss. In some cases, the indirect losses may even exceed those suffered directly.

But imports also bring gains. By displacing domestic production, they bring about shifts in labor and capital from less effective to more effective uses. Consumers get goods at lower prices and have more money to spend on a variety of commodities and services. Thus the gains are shared by an indefinite number of industries and occupations. Imports enlarge the supply of dollars in the hands of foreigners, enabling them to buy more American cotton, tobacco, automobiles, machinery and other export products. Likewise they stimulate all businesses connected with foreign trade. Here again we must take account of indirect effects. The increased business and personal incomes, like the ripples caused when a stone is thrown into a pond, transmit the gains widely.

In our present state of knowledge we cannot measure quantitatively either the gains or the losses resulting from tariff reduction. We can only estimate them, as I have attempted to do in the preceding chapters. Studies now in progress in universities and research institutions will make possible estimates more reliable than mine, covering a wider range of industries. Information of this sort is indispensable to framers of tariff policy, but it is not sufficient for their task. For statistical data, even estimates, can be based only on economic variables which are capable of measurement.

A true balance between the gains and the losses incident to tariff reduction must take into account intangible factors which defy measurement. Among the losses there is the distress, physical and psychological, of workers displaced by imports. Among the intangible gains should be reckoned the variety of style, design and material which imports introduce in consumers' goods. Import competition incites American manufacturers to adopt and improve on new techniques which have first been developed abroad. Foreign competition makes it difficult at times for domestic firms to maintain administered prices, and thus it helps to maintain one of the essential features of our free enterprise system.[5]

* * *

The task of this book was to discover what the tariff means to eight American industries, to estimate how far they are dependent on the continuation of import duties at their present level. We have dealt with the tariff as a local issue, but obviously it is also, and more importantly, a national issue. The makers of tariff policy must take into account the interests of the entire country, consumers as well as manufacturers. Our case studies should help the perplexed legislator, whom we introduced in Chapter 1, to decide between conflicting special interests, to determine whether or not tariff reduction would benefit or injure his community. But our studies are of less value in helping him identify the national interests affected by tariff changes. To strike a proper balance of gains against losses, national against local interests, is no mean task. The legislator must draw information and opinion from a wide range of sources. Much of what he gathers will be contradictory and much irrelevant. Evaluation and interpretation of this material will require all his skill in economic reasoning and all his capacity for sound judgment.

[5] For a fuller exposition of these and other gains from import trade, see my article on "Imports in the American Economy," *Foreign Affairs*, v. 24, no. 1 (October 1945), pp. 85-98.

APPENDIX

THE FOLLOWING persons assisted the author in the preparation of this volume, by advice and information. None of them, however, bears any responsibility for the accuracy of the facts as presented by the author or for his conclusions. A number of these persons also served as discussion leaders at meetings of the Council's study group; their names are marked by asterisks.

Glassware

BORCHERT, C. A.—Colonial Glass Company
BRODEGAARD, R. F.—R. F. Brodegaard & Company, Inc.
COLBURN, J. BRADLEY—Barnes, Richardson and Colburn
DALZELL, W. F.—Fostoria Glass Company
* DILLINGHAM, H. L.—American Glassware Association
* ENRIGHT, M. J.—Enright-LeCarboulec, Inc.
* GUSTKEY, CARL W.—Imperial Glass Corporation
* HADEN, SAMUEL K.—Morgantown Glassware Guild
* HANNUM, ROBERT F.—Fostoria Glass Company
HORTON, FURMAN C.—S. H. Kress & Company
HOUGHTON, ARTHUR A., JR.—Steuben Glass
KOLB, FRED—George Borgfeldt Corporation
LEAVY, ROBERT J.—Corning Glass Center
McCARL, J. W.—Duncan & Miller Glass Company
MILLER, JOHN—B. Altman & Company
* RUHE, FRANCIS H.—Francis H. Ruhe, Importers
* SCHMIDT, F.—F. Schmidt & Company
SMITH, KENNETH B.—U. S. Tariff Commission
STENGER, LOUIS W.—Seneca Glass Company
WEBER, JOHN C., JR.—West Virginia Glass Specialty Company

Chinaware

ALBERTSON, J. MARK—U. S. Tariff Commission
MARTIN, ROBERT F.—Robert Martin Associates

* MATSUSHITA, RUITARO—Noritake Company, Inc.
* MILLER, DONALD—Maddock & Miller
SUGIHARA, K.—Noritake Company, Inc.
SULLIVAN, ROBERT J.—Lenox, Inc.
* TORBERT, E. L.—Onondaga Pottery Company
* WARREN, LYNNE A.—Shenango Pottery Company
WELLS, J. M.—Homer Laughlin China Company
WEST, GEORGE—Fondeville & Company, Inc.

Bicycles

* AUERBACH, JOHN—Bicycle Institute of America, Inc.
CHICKERING, W. E.—American Machine & Foundry Company
* CLARKE, N. A.—Westfield Manufacturing Company
FISHER, ANDREW—Andrew Fisher Cycle Company, Inc.
GUTTER, ROBERT—R. H. Macy & Company, Inc.
HISS, DONALD—Covington & Burling
* OSGOOD, HAMILTON—Raleigh Industries of America, Inc.
PRICE, C. B., JR.—Belknap Hardware and Manufacturing Company

Watches

BULOVA, ARDE—Bulova Watch Company
CALVERT, MORTON E.—Win Nathanson and Associates, Inc.
DORFMAN, BEN—U. S. Tariff Commission
DRAPER, CHARLES—Massachusetts Institute of Technology
* GSELL, ROLAND—R. Gsell & Company, Inc.
* RUML, BEARDSLEY—Bulova Watch Company
SILVERSTEIN, ADOLPH—Win Nathanson and Associates, Inc.
SIMON, STANLEY—Bulova Watch Company
* SINKLER, ARTHUR B.—Hamilton Watch Company
WIESNER, JEROME—Massachusetts Institute of Technology

Woolens and Worsteds

ALMY, SAMUEL C.—Herbert Lawton & Company
* BLANCHARD, FESSENDEN
BROWN, GLEN F.—National Association of Wool Manufacturers
* BUTLAND, RALPH A.—J. P. Stevens & Company, Inc.

* HALE, RUFUS—Pacific Mills
HURWOOD, DAVID L.
KESTNBAUM, MEYER—Hart, Schaffner & Marx
LAWRENCE, JOHN—Folkard & Lawrence, Inc.
LAWTON, STANLEY—Herbert Lawton & Company
LOGIE, JAMES A.—Hickey-Freeman Company
* MILBANK, ROBERT W.—Milbank, Leaman & Company
ROHRBACH, EDWARD D.—Botany Mills, Inc.
UDELL, JEROME—Lester Udell, Inc.
WALEN, E. D.—Pacific Mills
WILKINSON, EDWIN—National Association of Wool Manu-
facturers

Iron and Steel

* HOWELL, MAX D.—American Iron and Steel Institute
* JOHNSTONE, W. H.—Bethlehem Steel Company, Inc.
* WOODWARD, ROBERT D.—Bethlehem Steel Company, Inc.

Chemicals

CABOT, THOMAS—Godfrey L. Cabot & Company
FOSTER, WILLIAM C.—Manufacturing Chemists' Associa-
tion, Inc.
FUNKE, R. H.—Nova Chemical Corporation
GIBBONS, DONALD R.—Arthur D. Little, Inc.
GILLIS, JOHN L.—Monsanto Chemical Company
GRAFF, STEPHEN—Synthetic Organic Chemical Manufac-
turers Association
HAINES, T. F. DAVIES—Ciba Pharmaceutical Products, Inc.
HALLBACH, ERNEST—Verona Dyestuffs Corporation
HORNER, KEITH R. J.—Ciba Company, Inc.
* KERTESS, F. A.—Terra Chemicals, Inc.
KIRKPATRICK, SIDNEY D.—*Chemical Engineering* and *Chem-
ical Week*
* LENHER, SAMUEL—E. I. du Pont de Nemours & Company,
Inc.
MACLEAN, H. S.—Imperial Chemical Industries, Ltd.
MARKWOOD, L. N.—Markwood Trading Company
* MAY, ERNEST B.—Otto B. May Company
MENNE, W. A.—Verband der Chemischen Industrie

MILLER, T. T.—W. R. Grace & Company
* MOODY, S. C.—American Cyanamid Company
PARK, JAMES G.—Standard Oil Company of New Jersey
SINGER, FRED G.—E. I. du Pont de Nemours & Company, Inc.
SMITH, JULIAN F.—Lenoir Rhyne College
WAGNER, CARY R.—Synthetic Organic Chemical Manufacturers Association

Electrical Manufacturing

BAKER, IVAN
* BARRACLOUGH, A.—English Electric Export & Trading Company, Ltd.
BELL, WILLIAM—United Illuminating Company
BLACK, FISCHER—*Electrical World*
BURR, ROBERT M.—National Electrical Manufacturers Association
CACCIAPUOTI, G. A.—Legnano Electric Corporation
* CRAWFORD, JAMES M.—General Electric Company
* DAVIES, R. H.—Ferranti Electric, Inc.
* ELLIOTT, W. A.—Elliott Company
FORT, TOMLINSON—Westinghouse Electric Corporation
FRYE, EDWARD D.—U. S. Department of the Interior
GREENWOOD, JOSEPHINE—Library, Consolidated Edison Company of New York, Inc.
HEROD, W. R.—International General Electric Company
* HOWLAND, J. L.—Westinghouse Electric Corporation
JACOBSON, JEROME—Jerome Jacobson Associates
MARVIN, BRYAN A.—Consolidated Edison Company of New York, Inc.
* MEIXNER, A. C.—Westinghouse Electric Corporation
METZ, A. F.—Okonite Company
MOREHOUSE, E. W.—General Public Utilities Corporation
* SIDLER, PAUL R.—Brown Boveri Corporation
STEMPLER, JACK L.—U. S. Department of Defense
WITHINGTON, SIDNEY
* WOOD, LAURENCE I.—General Electric Company

General

ABT, HENRI A.—German-American Trade Promotion Office

* BARRIE, ROBERT W.—Legislative Assistant to Representative Harrison A. Williams, Jr.

BATT, WILLIAM L., JR.—Toledo Industrial Development Council, Inc.

BENT, DONN N.—U. S. Tariff Commission

ELY, J. EDWARD—U. S. Bureau of the Census

LAMAR, HAROLD T.—U. S. Library of Congress

RADCLIFFE, HARRY S.—National Council of American Importers, Inc.

RASHISH, MYER—Committee for a National Trade Policy, Inc.

* RUTTENBERG, STANLEY H.—Congress of Industrial Organizations

SIMPSON, R. E.—U. S. Bureau of Foreign Commerce

INDEX

Ackerman, Harold, 145n
Allied Chemical & Dye Corporation, 186, 187
Allis-Chalmers Manufacturing Company, 219, 223, 224, 227n, 252, 253
American Bicycle Manufacturers Association, 69
American Cyanamid Company, 186
American Farm Bureau Federation, 90, 248
American Flint Glassworkers Union, 28
American Iron & Steel Institute, 172, 173n
American Machine & Foundry Company, 70, 75
American selling price, chemicals, 189-192, Tariff Commission opinion, 191; chinaware, 56
American Tariff League, 90
American valuation, *see* American selling price, U. S. value
American Woolen Company, 134, 156
Antidumping Act of 1921, 182, 257
Antitrust suits, chemicals, 208; electrical manufacturing, 226-227; watches, 100, 100n
Arnold, Schwinn & Company, 69
Austria, bicycles, U. S. imports from, 76 (table); glassware, U. S. imports from, 23 (table)

Barkin, Solomon, 135 140n, 150n, 157n
Bauer, Raymond, 259n
Bayer, Friedrich, 208
Belgium, glassware, U. S. imports from, 23 (table)
Belgium-Luxembourg, iron and steel, production, 173 (table)
Benrus Watch Company, 99
Berglund, Abraham, 165n
Bicycles, business organization, 69; comparability of product, 78; competitive conditions, 82-83, 285; description, 78, 83; diversification, 69; economic adjustment, 87; employment, 69-70, 73; history, 74; import competition, 71, 78-81, 83; importing by manufacturers, 80; imports, 71 (table), 72 (chart), 73 (table), 76 (table), balloon-tire, 80-81, 81 (table), 86, causes of increase, 76-79, lightweight, 76, 78-79, 81 (table), 86; inventories, 74; investment, 75; labor costs, 70, 283n; market, 68, 70, 73 (table), 75-76, 80, 82, future expansion of, 85-86; merchandising, 80; prices, 79; process of manufacture, 70; production, 71 (table), 72 (chart), 73 (table), 85, lightweight, 83, middleweight, 83-84; profits, 73, 75; tariff change, effects of, 84-85, 288; tariff rates, 77 (table), 84; wages, 82; *see also* Eisenhower, escape clause decisions; individual countries; quotas; Tariff Commission, escape clause action; tariff protection, manufacturers' attitude toward; trade agreements
Brown, Boveri & Company, Ltd., 227, 235, 236, 241n, 243
Bulova, Arde, 110-111
Bulova Watch Company, 92, 99, 100n, 111n, 115, 116, 117
Burgess, William F., 51n
Burlington Mills, 135
Burlington Industries, 156
Buy American Act (electrical manufacturing), 228, 235, 287; awards under, 215-217; cost of, 248-250; criticism of, 216-217, 235, 247-251; Defense Department directive, 246; history and purposes, 244-245; interpretation, 245-247; and national defense, 241-252, 281-282; proposed reforms, 239, 249; pro-

visions, 244-247; 1954 directive, 251-252

Canada, chemicals, production, 212; electrical manufactures, U. S. exports to, 224-225, 225 (table), U. S. imports from, 228-229, 229 (table), 230 (table)

Chemicals, synthetic organic, antitrust suits, 208; competitive conditions, 203, 211-213, 285; defense aspects, 178, 188-189, 210-213, 281; diversification, 182; domestic industry, 179-183, 186; dutiable value, 189; dyes, 182-183, consumption, 195 (table), 197, exports, 195 (table), 196, imports, 194 (table), 195 (table), 196, 198 (chart), production, 184 (chart), 185 (table), sales, 185 (table), 195 (table), tariff rates, 192 (table); foreign investment by U. S. firms, 209-210; growth, outlook for, 183, 186; import competition, 201, 211; imports, 194 (table), 195-200, competitive and noncompetitive, 189-192, effects on prices, 205; and inorganic chemicals, 180; intermediates, 181, consumption, 197, imports, 194 (table), 197, production, 184 (chart), 185 (table), 197, sales, 185 (table), tariff rates, 192 (table); intra-industry competition, 205; mechanization, 182, 202; merchandising, 203; mergers, 182; output per employee, 202; petrochemicals, 187-188, 203; phthalic anhydride, 199-200; prices, 286; production, 181 (table), 183, 184 (chart), 185 (table), 186, by foreign firms in U. S., 208-209; products, 180, 183, 186-187; research, 203-204; sales, 181 (table), 185 (table), 186; stockpiling, 211, 213; subsidies, 213; tariff change, effects of, 200-201, 287; tariff history, 182, 188-194; tariff rates, 192 (table); wages, 201; see also American selling price; individual countries; tariff protection, manufacturers' attitude toward; trade agreements; U. S. value

Chinaware, hotel, 41, 42, 43-44

Chinaware, household, comparability of product, 56, 62-63; consumption, 42, 45, 48 (chart), 50 (table), 64; diversification, 66; earthenware, distinguished from, 42n; economic adjustment, 63-65; employment, 45; geographical location, 44; history, 42-44; import competition, 39, 47, 50 (table), 52, 57, 58-61; imports, 46, 48 (chart), 49 (table), by returning tourists, 46n; income, national, and consumption, 64-65, and imports, 59; labor costs, 39, 283; market, 56; mechanization, 63; merchandising, 63-64; prices, 47, 62; process of manufacture, 40-41; production, 43, 43 (table), 44, 48 (chart); profits, 45-46; tariff change, effects of, 52, 54-55, 65-67, 287; tariff history, 51-55; tariff rates, 53 (table), 58; see also American selling price; competition, inter-industry; individual countries; quotas; Tariff Commission, escape clause action; tariff protection, manufacturers' attitude toward; trade agreements

Ciba, Ltd., 207, 209
Clarke, N. A., 83
Cleveland Welding Company, 70, 74, 75
Coleman, John S., 269n
Colson Corporation, 74
Commission on Foreign Economic Policy (Randall Commission), 248-249, 265, 268n, 269n, 271, 273-274
Committee on the New England Economy, Council of Economic Advisers, 269n
Competition, inter-industry, chinaware, 43, 63; woolens and worsteds, 149-150, 157
Competitive conditions, see individual commodities
Congress of Industrial Organizations, 90
Cordiner, Ralph J., 223n
Corning Glass Works, 15
Customs administration, 257-258; see also American selling price; Buy American Act; U. S. value; watches, customs administration